Cinema of Discontent

THE SUNY SERIES
HORIZONS OF CINEMA
MURRAY POMERANCE | EDITOR

RECENT TITLES

Mary Ann McDonald Carolan, *Orienting Italy*

Matthew Rukgaber, *Nietzsche in Hollywood*

David Venditto, *Whiteness at the End of the World*

Fareed Ben-Youssef, *No Jurisdiction*

Tony Tracy, *White Cottage, White House*

Tom Conley, *Action, Action, Action*

Lindsay Coleman and Roberto Schaefer, editors, *The Cinematographer's Voice*

Nolwenn Mingant, *Hollywood Films in North Africa and the Middle East*

†Charles Warren, edited by William Rothman and Joshua Schulze, *Writ on Water*

Jason Sperb, *The Hard Sell of Paradise*

William Rothman, *The Holiday in His Eye*

Brendan Hennessey, *Luchino Visconti and the Alchemy of Adaptation*

Alexander Sergeant, *Encountering the Impossible*

Erica Stein, *Seeing Symphonically*

George Toles, *Curtains of Light*

Neil Badmington, *Perpetual Movement*

Merrill Schleier, editor, *Race and the Suburbs in American Film*

Matthew Leggatt, editor, *Was It Yesterday?*

Homer B. Pettey, editor, *Mind Reeling*

Alexia Kannas, *Giallo!*

A complete listing of books in this series can be found online at www.sunypress.edu

Cinema of Discontent

Representations of Japan's High-Speed Growth

Tomoyuki Sasaki

SUNY PRESS

Cover illustration: Shimakawa Masashi
Source photo for cover illustration: Aoki Katsuyuki
Map production: True Vision

Published by State University of New York Press, Albany

© 2022 State University of New York

All rights reserved

Printed in the United States of America

No part of this book may be used or reproduced in any manner whatsoever without written permission. No part of this book may be stored in a retrieval system or transmitted in any form or by any means including electronic, electrostatic, magnetic tape, mechanical, photocopying, recording, or otherwise without the prior permission in writing of the publisher.

For information, contact State University of New York Press, Albany, NY
www.sunypress.edu

Library of Congress Cataloging-in-Publication Data

Name: Sasaki, Tomoyuki, author.
Title: Cinema of discontent : representations of Japan's high-speed growth / Tomoyuki Sasaki.
Description: Albany : State University of New York Press [2022] | Series: SUNY series, horizons of cinema | Includes filmography.
Identifiers: LCCN 2022013458 | ISBN 9781438490991 (hardcover : alk. paper) | ISBN 9781438491011 (ebook) | ISBN 9781438491004 (pbk. : alk. paper)
Subjects: LCSH: Japan—In motion pictures. | History in motion pictures. | Economics in motion pictures. | Motion pictures—Japan—History—20th century.
Classification: LCC PN1995.9.J34 S275 2022 | DDC 791.430952—dc23
LC record available at https://lccn.loc.gov/2022013458

10 9 8 7 6 5 4 3 2 1

Contents

List of Illustrations   vii

Acknowledgments   ix

Introduction: Narrating High-Speed Growth through Film   1

1. Drifting in Tokyo: Reconstruction and Uneven Development in Kawashima Yūzō's *Susaki Paradise Red Light* (1956)   25

2. A Girl from Izu: Labor Migration and Modern Subjectivity in Masumura Yasuzō's *Blue-Sky Girl* (1957)   61

3. Osaka, City of Spies: The Powerless Worker in Industrial Society in Inoue Akira's *Black Weapon* (1964)   103

4. Yokohama Romance: The Cold War, Revolution, and Asian Solidarity in Ezaki Mio's *A Warm Misty Night* (1967)   141

5. Waiting for Spring in Shiretoko: A Postscript to High-Speed Growth in Kumashiro Tatsumi's *The Light of Africa* (1975)   177

Coda   213

Notes   219

Bibliography 235

Filmography 255

Index 261

Illustrations

Figures

1.1	*Susaki Paradise Red Light* (1956)	41
1.2	*Susaki Paradise Red Light* (1956)	49
1.3	*Susaki Paradise Red Light* (1956)	49
1.4	*Susaki Paradise Red Light* (1956)	53
1.5	*Susaki Paradise Red Light* (1956)	55
2.1	*Blue-Sky Girl* (1957)	68
2.2	*Blue-Sky Girl* (1957)	73
2.3	*Blue-Sky Girl* (1957)	80
2.4	*Blue-Sky Girl* (1957)	98
2.5	*Blue-Sky Girl* (1957)	98
2.6	*Blue-Sky Girl* (1957)	99
3.1	*Black Weapon* (1964)	123
3.2	*Black Weapon* (1964)	123
3.3	*Black Weapon* (1964)	133
3.4	*Black Weapon* (1964)	137
3.5	*Black Weapon* (1964)	139
3.6	The Daiki building	140
4.1	*Red Handkerchief* (1964)	149

4.2	*A Warm Misty Night* (1967)	153
4.3	*A Warm Misty Night* (1967)	153
4.4	*The Wharf of No Return* (1967)	154
4.5	*A Warm Misty Night* (1967)	164
4.6	*A Warm Misty Night* (1967)	172
5.1	Hagiwara Ken'ichi	183
5.2	*The Light of Africa* (1975)	198
5.3	*The Light of Africa* (1975)	199
5.4	*The Light of Africa* (1975)	204
5.5	*The Light of Africa* (1975)	204
5.6	*The Light of Africa* (1975)	207

Maps

I.1	Places discussed in *Cinema of Discontent*	20
1.1	Eastern Tokyo (circa 1956)	31
3.1	City of Osaka and Senri New Town (circa 1964)	132

Tables

1.1	Opinion survey on citizens' daily lives (selected questionnaire)	36
2.1	Populations of selected prefectures with major cities	70
2.2	Populations of selected rural prefectures	71
3.1	Daiei's "Black" series	110
3.2	Penetration rates of appliances in the household	114
5.1	Number of unemployed and unemployment rate in Japan	190

Acknowledgments

The Department of Modern Languages and Literatures and the Dean's Office of the College of William & Mary provided me with generous financial support. Thanks to them, I was able to make multiple research trips to Japan while preparing this book until the COVID-19 pandemic made international travel almost impossible in 2020. Also, the university's Swem Library has been very supportive in the acquisition of sources.

The Kansai University Division of International Affairs invited me to their campus in beautiful Senri, in Osaka, as a visiting scholar in May and June of 2017. It was my first long-term stay in Japan in almost ten years and the first long-term stay in my native Kansai since I moved to the United States in the early 2000s. The great degree of freedom they gave me during my stay allowed me to explore various familiar and unfamiliar neighborhoods in Osaka, Kobe, the Hanshin-kan, and Hokusetsu and to think earnestly about the meanings of places in cultural representation. This experience greatly contributed to shaping the general framework of my argument in this book.

Sasagawa Keiko of Kansai University kindly served as faculty host during my stay in Osaka. Kanno Yuka of Doshisha University tirelessly answered many questions about films, sharing her deep knowledge and insights. Micah Auerback of the University of Michigan facilitated the collection of numerous sources at every stage of the preparation of this book. The two anonymous reviewers provided valuable and extremely encouraging feedback.

In addition to these organizations and individuals, I also want to acknowledge the many film directors, actors, and actresses of whom I have been enamored since I was a teenager. This may not be a common way of using the acknowledgments section of a book, but they have all helped me cope with a number of difficulties throughout my life, and they are one main reason that I wanted to write this book. The complete list of these people would be too long, but all the people discussed or even briefly mentioned in this book are people I respect and care for deeply.

Lastly, I thank my family in Richmond—one human and one dog—for listening to me and talking to me all the time. Thank you.

November 2021
Richmond, Virginia

Introduction

Narrating High-Speed Growth through Film

> Suntanned girls are playing on the beach
> I am transporting cars to the factory for repair
> But I am caught in traffic
> The TV says this country worries it's too rich
> But my life hasn't changed at all
>
> —"An August Song" ("Hachigatsu no uta"),
> 1986, sung by Hamada Shōgo[1]

I GREW UP IN JAPAN IN THE 1980s, that is, on the eve of and during what we now remember as the "bubble economy," characterized by the sharp escalation of asset prices—probably the most prosperous time in the history of modern Japan. The marvelous high-speed train that we took every summer to go to my grandmother's house; the "Port Liner," the world's first driverless transit system, which connected downtown Kobe and the manmade Port Island; the gigantic Hankyū Osaka-Umeda Station's ten platforms and labyrinthine underground city; the department stores' mesmerizing variety of clothes, prepared foods, and appliances; and the electronics stores filled with gorgeous audio systems all made me somewhat aware of my country's material wealth and mature consumer culture. It was (and still is) common, in describing the experience of postwar Japan, to contrast this affluent time with the state of complete devastation in the immediate post–World War II years and to bridge these two periods with the extraordinary historical event of high-speed growth. The material comfort we enjoyed in the 1980s was supposed to be the result of the effort Japanese people had made during this historical event.

Later in life, I started watching seriously (and fondly, of course) Japanese films released during this supposedly glorious time of high-speed growth for personal pleasure and, later, for my work as a historian. But the images of postwar Japan that these films presented, or, more correctly, the impressions of postwar Japan that I received from these films, did not always align with and sometimes even betrayed the widespread bright, optimistic images of high-speed growth. Naruse Mikio's films of the 1950s and 1960s—for instance, *Flowing* (*Nagareru*, 1956), *When a Woman Ascends the Stairs* (*Onna ga kaidan o agaru toki*, 1960), and *Yearning* (*Midareru*, 1964)—seemed to communicate not the rapid reconstruction of the national economy but the persisting legacies of the war, the precarious nature of working women's everyday lives, and their emotional despair and resignation. Imamura Shōhei's films of the 1960s—*Pigs and Battleships* (*Buta to gunkan*, 1961) and *The Insect Woman* (*Nippon konchūki*, 1963)—conjured the chain of poverty, the violence of capital, and the cunning required for daily survival rather than the affluence of a society amid the Ikeda cabinet's "income doubling plan" and anticipation of the 1964 Tokyo Summer Olympics. In Yamada Yōji's films of the 1970s, including *Where Spring Comes Late* (*Kazoku*, 1970) and *Home from the Sea* (*Kokyō*, 1972), I found not so much the prosperity of urban centers in Tokyo and Osaka as the disquiet generated by the fundamental structural change in the economy of rural Japan amid massive industrialization throughout the archipelago.

Watching these and other films again and again, I became fascinated by the inconsistency between what we are commonly told or encouraged to believe about high-speed growth and how the people who lived and worked then might have actually experienced this historical event. It looked to me as though diverse sentiments, negotiations, and responses back then had somehow converged into a few, far simpler narratives that disguised that diversity. This led me to the broader questions of the relation between history and narratives. What language can we employ to narrate past events? By choosing one narrative, what other narratives do we sacrifice? What are the politics behind such choices? And is it possible to change, through narratives, our perceptions of the past? This book is an attempt to examine these questions through the use of popular films as historical sources and to explore the possibilities of counternarratives that help us better understand the heterogeneity of experiences during the era of high-speed growth. As the rest of this book demonstrates, cinematic texts are part of a contemporary intellectual and cultural discourse contesting a variety of concerns and interests and therefore reveal much about the society that produced them.

Historical Narratives of Postwar Japan

The linguistic turn in the humanities and the social sciences persuasively established that there is no single true history waiting to be recuperated by historians. The writing of history is a subjective and ideological act that reflects the historian's belief, values, and worldview—as well as, we hope, their conscience and commitment to accuracy. We can write history from a variety of perspectives, incorporating various analytical categories, depending on the positionality that each of us assumes. History writing is a process of signification in which "the world has to be made to mean" through the employment of "language and symbolization" (S. Hall 1982, 63). It is the practice by which we identify certain events in the past as worth remembering, documenting, and disseminating; give specific meanings to those events; articulate causal relations among them; put them in a chronology; and then turn them into a coherent narrative. Not all historical narratives, however, exist equally. Certain historical narratives occupy hegemonic positions and present themselves as the natural way of understanding the past, whereas other narratives may be relegated to positions supplementary to more dominant narratives or even eradicated as unimportant, irrelevant, or erroneous.

In the modern world, the nation-state has served as one of the most powerful frameworks for historical narratives. As nationalism swept across much of the world in the nineteenth century, the ruling elites in newly emerging or reorganized states—whether in Asia, Europe, or the Americas—expected their shared history (or their conviction in such a history, more precisely) to make up for the absence of temporal continuity, cultural consistency, emotional solidarity, and collective memory in their anonymous and intangible national communities and also, to borrow Anthony Giddens's expression, to provide "an anchorage for anticipated developments in the future" (1987, 212). Since the nineteenth century, political leaders, intellectuals, educational institutions, the mass media, and so on have created a set of narratives designed to give legitimacy and credibility to their nation-states, to enlighten the masses, and to make them loyal and conscious citizens. Although the prominence of multinational corporations and global media in the world today might convince us that national borders are gradually losing their significance, historical narratives are still commonly used to warrant the collective experience of the nation-state and induce a sense of belonging among its people.

In the case of modern Japan, until defeat in World War II and the fall of empire in 1945, the emperor and the national polity, or *kokutai*, that he was thought to embody worked as the most influential set of ideologies upon which the history of the nation-state was written. For this narrative, the emperor, who had been deprived of political authority during the Tokugawa era and was not registered in regular people's minds, had to be revitalized as the sovereign of the newly born Meiji state and symbol of the cultural and spiritual unity of national subjects (Fujitani 1996). The historical view that placed the emperor at its center, while competing with other historical views such as historical materialism during the Taishō democracy era, came to earn the predominant position in both academic and popular discourse in the 1930s as Japan's imperial expansion to Manchuria and China accelerated and as military intrusion into parliamentary politics, academia, school education, and people's everyday lives intensified. The famous 1935 "emperor organ theory" incident—right-wing nationalists' fierce attack on Minobe Tatsukichi's well-accepted theory that the emperor was only an organ of government and their insistence on the emperor's divinity—and the subsequent state campaign to glorify *kokutai* must be remembered as an effort to impose this historical view over alternatives through threats, violence, and the rejection of dialogue.[2]

It may be difficult to find a historical view as powerful as this emperor-centered view when we shift our attention to postwar Japan, where a new constitution stipulated the principle of popular sovereignty (in the preamble); guaranteed freedom of thought, religion, conscience, and speech (in articles 19, 20, and 21) as well as academic freedom in education (in article 23); and thereby endorsed pluralist democracy. Though it is true that the emperor remained an influential cultural symbol (Ruoff 2001), the state generally refrained from overtly coercive methods to impose a single historical view. This does not imply, however, an absence of hegemonic historical views. As economic reconstruction steadily advanced and as Cold War uncertainties quickly spread, "modernization" came to serve as a key organizing concept for a coherent narrative of the history of modern Japan. Modernization theory, first developed in the United States as an alternative to Marxism, was introduced to Japan by such scholars as Edwin Reischauer, John Hall, and Marius Jansen in the 1960s. Amid the tense ideological conflict incited by the anti–Security Treaty protest and the anti–Vietnam War movement in Japan, these and other scholars of Japanese studies enthusiastically promoted modernization theory as that which would help to reinterpret and rewrite the history of modern Japan as the nation's continued progression toward greater economic rationality, material affluence, and political liberalism without radical and violent revolution.[3] This was an appealing theory in that it used growth, which could be demonstrated with concrete and objective data (such as GNP, GDP, and household income), as an analytical category and naturalized it as a permanent and indispensable condition for the existence of human societies. It played on Japanese people's self-esteem by allowing them to recognize the relevance of modern Japan's experience within the context of world history as a successful case of social transformation in the non-West.[4] As Harry Harootunian (1993) argues, this American-born narrative, or "America's Japan," had become "Japan's Japan" by the 1970s.

To this day, modernization theory remains influential in academia and beyond as a way of organizing past events and making connections among them (even if it has become increasingly difficult, in academia at least, to maintain blanket support for the concept of modernization based on economic development as we are now cognizant of its harmful consequences). Within the perception of history guided and dictated by it, high-speed growth is presented as a central event. The stories of the astounding growth of Japan's GDP, the success of the 1960s "income doubling plan," Japanese companies' innovations and technologies, and the prominence of Toyota, Honda, Sony, and Nintendo overseas are all familiar to those living in Japan and those who have studied Japanese history even cursorily. All have contributed to representing the history of postwar Japan as a narrative of great triumph and accomplishment, or, to use an expression familiar in both English and Japanese, a narrative of the "economic miracle," or *keizai no kiseki*. This kind of economic miracle narrative highlights the extraordinary and unprecedented nature of the growth that Japan managed to achieve in just a few decades from the end of World War II.

On the one hand, high-speed growth is of course an irrefutable historical fact. Triggered by the revival of the ammunitions industry during the Korean War, the Japanese economy began to demonstrate conspicuous signs of recovery and experienced its first postwar economic boom. From the mid-1950s to 1973, it grew at an average annual rate of 10 percent. By the mid-1960s, Japan turned from a debtor to a creditor nation. In 1965, Japan ran a trade surplus with the United States for the first time in postwar history, which would lead to intense trade friction between the two countries in the 1970s and 1980s. In 1968, it became the second-largest economy in the capitalist world, behind only the United States. Japan was an original member of the current G7 when it launched as the G6 in 1975. By this time, the economic power of the country defeated in World War II had far exceeded the expectations of its former occupier.[5]

The quality of Japanese people's daily lives dramatically improved during this period, too: cars, televisions, washing machines, vacuum cleaners, air conditioners, dinners at fancy restaurants, vacations abroad, and designer clothes, none of which had been easily attainable for a regular working person at the beginning of the high-speed growth, lost their novelty by the end of the 1970s. Accordingly, a large majority of Japanese people came to identify themselves as middle class in that decade. In a national survey conducted by the *Asahi* newspapers in 1985, 36 percent of the 2,310 respondents said that they were "satisfied" with their current lives, and 41 percent were "more or less satisfied." This survey also showed that while not entirely satisfied with incomes and savings, a large majority of the respondents believed their needs for housing, "delicious food," and "good clothes" to be well fulfilled ("Sengo yonjūnen no Nihon" 1985, 11).

On the other hand, high-speed growth is not simply a historical fact but also a prescriptive and disciplinary cultural discourse, or what Herbert Marcuse ([1965] 1968) called "affirmative culture," removed from social reality and aimed at helping people achieve fulfillment and satisfaction in the spiritual realm. Here, I am referring to the fact that the ruling elite in postwar Japan have often discussed high-speed growth in such a way as to foster national pride, identity, and dignity. The narrative of the economic history of postwar Japan that the Economic Planning Agency compiled for its fiftieth anniversary provides an excellent example. It begins, "The era of high-speed growth of the Japanese economy from the immediate aftermath of World War II to the first half of the 1970s was a period of dramatic development [*gekiteki na tenkai*] rarely observed, not only in the history of Japanese economy but even in the history of the world economy. It must be the case that [Japan's] experience will be analyzed repeatedly and handed down [*katari tsugarete iku*] both inside and outside [Japan]" (Keizai Kikakuchō 1997, 5). This narrative describes the overall history of postwar Japan as a splendid drama in which the Japanese, who found themselves in "ruin and despair" ("haikyo to zetsubō") just after defeat in war, miraculously rebuilt their homeland and transformed it into "one of the world's top economic powers" ("sekai yūsū no keizai taikoku"; 5).

The narrative of postwar history promoted by the Liberal Democratic Party (LDP) is a good example, too. It starts with the following statement:

> When we look back, the thirtieth year of Shōwa [1955] was the time when Japan, which had become scorched earth [*shōdo*] through war, was getting on track for a miraculous recovery [*kisekiteki na saikō*] and reconstruction of our homeland [*sokoku*], thanks to the effort of forerunners who would continue to our party. Our predecessors desired development and prosperity as well as peace and stability, bravely shaped the form of our country, achieved high-speed economic growth, and established [Japan's] place within the international community. (Jiyū Minshutō 2006, preface).

While these narratives may embrace high-speed growth more explicitly than most, it is not uncommon for narratives of high-speed growth to employ this historical event to remind the Japanese of the material and psychological devastation that they or their forefathers overcame (I use this gendered term because most of those who play critical roles in these narratives are men) as well as the collaboration, industriousness, and patience they demonstrated for the common goal of making economic growth happen, resorting to such a language as "ashes" (*yakeato*), "hardship" (*kunan*), "turbulence" (*gekidō*), and "miracle" (*kiseki*). In other words, this type of narrative not only describes what happened but also appeals to Japanese people's sense of solidarity at the national level about their supposedly shared past.

In popular culture of the past two decades or so, there have been occasional "Shōwa retro booms"—elevated interest in those years that roughly coincide with high-speed growth and its aftermath, from the mid-1950s to the 1980s. The 2005 film *Always: Sunset on Third Street* (*Always san-chōme no yūhi*), which, using numerous computer-graphics images of 1958 Tokyo, portrays heartwarming interactions between a family that owns a small garage and a girl who moves from Aomori to work for them, was one harbinger of such a boom (Katagiri 2007; Morinaga 2007; Ichikawa 2010). Its enormous popularity resulted in the production of two sequels, in 2007 and 2012, both of which dealt with the same Tokyo family and rural girl but were set in 1959 and 1964 respectively. Although the representations of the "good old days" in these and other cultural productions may seem simply to reflect benign nostalgic longing for things already lost—whether foods, fashions, houses and homes, lifestyles, neighborhoods, streets, personal relations, or affects—they certainly help constitute a prescriptive narrative of high-speed growth in that they serve to foster the audience's sense of collective belonging as Japanese by highlighting those days when the Japanese people might have been still struggling materially but were supposedly working together with hope and optimism for better lives.[6] As the Japanese economy has stagnated and as neoliberal policy has justified growing economic polarization in the last few decades, this type of historical narrative appears to have acquired greater appeal as a convenient tool for shifting the locus of solidarity from the socioeconomic to the cultural sphere. It is not a mere coincidence that Abe Shinzō of the LDP, who, during his tenure as prime minister from 2012 to 2020, demonstrated little intention to assert the state's constitutional responsibility for the welfare of the people while eagerly dismantling the notion of the social, highly praised *Always: Sunset on Third Street* (Abe 2006).

The goal of *Cinema of Discontent* is to construct diverse counter-narratives that cannot be co-opted by or absorbed into the conventional narrative that represents high-speed growth as a grandiose national project. This book sheds light on the heterogeneity of experiences generated by high-speed growth and examines what it meant to undergo this historical event, without reducing it to either a self-congratulatory story of success or a redemptive story of patience. For this, we must first acknowledge a simple fact: high-speed growth was a massive and rapid capitalist expansion. During this period, the Japanese state fully committed itself to the reconstruction and growth of its economy in Cold War Asia under American tutelage (e.g., the singing of the Security Treaty in 1951 and participation in the Mutual Security Act program in 1954). Corporate managers mobilized men and women from cities, suburbs, and villages and galvanized them to compete in the market while the LDP, central and local governments, bureaucrats, academics, and others facilitated this process through various economic, social, and educational policies (e.g., "mass employment," or *shūdan shūshoku*, from the 1950s to 1970s; the New Life campaign in the 1950s; and the discourse of "industrial society" in the 1960s). These men and women were encouraged (or required) to act not only as workers willing to serve employers diligently but also as consumers eager to spend money on personal and familial needs and pleasures (e.g., the TVs, washing machines, and refrigerators promoted as "three sacred treasures" in the 1950s) and as patriotic and disciplined citizens committed to contributing to the national good (e.g., the state-led "income doubling plan" in the 1960s). High-speed growth was frankly an intense form of accumulation through the intense enhancement of the production of surplus value, carefully arranged by the joint forces of the state and the business world.[7] As such, it was fundamentally a contradictory process accompanied by numerous tensions and anxieties related to, for example, the uneven distribution of wealth within society, the economic and cultural gap between the city and the countryside, the alienation and powerlessness of individual workers, growing and irreversible corporate control over everyday life, militarized peace and prosperity, the overgrowth of metropolises, and precarious and contingent work.

If we place these problems within the conventional narrative of high-speed growth, they look like obstacles that people in Japan had to overcome or simply come to terms with as the society became affluent and as the nation acquired the status of a global economic power. In other words, by adopting the conventional narrative of high-speed growth as the basic framework for remembering postwar history, we might end up interpreting these problems at most as secondary issues that bring complexity, nuance, and a bit of drama to this narrative, thereby concealing the contradictions and violence structurally embedded in the economic and political system of postwar Japan. But, of course, the people who were living through high-speed growth, especially in its early phase in the 1950s, did not possess such a grand narrative with which to construe (or glamorize) the tensions and anxieties they were facing. It is possible that the immense social changes that were occurring back then were more confusing and disquieting than promising and exciting. People were likely more concerned about how these changes were affecting their immediate lives and livelihoods and how to protect themselves from these changes than how the changes would be remembered. If we are to understand the experiences of high-speed growth earnestly, we must acknowledge these points and consider how to construct a set of narratives that permits us to represent the tensions and anxiety of this historical event without trivializing them.

Methodology: Historicization of Cinematic Texts

To achieve this purpose, *Cinema of Discontent* analyzes cultural texts, particularly feature-length fictional films produced in the two decades between the 1950s and 1970s. In making this decision to focus on cultural history, I agree with such historians of modern Japan as Yoshikuni Igarashi and Miriam Silverberg in their insistence upon treating culture as a historically constituted, inherently political, and above all potentially subversive category. In *Bodies of Memory*, Igarashi (2000) analyzes the "absent presence" of Japan's war memory that appeared in various cinematic and literary representations and intellectual discourses between 1945 and 1970. In *Erotic Grotesque Nonsense*, Silverberg (2006) deals with cultural production in the interwar years and points out the new modern sensibilities that the masses had come to share, which did not always conform to emperor-centered statist ideology. *Cinema of Discontent* participates in the discussion advanced by these historians regarding the entangled links between culture and politics, or more precisely the politically engaged reading of cultural texts. This book seeks to demonstrate how the study of culture, which tends to be addressed within an abstract, ahistorical, and essentialized national context, can contribute to challenging and destabilizing the knowledge of postwar history that is widely accepted at the national level.

While there are many ways of studying cinematic texts, the approach I employ for this book is the close reading of these texts based on careful historicization. That is, I examine what narratives of high-speed growth I can extract from cinematic texts by considering their historical significance in conjunction with contemporary political, socioeconomic, and cultural conditions as well as intertextual relations with intellectual discourses and other cultural artifacts, such as literary works and popular songs. The work of film scholars Mitsuyo Wada-Marciano (2008) and Misono Ryōko (2012) on Shōchiku *gendaigeki* ("contemporary drama") in the interwar years provides critical insight into this effort. Resorting to the analytical concepts of "modernity" (Wada-Marciano) and "the nation-state" (Misono), they have unraveled and articulated the meanings and roles of seemingly apolitical *gendaigeki* texts within the context of such events as industrialization, Westernization, urban development, colonialism, and imperialism. Inspired by and building upon their historically oriented approaches, *Cinema of Discontent* brings historical specificity to the readings of postwar films and places them in a dialogue with the events, concerns, ideas, ideologies, and trends that prevailed in contemporary Japanese society.[8]

This is to say, I use cinematic texts as primary sources for the study of postwar history. But a cautious reader may point out that the cinematic texts I am dealing with are all fictional and that it is inappropriate for a historian to rely on these sources to tell the stories of what really happened and how it happened. My response is that I am not using these as sources that document historical figures, events, and statistics with accuracy as one of the primary criteria. To me, the value of these sources lies in the possibilities they open up for scrutiny of the people and society that produced them. A film text, as a cultural artifact produced collectively by a multitude of people, interweaves multivalent observations and commentaries on the transformations that a society experiences (though these observations and commentaries may not always be intentional), exhibiting in itself a specificity rooted in the social relations of the time when it is made. As such, film constitutes a part of the broader contemporary cultural and intellectual discourse, in the same way that, for instance, literature and literary criticism, history and historiography, philosophy, journalism, sociology, anthropology, art, and music do. My purpose in using films as sources is to identify these historically mediated, conditioned, but also limited observations and commentaries. I will attempt to descry, borrowing French historian Marc Ferro's expression, "what is latent behind what is apparent" and "the nonvisible by means of the visible" ([1977] 1988, 30) and thereby diversify the ways of remembering and narrating the events of the past—in this book's case, high-speed growth.

Let me offer a widely familiar example to clarify this point. Ozu Yasujirō's 1953 film *Tokyo Story* (*Tōkyō monogatari*), a film about the journey of an old married couple from Onomichi in Hiroshima Prefecture to see their children living and working in Tokyo, is probably one of the Japanese films best known and most acclaimed outside Japan, as well as being representative of Japanese cinema's postwar "golden age." The director's unique stylistic camerawork, including "tatami shots" (taken by a low-positioned camera) and "pillow shots" (brief shots of static objects that do not seem particularly relevant to the main plot), has commonly led critics to discuss this film (and Ozu's oeuvre broadly) within the framework of auteurism and national aesthetics, as if it represented some sort of cultural and spiritual value system shared by people in Japan.[9] If I were to use *Tokyo Story* as a historical source, however, my approach would be quite different (though I do not discuss this film extensively in this book). First, we would need to identify key themes and motifs addressed in the film—for instance, Tokyo as a major destination of labor migration since the prewar era, the reconstruction of the urban middle class in the early postwar years, and economic and cultural unevenness between the capital (Tokyo) and a provincial city (Onomichi). Next, we would gather sources that help us better appreciate these themes and motifs within the historical context of Japan circa 1953, which might include statistics on the recovery of Tokyo's economy and the movement of people from the countryside to Tokyo; contemporary analyses of these issues, such as white papers; the media coverage of these issues; and films, novels, and popular songs on the topic of "going up to the capital," or *jōkyō* (as chapter 2 shows, this topic had been depicted again and again in cultural representations since the prewar era). Throughout this process, we would ask what observations of Japanese society on the eve of high-speed growth we can read into this film, whether at the level of plot or cinematography, and what historical narrative we can construct by combining these observations with other available discourses of contemporary Japanese society. In sum, to use *Tokyo Story* as a historical source is to articulate in detail the significance of the fact that it was made not in, say, 1949 or 1958 but in 1953 and to incorporate this historical specificity into our appreciation of this film.

Maruyama Masao and the History of Ideas

Maruyama Masao's discussion of methodologies for *shisōshi*, or "the history of ideas" ([1961] 1996), based on a lecture that he had delivered in 1960, has helped me conceptualize this task of constructing historical narratives through the analysis of cinematic texts. Defining himself as a specialist in the field of the history of ideas, Maruyama distinguishes his own field from two other related fields. First is what he calls *shisōron*, or the "theory of ideas." He explains that people in this field generally aim to construct their own philosophies. Although their philosophies may derive from the examination of historical sources, it is not unusual for them to use ideas from the past without considering the contexts from which they emerged. Maruyama does not talk much about this field, but one suspects that he has in mind those, probably outside academia, interested mainly in applying historically specific ideas, whether from China, India, Greece, or France, to contemporary Japanese society for practical purposes. The other field he distinguishes his own from is positivist history. Here, he is clearly referring to those historians who believe that they can tell stories about the past free from subjective judgments through the careful selection and presentation of primary sources. Maruyama positions his own work in between these two fields and argues that a historian of ideas is just like an "instrumentalist" (*ensōka*) in the field of music. Just as the instrumentalist is expected to express their own imagination and creativity through performance but is also constrained by the scores that composers of the past wrote, the historian of ideas seeks to provide their own ideas and interpretations through narratives but must also reference historical sources to corroborate these ideas and interpretations. Maruyama sees the essence of the work of the historian of ideas in its dual nature—proactive and creative engagement with sources from the past and recognition of limits imposed by the same sources—and the dialectic interaction between the two. Like Maruyama, I see myself as a historian of ideas (or, using his metaphor, an instrumentalist), and as such I employ my own imagination to construct historical narratives based on my own readings of cinematic texts, but I also ensure that my readings are not arbitrary and random but are validated through the incorporation of relevant and responsible sources.

To me, one of the greatest allures of this approach is that it permits me to analyze cinematic texts with a degree of nuance, subtlety, and sensitivity. The films that I analyze in *Cinema of Discontent*, which include a light romantic comedy (chapter 2), a spy film (chapter 3), and an action film (chapter 4), do not always address the anxieties and tensions of high-speed growth explicitly. Some might point out that there are films produced during the same period that tackled these issues more directly. For example, Kobayashi Masaki's *Black River* (*Kuroi kawa*, 1957), set in a town adjacent to a US base, depicts the resistance of destitute residents in a shabby old tenement to the greedy landlord's proposal to sell it to a developer who plans to build a cabaret for American GIs there. Urayama Kirio's *Foundry Town* (*Kyūpora no aru machi*, 1962) portrays the everyday life of a schoolgirl, played by a young Yoshinaga Sayuri, living in a working-class neighborhood in the industrial city of Kawaguchi in Saitama Prefecture. Ōshima Nagisa's *Death by Hanging* (*Kōshikei*, 1968), inspired by the rape and murder of a schoolgirl by a Korean Japanese man, sheds light on the poverty and racism faced by the *zainichi* Korean community in postwar society. But I have consciously chosen to examine films that seem made primarily to entertain a mass audience instead of such films designed to raise awareness of social problems. This is because Maruyama's methodology, which values the balancing of one's imagination and the historicization of texts, urges us to direct our attention not only to the main plots of cinematic texts but also to characters' seemingly trivial dialogue, their unspoken backstories, their bodies and movements, their occupations, the sites of location shooting, the music, and the items in the mise-en-scène, and thereby make meanings and ascertain relevance where we might not ordinarily expect to do so. For example, when the heroine in Masumura Yasuzō's *Blue-Sky Girl* (*Aozora musume*, 1957), discussed in chapter 2, engages in various physical activities, such as Ping-Pong and dance, I ask what these activities could have meant within the contexts of gender relations and patriarchy in the 1950s. When two men in Kumashiro Tatsumi's *The Light of Africa* (*Afurika no hikari*, 1975), discussed in chapter 5, share an apartment in a small fishing town in Hokkaido, that prompts me to consider how we can link their cohabitation and homosocial affect to the economic recession brought on by the 1973 oil crisis.

Furthermore, Maruyama's methodological discussion invites me to be conscious of the historicity or historically conditioned and restricted nature of my own desire to study postwar history through engagement with cinematic texts. In the lecture mentioned above, as an example of his scholarship as a historian of ideas, Maruyama talks about the reexamination of the notion of loyalty to a master in feudal relations since the Warring States period in Japan. While this notion has commonly been understood as one's absolute and blind obedience to one's master, Maruyama, through the reading of various historical sources, argues that the recognition that one was tied to a master by fate and therefore could not leave him under any circumstances could actually result in one's strong commitment to correcting the master's wrongdoings, if necessary, and that it was exactly this ethos shared by concerned warriors that worked as a driving force for the Meiji Restoration.[10] When he spoke about this in October 1960, Japanese society was in the immediate aftermath of the massive nationwide protest against the signing of the revised US-Japan Security Treaty, or Anpo. Just like many other intellectuals, students, and workers in contemporary Japan, Maruyama took the LDP's railroading of the revised Anpo in the Diet as an indefensible challenge to democracy and supported the protest, finding in it the possibility for Japanese people to further cultivate democratic consciousness (Maruyama [1960] 1996b, [1960] 1996c). This political condition undoubtedly fueled his wish to understand through the reassessment of historical sources the ethos of social transformation (or revolution) not simply as an import from the modern West but as something rooted in Japan's own history and thereby to validate and empower the popular movement for democracy.

Similarly, my attempt to construct alternative narratives of high-speed growth is a product of the political and social environment that permeates present-day Japan (and beyond). I am referring especially to the rise of neoliberalism as the dominant ideology of social governance. Japan's ruling elite in the past two decades or so actively propagated such ideas as "structural reform" (*kōzō kaikaku*), "deregulation" (*kisei kanwa*), "reform of the ways of working" (*hatarakikata kaikaku*), "a society where all one hundred million people participate actively" (*ichioku sōkatsuyaku shakai*), and "the energy of the private sector" (*minkan katsuryoku*) in order to further accustom current and future workers as well as already retired workers to the principles of competition. What is worse in Japan's case is that long-term rule by the LDP, while encouraging competition among workers, has also exacerbated grave cronyism, which prioritizes connections and personal friendship over merit and ability in the world of business and politics, invalidating the notion of a just society. The vivid images of Japanese society that the proponents of neoliberal policy foreground—freed from conventions and restrictions and rife with possibilities and opportunities—work to conceal the uncertainty and unpredictability brought about by the current political and socioeconomic system, or in some cases even identify them as stepping-stones for the nation's financial health and economic survival ("reforms accompanied with pain," or *itami o tomonau kaikaku*, in the common formulation). It is this type of glorification of the social reality that has driven me to the study of historical narratives. I hope that this book, by detailing anxieties and tensions during high-speed growth as problems intrinsic to the system of capitalism (rather than contingent and temporary), will contribute to critiquing the forces that seek to impose specific ways of narrating what is happening in Japan today and thereby to foster specific thinking and behavior that conform to such narratives.

"Place" as an Analytical Category

One thing I cannot help noticing when watching films made around the time of high-speed growth is their remarkable sensitivity to various places in Japan. Filmmakers back then conducted location shootings in many places and made actors and actresses learn the dialect of each place, through which they tried to convey to the audience the landscapes, cultures, communities, and ambience characteristic of those places. Kinoshita Keisuke's *Twenty-Four Eyes* (*Nijūshi no hitomi*, 1954), shot on idyllic Shōdo Island in the Seto Inland Sea, portrays the interchange between a schoolteacher, played by Takamine Hideko, and her twelve students, played by local children, over eighteen years from the 1920s to the immediate postwar era (though not all these students survive poverty and the war). In the same director's *Immortal Love* (*Eien no hito*, 1961), the unchanged nature of Mount Aso in southern Japan is effectively contrasted with the distress and sorrow of the heroine, again played by Takamine, who has no choice but to marry the man who raped and impregnated her, while giving up the man she truly loves. In Nakamura Noboru's *Ki River* (*Ki-no-kawa*,

1966), adapted from Ariyoshi Sawako's ([1959] 2006) well-known novel, this splendid river flowing through Wakayama Prefecture provides an important backdrop for the main motif of the tension between a traditional mother (Tsukasa Yōko) and a rebellious daughter (Iwashita Shima) from the Meiji to the Shōwa era. Kuroki Kazuo's *Preparation for the Festival* (*Matsuri no junbi*, 1975), based on the experience of screenwriter Nakajima Takehiro, depicts the life of a young man in a provincial town in Kōchi Prefecture (Etō Jun) and his boredom, sexual curiosity, longing for Tokyo, and dream of becoming a screenwriter. Of course, we can also think about Yamada Yōji's "Tora-san" series with Atsumi Kiyoshi and Nikkatsu's "Rambler" (*Wataridori*) series with Kobayashi Akira. These are just a few examples, but what I want to point out is that those involved in filmmaking back then were extremely conscious of the power that place possessed—that is, the specific images, affects, and moods that a specific place could induce—and regarded it as a crucial attraction that film could offer. When a 1957 *Asahi* newspaper article praised the large-scale location shooting conducted by Kinoshita Keisuke for his *Times of Joy and Sorrow* (*Yorokobi mo kanashimi mo ikutoshitsuki*, 1957), saying that people would become bored of Japanese cinema if it depicted only Ginza ("Nihonjū o roke suru" 1957), it was clearly referencing the regular audience's growing interest in discovering and learning about different places on screen at the onset of high-speed growth.

With this fact in mind, I have chosen as objects of study for this book films that are set in a variety of places in Japan and have adopted "place" as a useful analytical category. Whereas high-speed growth is often narrated and remembered as a collective and shared experience of the nation, if we shift our attention to different places within the nation-state, including the metropolis, suburb, port city, countryside, resort town, and "periphery," we can effectively complicate the dominant mode of narrating this historical event. In other words, by complementing and relativizing the common analytical category of the nation-state, which certainly has its own merits but easily falls into the problems of overgeneralization and abstraction, place can bring more concreteness to our analysis and make us more cognizant of the difference, conflict, and unevenness that exist within the nation-state. Once we focus on place, we can no longer speak about high-speed growth simply as a national event but are compelled to consider seriously such issues as whether this process is applicable to all places within the nation-state, how the experiences of major cities like Tokyo and Osaka differed from those of farming and fishing communities in rural Japan, and how we can fathom the relations between places with different socioeconomic backgrounds.

When I say *place* in this book, I do not mean simply a geographical point or physical setting. As geographers and urban historians alike have indicated, a place is a social construct—that is, a space that has been (re)organized through activities, whether physical or intellectual, social or personal, for specific purposes and uses and into which specific meanings have been woven accordingly. These meanings are established and solidified by the entwined interactions between those who develop, control, and manage that place; those who live and work there; and those who visit, imagine, and tell stories about it and, in turn, contribute to shaping people's perceptions, experiences, desires, and memories regarding that place. Furthermore, whereas a place often has a set of prevailing meanings broadly recognized at the global, national, or regional level (or what one might call public images), it is often the case that the same place implies multifaceted, multilayered, and sometimes conflicting and hierarchical meanings and images depending on class, birth and origin, status, occupation, race, ethnicity, gender, sexual orientation, and many other personal and social factors of those involved with that place (Jones and Evans 2012; Hayden 1997; Tuan 1977; Relph 1976). If we think about, for instance, Kobe, the widely shared public image of this major city in the Kansai region may be that of an exotic and stylish port city, but some people may imagine it primarily as the site of the catastrophic Hanshin-Awaji earthquake of 1995. While art historians may associate Kobe with modernist art and architectural movements in the interwar years, so-called Hanshin-kan modernism, researchers of immigration and diaspora may think about its large Chinese and Korean communities. Or, for a person like myself, raised in a small, insipid suburban town in Hyogo Prefecture, downtown Kobe—Sannomiya and Motomachi—may signify an urban center where excitement and anonymity are guaranteed.

The conceptualization of place as socially constructed and culturally polysemous is important for the argument in *Cinema of Discontent* for the following two reasons. The first is that the representations of places in the cinematic texts examined in this book are grounded upon the historically accumulated knowledge of these places that had been disseminated in Japanese society by then. For example, Kawashima Yūzō's *Susaki Paradise Red Light* (*Susaki Paradaisu aka-shingō*, 1956;

discussed in chapter 1) is set in two neighborhoods in the central part of Tokyo: Susaki and Akihabara. Their representations derive from the images of these two places familiar to contemporary viewers, at least in Tokyo and its metropolitan region: the former as a declining red-light district faced with the upcoming enforcement of the Anti-Prostitution Law and the latter as a neighborhood metamorphosing into a vibrant "electric town." By juxtaposing these two places, the film effectively draws attention to uneven development within the city. In Masumura's *Blue-Sky Girl*, the appreciation of the main plot of the heroine's movement from a small town in Izu to Tokyo requires an understanding of the contrasting images of the countryside as a supplier of workers and the city as a place for the achievement of professional and personal success—images that became popularized in the interwar years and were further reinforced in the postwar era. The representations of Yokohama in Ezaki Mio's *A Warm Misty Night* (*Yogiri yo kon'ya mo arigatō*, 1967; discussed in chapter 4) presuppose the audience's shared knowledge of this place as a cosmopolitan trade port as well as a military town with large American bases. In sum, filmmakers did not pick these places (and the locations of the other films examined in this book) randomly or simply as a matter of convenience but by deliberating upon the cultural meanings ascribed to them; my effort to historicize these films therefore unavoidably requires an appreciation of these meanings.

The second reason to adopt the perspective of place as socially constructed and culturally polysemous is that these films also sought to create new meanings for places. For example, the representations of Osaka in Inoue Akira's *Black Weapon* (*Kuro no kyōki*, 1964; discussed in chapter 3) betray viewers' common expectations because this metropolis does not appear as a vital merchant city with a long history or a city of *ninjō* (human warmth and kindness)—associations conventionally applied to Osaka. Quite the contrary; by showing repeatedly the artificial landscape of the newly launched suburban community in northern Osaka, the film brings to light the anonymity, standardization, and what Edward Relph (1976) calls "placelessness," characteristic of highly industrialized societies such as postwar Japan. When Kumashiro's *The Light of Africa* portrays a small fishing community in eastern Hokkaido, it does not stress the serene and innocent nature of rural Japan, which the National Railway's "Discover Japan" campaign was enthusiastically promoting at that time, but redirects viewers' attention to the exhaustion and frustration of a provincial community left behind by high-speed growth. By assigning new meanings to these places, these films transmuted, challenged, and destabilized the existing meanings and thereby constructed a constellation of more complex meanings, which urges us to consider what political and socioeconomic factors prompted these new meanings and how we can incorporate them into our narratives of high-speed growth (see map I.1).

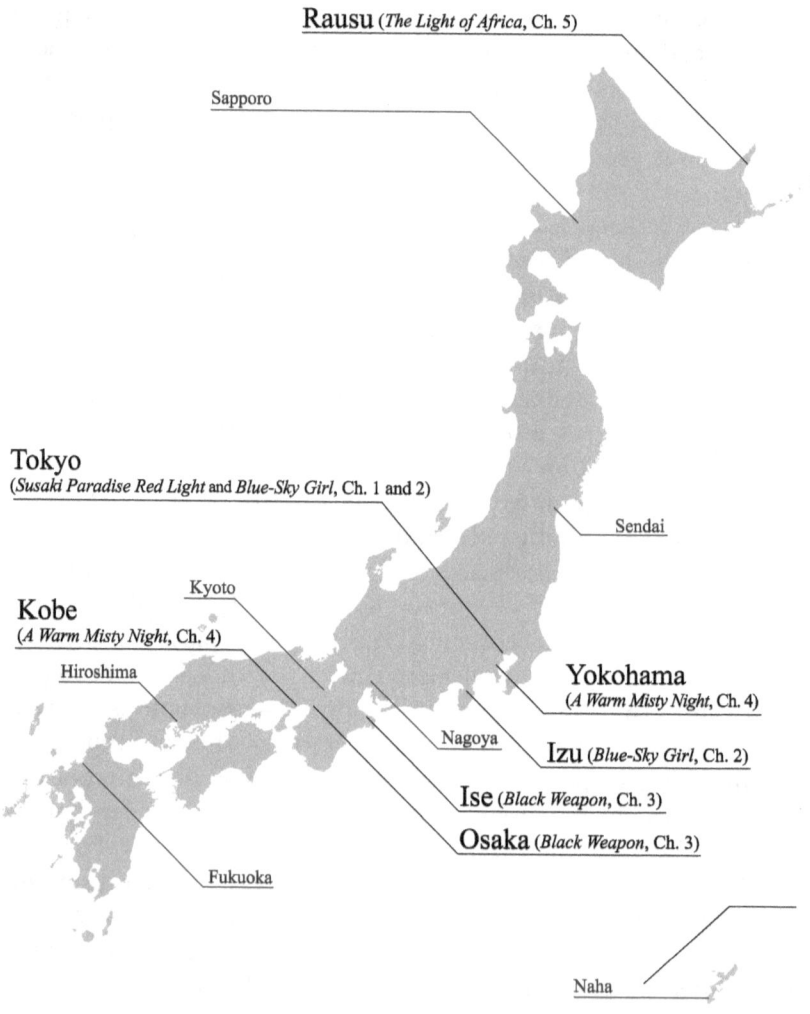

Map I.1. Places discussed in *Cinema of Discontent*.

Chapter Organization

Cinema of Discontent comprises five chapters. These are organized chronologically, covering the period between 1956 and 1975, which roughly coincides with the two decades of high-speed growth and its immediate aftermath—that is, from the so-called Jinmu boom to the oil crisis and recession. Each chapter analyzes one film thoroughly and offers a historically contextualized close reading while also paying attention to other relevant films and forms of cultural representation.

The first chapter, "Drifting in Tokyo," discusses Kawashima Yūzō's *Susaki Paradise Red Light* (1956). This film was released at the very beginning of high-speed growth, the same month as the Economic Planning Agency's white paper that included the famous statement "It is no longer the 'postwar'" ("mohaya 'sengo' dewa nai"), indicating that postwar reconstruction had been completed (Keizai Kikakuchō 1956). While Kawashima's films have often been treated lightly as *fūzoku* films—films that depict the inconsequential everyday lives of ordinary people—my goal in this chapter is to read *Susaki Paradise* as a critical counterpoint to the discussion incited by the Japanese state's confident assertions in this white paper about the state of the Japanese economy. This film's depiction of the precarious life of a penniless young man and woman (Mihashi Tatsuya and Aratama Michiyo), rather, highlights the legacies of wartime destruction and the tardiness of reconstruction. Furthermore, through the analysis of the characters' movements through Tokyo neighborhoods and their negotiations, this chapter also examines the spatial manifestation of the uneven recovery from wartime damage in the mid-1950s.

The second chapter, "A Girl from Izu," focuses on Masumura Yasuzō's *Blue-Sky Girl* (1957). This director's second film deals with a young woman's pursuit of romantic love and search for her biological mother after she moves to Tokyo from a rural fishing town in Izu in Shizuoka Prefecture. While its bright cinematography and positive, outgoing heroine, played by Wakao Ayako, project the arrival of a new era of peace, democracy, and growth, this chapter locates the film within the context of the contemporary migration of young rural workers to cities, or more correctly their displacement from their hometowns for the sake of urban industrial development, entailed by demands from the business world and the state. In so doing, it interprets the heroine as speaking on behalf of these numerous nameless wage laborers, expressing their predicament and loneliness, and explains how the protagonist's seemingly unconstrained, liberated body also stands for the disciplined body required for social success within the particular gender order of 1950s Japan.

The third chapter, "Osaka, City of Spies," concerns Inoue Akira's *Black Weapon* (1964). In the conventional narrative of postwar history, the year 1964 is remembered as the height of high-speed economic growth. The country's GDP was rising rapidly. Tokyo hosted the Summer Olympics. The Shinkansen, the world's first high-speed train, started service between Tokyo and Osaka. *Black Weapon*, however, presents an extremely grim and depressing image of economic growth. Set and shot in Osaka, which is represented as a modern industrial city devoid of geo-cultural and historical particularities, the film depicts brutal corporate espionage and the fate of a young factory worker (Tamiya Jirō) whose dream of a stable, middle-class life has been destroyed by it. Detailing the course of this protagonist's transformation into an industrial spy himself and his revenge on the company executives, this chapter discusses the powerlessness and atomization of individual workers and how spies are imagined as those free from social constraints in the ever-swelling corporate society of the 1960s.

The focus of chapter 4, "Yokohama Romance," is Ezaki Mio's *A Warm Misty Night* (1967). This film is set in contemporary Yokohama, and the protagonist (Ishihara Yūjirō) is a former sailor who runs a nightclub at the city's harbor but also engages in the clandestine business of helping those who have to flee Japan for various reasons. The story develops around the triangular relationship of this nightclub owner, his former lover (Asaoka Ruriko), and her husband (Nitani Hideaki), who is from an unidentified Southeast Asian country and needs the protagonist's support to return to his homeland to lead a revolution that has just started there. This chapter incorporates into its reading of the film the politics of contemporary Japan, particularly its complicity with the United States' war in Vietnam, and the history of modern Yokohama as a vibrant port city for international trade since the Meiji era and as a host to American military bases in the postwar era. I draw attention to the tension that the protagonist faces as he benefits economically from the presence of American troops in Yokohama but simultaneously attempts to demonstrate his pan-Asian solidarity by ceding his former lover to the Southeast Asian revolutionary.

Finally, chapter 5, "Waiting for Spring in Shiretoko," analyzes Kumashiro Tatsumi's *The Light of Africa* (1975). The film was released two years after the 1973 oil crisis that brought an end to high-speed growth and led to a large-scale recession. In the film, two jobless friends (Hagiwara Ken'ichi and Tanaka Kunie) come to a small fishing town on Shiretoko Peninsula in eastern Hokkaido in the winter, planning to work and save money until the spring, when they hope to board a ship to Africa. However, the two men encounter various obstacles—poverty, deteriorating health, and ostracism—and eventually give up their dream. Together with this plot, the images of dark, snowy Hokkaido create a despondent atmosphere. I link this atmosphere to the sense of malaise that caught Japanese society during the oil-crisis recession by examining the two men's precarious work conditions, the fishing town as a rural community distressed by a long-term state policy that prioritized the growth of the metropolitan regions, and the idea of Africa not so much as a concrete destination but as a fantasy that permits the two men to transcend their hopeless economic reality.

Note on Japanese Names and Titles

Macrons are used to indicate long vowels, such as Tamiya Jirō, Kyō Machiko, and Susaki-Bentenchō. But they are not used in the commonly recognized names of regions, prefectures, and major cities, such as Hokkaido (instead of Hokkaidō), Osaka (instead of Ōsaka), and Kobe (instead of Kōbe).

There seems to be no generally agreed upon way of rendering the titles of Japanese films, novels, songs, and other cultural artifacts in English. Assuming that some readers do not have any knowledge of the Japanese language (and hoping that this book reaches readers interested in Japanese culture broadly), I have put titles in English translation first and then the Japanese original title in parentheses. If the work has circulated widely in the United States and/or other English-speaking countries under a certain title (e.g., if the film was officially released with English subtitles), I use that title even if it is not a literal translation of the original title. If the literal translation seems helpful for the appreciation of that work or is central to my argument, I give it in parentheses after the original title. If it is impossible to translate the film's title into English, only the original title is used, but this is followed by an explanation of the meaning of the title in parentheses. For example:

- *Black Weapon* (*Kuro no kyōki*, 1964)
- "Sentiment of Travel in Shiretoko" ("Shiretoko ryojō," 1970)
- *Street of Shame* (*Akasen chitai*, 1956; literally "red-line district")
- *Bonchi* (1960; the title refers to the young son and heir to a merchant family in Osaka)

1

Drifting in Tokyo

Reconstruction and Uneven Development in Kawashima Yūzō's *Susaki Paradise Red Light* (1956)

If you are a fool, so am I
If you knew I was a fool, why did you fall in love?
We fell and drifted to this back street
This is now our temporary home

>—"Back Street Nocturne" ("Uramachi yakyoku"),
>sung by Kasuga Hachirō, 1954

I, too, am one of the buddies
When the sun sets, I always come to
Twilight Tavern
Sit on a broken stool
Drink the stuff as hot as fire

>—"Twilight Tavern" ("Tasogare sakaba"),
>sung by Frank Nagai, 1958

JAPAN FOUND ITSELF IN AN economic quandary in the first five years after defeat in World War II. Bombings by the United States had destroyed major cities. Production halted. The reconstruction of industrial infrastructure proceeded only slowly. As the empire was dismantled, more than six million Japanese—both civilians and military personnel—began repatriating from the former colonies and other parts of Asia and the Pacific, causing a sharp increase in population on the archipelago. Food production could not keep up with this growth. Many, particularly those in cities, suffered from malnutrition, starvation, and poor health. Urban streets and train stations filled with children who had lost parents, many of whom eventually starved to death. The Dodge Plan, which the US occupation forces enforced in 1949 to curb the persistent inflation, resulted in a deep recession, as unemployment and bankruptcies soared.

The Korean War provided an unexpected opportunity for the Japanese economy. The massive procurement orders that Japanese companies received from the US military triggered the rapid revival of the textile, metal, construction, and service industries. This war also made the United States aware of the geopolitical importance of Japan in an Asia-Pacific region troubled by the Cold War, forcing it to rehabilitate its former enemy as a stable military ally and to integrate Japan into its capitalist bloc. In 1954, Japan participated in the United States' Mutual Security Act program, a foreign aid program designed to contain the waves of revolution. Through this program, Japan secured economic support from the United States in exchange for a commitment to the continued pursuit of rearmament, which led later the same year to the creation of the Self-Defense Forces, a full-fledged military organization developed out of the National Police Reserve (established in 1950) and the National Safety Force (1952).[1] In the same year came the Jinmu boom, its name implying a scale unprecedented in the history of Japan since the legendary first emperor. Retrospectively, this was seen as the very beginning of the era of high-speed economic growth that lasted for about two decades, until the 1973 oil crisis.

When narrating history, designating the start of a historical event as such can give the impression that many dramatic, visible changes subsequently unfolded. But this is not always the case. Historical changes and transitions can be sluggish, inconsistent, and halting. It is possible that people living amid that historical event are not fully aware that significant changes are taking place but realize it only retrospectively through the historical narratives that become available later. High-speed growth is one such event. Even after high-speed growth supposedly started in the mid-1950s, many working people remained concerned about their everyday recovery from the various losses and damages caused by the war. It took far longer than the conventional narrative of postwar history suggests for regular people living in Japan to enjoy the perks of the growing national economy.

The aim of this chapter is to examine cultural representations of Japanese society at the very beginning of this era of growth. It does so through the analysis of *Susaki Paradise Red Light* (*Susaki Paradaisu aka-shingō*, hereafter *Susaki Paradise*), directed by Kawashima Yūzō and released in July 1956. "Susaki Paradise" is the name of a licensed quarter that existed in a neighborhood called Susaki-Bentenchō (now Tōyōchō in Kōtō Ward) on a small artificial island in the southeastern part of Tokyo and remained active until the full enforcement of the Anti-Prostitution Law in 1958.[2] Kawashima's film is set in a neighborhood just outside this licensed quarter, or more precisely the neighborhood right by the bridge that leads into the quarter. It depicts a twisted romantic relationship between a woman who used to be a prostitute in Susaki Paradise and a jobless and exhausted man, the former played by Aratama Michiyo, previously a star of the Takarazuka Revue, and the latter played by Mihashi Tatsuya, a regular of Kawashima's films.

At first glance, *Susaki Paradise* may not seem particularly relevant to a discussion of such a momentous historical event as high-speed growth since the man, the woman, and the others in the film are simply concerned with personal matters in a small neighborhood in Tokyo. To highlight its historical relevance, I contrast this cinematic text to another text released coincidently around the same time as *Susaki Paradise*, namely the Economic Planning Agency's annual white paper. In today's Japan, this white paper constitutes a part of the national memory of postwar history and is frequently referenced by historians, journalists, and commentators alike, for it pointed out the nation's swift economic recovery from the war and proclaimed the completion of postwar reconstruction. When we examine *Susaki Paradise* in comparison to this white paper, it becomes evident that this film by Kawashima presents a narrative that counters or at least diverges from the positive interpretation of the nation's economic performance promoted by the state bureaucrats.

I first situate Kawashima as a director of *fūzoku* films who vigorously depicted the social and cultural atmosphere of contemporary Japan and consider the implication of this labeling. Second, I demonstrate how *Susaki Paradise*, through its representations of the penniless couple and the neighborhood in which they try to settle, draws attention to the persistent legacies of the war, the difficulty in overcoming them, and the economic struggle of everyday life in a society that is supposedly entering a new phase of growth. I also compare this neighborhood's representation to that of a few other places observed in the film as well as the movement of some characters between them, thereby examining the process by which uneven development was intensifying at the spatial level within the city of Tokyo. Finally, I articulate the seductiveness of the liminality offered by the neighborhood by the bridge, resorting to the concept of *muen*, or "no ties," and demonstrate how it is represented as an urban space where various social constraints are suspended—if only temporarily.

Kawashima Yūzō and *Fūzoku* Films

Kawashima often set his films in urban sites in contemporary Japan—that is, Japan between the mid-1940s and early 1960s (sadly, he passed away in 1963 at the age of 45)—and depicted the lives of people living and working in these places while addressing a variety of issues that people then were concerned about in a humorous, entertaining, and sometimes self-consciously vulgar manner. His 1955 *Tales of Ginza* (*Ginza nijūyonchō*) was set in neighborhoods in central Tokyo such as Ginza and Shinbashi; features Mihashi Tatsuya as Mr. Coney, a kind, handsome, modern-looking florist; and showed the underground world of drugs, crime, and money in early postwar Tokyo. *Burden of Love* (*Ai no onimotsu*, 1955) dealt with the issues of the baby boom and rapid population growth, centering on a minister of health and welfare (Yamamura Sō) who publicly promotes birth control and contraception but finds out that his forty-eight-year-old wife (Todoroki Yukiko) has accidently become pregnant. *The Kiss Thief* (*Seppun dorobō*, 1960), adapted from Ishihara Shintarō's novel, was a light, upbeat comedy about romance between a womanizing professional boxer (Takarada Akira) and a girl from a strict private high school (Dan Reiko) in a society where people were becoming increasingly hungry for the sensational and the exciting at the early stage of high-speed growth. *Susaki Paradise* can be situated in this line of works from his oeuvre.

Contemporary critics labeled films such as the above "*fūzoku* films." In present-day Japanese, the term *fūzoku* is most commonly associated with the sex industry and various types of work conducted in that industry (as we see in such usages as *sei fūzoku*), and therefore people now refrain from using it in other senses to avoid confusion. But this term, in its original sense, carries much broader implications that denote the realm of regular people's everyday lives, including but not limited to customs, manners, trends, pastimes, festivals, foods, fashions, and vernacular languages. If *dentō*, or "tradition," indicates the ideas and practices that people pass down generation after generation (or, more correctly, those they *want to believe* they have passed down and will pass down), *fūzoku* refers to that which is more transient and changeable and characterized by strong association with a specific historical moment. For example, if sake and Kabuki are considered aspects of Japan's "tradition," bubble tea and Japanese hip-hop belong to its *fūzoku*, the connotation of which is that the latter is less important and serious in that it can perish quickly and be replaced by other similar trends (and, indeed, it appears that the bubble-tea boom has already ended in Japan, though it still excites young consumers in North America).

It was in this original sense of the term that contemporary critics described Kawashima's works as *fūzoku* films. They definitely shared a slight, though not always explicit, contempt and an impulse to trivialize his films as superficial, undeserving of deep examination, and serving primarily for entertainment (Ogura 2006; Ku 2018). This is evident when we consider the fact that the films made by those established and renowned directors such as Mizoguchi Kenji and Ozu Yasujirō (particularly in their later years) were seldom labeled by critics as *fūzoku* films even though they did address the *fūzoku* of contemporary Japanese society. The assumption behind this is that the films of these "giants" cannot be simply about the ephemeral phenomena of the time but must deal with deeper, more universal philosophical and spiritual themes that transcend their particular historical and cultural contexts.

Fūzoku, however, is not a discrete category insulated from more "serious" issues such as politics and the national economy. In this regard, Tosaka Jun's ([1936] 1966) discussion of the term is useful. Writing in the interwar period, which saw the rapid rise of modern *fūzoku*, he defined the phenomenon as an effect of the relations of production. That is, *fūzoku* is not simply a synonym for what people crave, practice, or consume in a given society; it is related to and transformed by the material conditions of the time under which people work and struggle for their livelihood. According to him, *fūzoku* is like "clothing" (*ifuku*) put on by "each phase or part of the essential structure of the society" ("shakai no honshitsuteki na kōzō no sorezore no dankai ya bubun"; 274). Therefore, when we observe the rise of a new phenomenon of *fūzoku*, we need to inquire into the social relations that operate under that clothing.[3] Although writing within the context of interwar Japan, Tosaka was clearly concerned about how *fūzoku* was generated and reified within the broader framework of the capitalist economy. Indeed, there is a great deal of commonality between his concerns in the interwar period and those of cultural studies scholars in the post–World War II period, such as Stuart Hall (1981), who rejected an essentialist understanding of popular culture and insisted on investigating it in connection to power relations of domination and subordination. Our analysis, too, must treat *fūzoku* not exclusively as a focus of observation but also as a symptom that allows us to probe the organization and configuration of contemporary Japanese society, investigating the political economy and power relations within which the *fūzoku* in question was produced and disseminated.

If we are to understand *Susaki Paradise* as a *fūzoku* film of the mid-1950s, we first need to locate the social and cultural meanings of Susaki Paradise within the historical context of modern Japan. Major cities in prewar Japan maintained state-authorized licensed quarters for legal prostitution. Susaki Paradise was one such licensed quarter, originally located in Nezu in Tokyo, not far from the Imperial University (present-day Tokyo University) in Hongō. Fearful that this proximity might have a corrupting influence on the elite students enrolled in the university at the state's expense, the Tokyo prefectural government decided to relocate the licensed quarter and ordered the building of an artificial island on landfill in Tokyo Bay. Construction was completed in 1887. The next year, the licensed quarter was moved to this island, to a new town named Susaki-Bentenchō, about 4.5 miles southeast of its original location, and prospered there as one of the most famous licensed quarters in Tokyo. The quarter was closed during the Pacific War as the buildings in this neighborhood were used as dormitories for workers at the munitions factories of such companies as Ishikawajima Shipyard, and then it was destroyed completely in the bombings by the US Air Force in March 1945. Soon after the end of the war, however, the quarter was revived as "Susaki Paradise" (Tōkyō Kyōshokuin Kumiai Kōtō Shibu 1987, 96–97; Kōtōku 1997, 25–26; see map 1.1).

Although the US occupation forces ordered the abolition of state-authorized prostitution in 1946, many of those who lost their jobs in the licensed quarters continued working as prostitutes on the street.[4] As the spread of venereal diseases became a serious concern for both the Japanese authorities and the US occupation forces late in 1946, the former designated certain neighborhoods as "special restaurant areas" (commonly known as *tokuingai*, an abbreviation of *tokushu inshokutengai*) where prostitution was tolerated. The designation

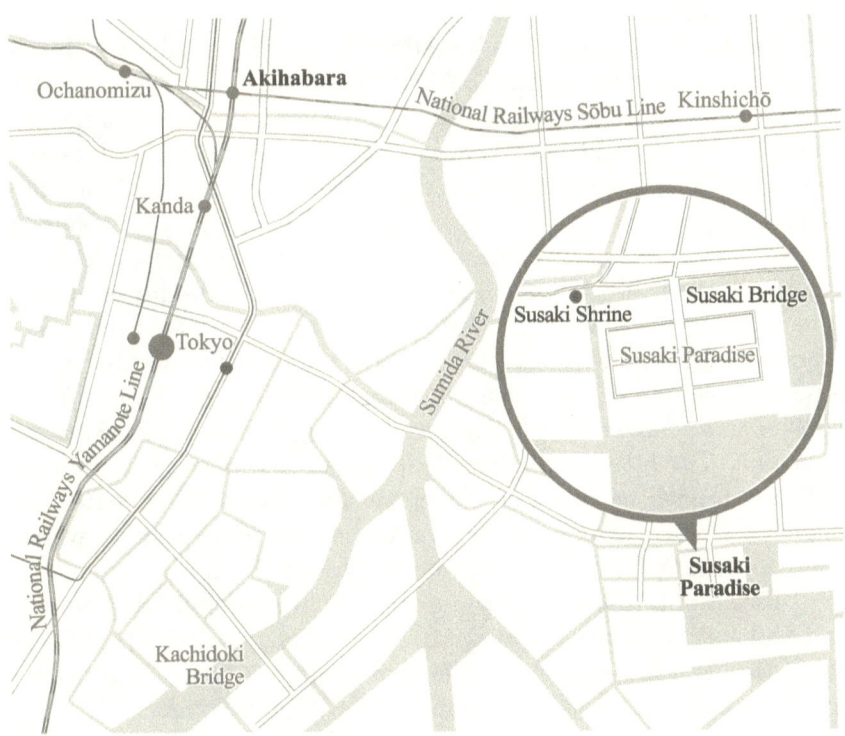

Map 1.1. Eastern Tokyo (circa 1956).

of these areas, which came to be known also as *akasen chitai* (red-line districts), marked the revival of state-authorized prostitution. Meanwhile, prostitution tailored for US military personnel in base towns also continued to flourish, and this generated moral and educational concerns among people in these communities. Accordingly, opposition emerged among Diet members—especially the Socialists—and women's organizations, which saw prostitution as immoral, antisocial, and uncivilized. In May 1956, the Diet passed the Anti-Prostitution Law (while the law came into effect in April 1957, the criminal punishment of those who violated the law was eventually postponed until April 1958).[5] But the problem with this law was that since it was written by parties hostile to prostitution, it was meant to criminalize the practice without offering any solution to the fundamental problem of poverty and gender-based discrimination that forced working-class women into it. Many women would continue to engage in prostitution illegally after the enforcement of this law, often manipulated by organized crime syndicates and pimps.[6]

As prostitution became a heated topic of public debate, its cultural representations thrived, too. Yoshiyuki Junnosuke's novellas *The City of Primary Colors* (*Genshoku no machi*) and *Sudden Shower* (*Shūu*) were published in 1951 and 1954, respectively—the former set in Hato-no-machi, or "dove town," a *tokuingai* that existed in east Asakusa, and the latter set in an unidentified *tokuingai* somewhere in Tokyo (Yoshiyuki 1966). *Sudden Shower* won the thirty-first Akutagawa Prize. Between 1954 and 1955, Shibaki Yoshiko, then already a well-known author who had won the fourteenth Akutagawa Prize in 1941 for her *Produce Market* (*Seika no ichi*; Shibaki [1941] 1997), published six novellas about Susaki Paradise: *Susaki Paradise* (*Susaki Paradaisu*), *Black Fire* (*Kuroi honō*), *Around Susaki* (*Susaki kaiwai*), *The City of Amusement* (*Kanraku no machi*), *Till I Become a Butterfly* (*Chō ni naru made*), and *Woman of Susaki* (*Susaki no onna*). In these novellas, Shibaki illuminates the plight of women working in or near Susaki Paradise, none of whom seem to benefit from the economic growth of the time.

Kawashima's *Susaki Paradise* is an adaptation of Shibaki's novellas, and Shibaki's work also inspired Mizoguchi Kenji, who directed *Street of Shame* (*Akasen chitai*, whose literal translation is "red-line district") in the same year that Kawashima made *Susaki Paradise*. Although Mizoguchi's film changed its setting to another *akasen chitai*, Yoshiwara, one of the most memorable characters in the film, Yumeko (Mimasu

Aiko), an old, worn-out prostitute who repatriated from Manchuria and ended up in Yoshiwara, is modeled after the protagonist of Shibaki's *Woman of Susaki*. Yumeko lost her husband in the war and raised her son with her own income, looking forward to living with him in a nice "reinforced concrete apartment" (*tekkin konkurīto no apāto*) someday. But her son, contemptuous and embarrassed of her occupation, abandons her, and she goes mad.[7] Unlike Mizoguchi's *Street of Shame*, Kawashima's *Susaki Paradise* hardly depicts the *akasen chitai*. While all the main characters in *Street of Shame* are prostitutes and almost the entire story takes place within their brothel, Yume-no-sato, or "Land of Dream," the young couple at the center of *Susaki Paradise*—Yoshiji and Tsutae—lives and works outside this quarter. The heavy presence of Susaki Paradise, however, is implied throughout the film, and declining state-authorized prostitution right before the enforcement of the Anti-Prostitution Law provides an important backdrop for the story. Below, I examine the *fūzoku* represented in this film—who these two drifters are, why they have ended up here, how the film represents the neighborhood right outside Susaki Paradise where they settle, and what relations exist between this neighborhood, Susaki Paradise, and the broader outside world—taking into account the discourses of the Japanese economy that arose in 1956.

July 1956: The Economic White Paper

In July 1956, a few months after the establishment of the Anti-Prostitution Law and the same month as the release of *Susaki Paradise Red Light*, the Economic Planning Agency published its annual economic white paper, with the subtitle "The growth and modernization of the Japanese economy" ("Nihon keizai no seichō to kindaika"). This white paper presented a positive and confident analysis of the Japanese economy, maintaining that 1955 had been the most prosperous year for the nation since the end of World War II. It pointed to the nation's growing exports, the improvement in the balance of payments, an increase in production, the stabilization of prices, and a rise in national income as well as per-capita income as conspicuous symptoms of economic recovery. By this year, the levels of industrial production and national income exceeded their pre-1945 peak levels, having grown at average annual rates of 22 and 11 percent respectively over the previous ten years (Keizai Kikakuchō 1956, 22–24). This allowed the Economic Planning Agency to conclude its discussion with the famous statement "it is no longer the 'postwar'" ("mohaya 'sengo' dewa nai"), indicating that economic reconstruction was complete (42). In Japan today, this statement is frequently cited in the narratives of postwar history and remembered as the proclamation of a new era of high-speed growth.

However, the tone of the white paper was in fact not optimistic but cautionary. The point of the statement "no longer the 'postwar'" was that Japan could no longer focus simply on the reconstruction of its economy but needed to think ahead, aiming for a true modernization of its structure for continued growth, which would be far more difficult than reconstruction. The white paper anticipated inevitable pain and resistance in this process and urged the nation to adapt quickly to "the technologies in the world that advance every day and the world environment changed by them" ("hibi ni susumi yuku sekai no gijutsu to sore ga kaete yuku sekai no kankyō"; 43). If the nation failed to do so, according to the white paper, Japan could not make up for the technological gap with advanced industrial countries and would be overtaken by underdeveloped countries in industrial production.[8]

This white paper met with intense criticism. Many did not accept its basic argument that now that national reconstruction had been completed, the Japanese economy needed to move to the next stage for global competition. In critics' views, national reconstruction was still far from completion and, therefore, *sengo*, or the "postwar," was persisting. Hanamori Yasuji (1956), the founder and chief editor of the women's magazine *Kurashi no techō*, candidly expressed his annoyance at the fact that the white paper focused on the supposed prosperity of the macro-level economy and ignored the plight of ordinary people. He asked how the white paper dared to say "no longer the 'postwar'" when many of those who had lost their houses during the war were still living in rented rooms, when many could not buy televisions on their own and were watching broadcasts through the windows of electronics shops, and when many could not even afford meat or eggs. For him, the white paper was trying to create a false image of the state of the Japanese economy by providing numbers but overlooking what those numbers truly meant to ordinary Japanese people or how those numbers were actually felt by them. A witty and humorous writer, Hanamori concluded that the white paper was actually an "empty paper," or *kūhakusho*, a pun on the Japanese term for "white paper," *hakusho* (4).

In a similar vein, the *Yomiuri* newspaper, explaining the main argument made in the white paper, pointed to the absence of an actual felt sense of economic recovery among the people, citing the shortage of housing, the low quality of clothing, and the accumulated debts under which many companies struggled. While the white paper promoted "high efficiency, high wages, and a high living standard" ("kō-nōritsu, kō-chingin, kō-seikatsu suijun"; "Chikayori-gatai yashinsaku" 1956, 3) as the ideal form of growth, the *Yomiuri* found this tenet—which was borrowed from American economic practices—unrealistic and unviable in contemporary Japan, where available capital for investment was still limited and many workers were being fired in the name of rationalization. Thus, these critics problematized the fact that the white paper, driven by a thirst for growth, glorified the success of a few sectors in Japanese society while ignoring the unresolved legacies of the war and the problem of class difference. Or, we can also argue that they were frustrated at the white paper's neat separation between the national and household economies and the deliberate refusal to address the latter.

According to an opinion survey on citizens' daily lives conducted by the Prime Minister's Office in February 1955, about one year and five months before the publication of the white paper, only a very small percentage of respondents (7.2 percent) felt that the quality of their lives had improved compared to the previous year. A large percentage felt that their lives either had not changed or had worsened (47.3 percent and 41.9 percent, respectively). As for their life prospects, only 11.9 percent expected them to improve, while 39.5 percent did not expect any change and 30.9 percent felt that they would worsen (see table 1.1). Another survey conducted three years later shows that a large majority had not yet seen any improvement in their lives compared to five or six years earlier (40 percent responded that their circumstances had not changed and 29 percent that they had worsened) and that nearly half (46 percent) still felt they had been better off in the prewar era.[9] It is safe to maintain that the critics of the white paper were indeed speaking for the regular working people of Japan back then. Although the year 1956 is often linked with that famous statement in today's conventional historical narrative, we should not forget that there still existed a deep sense of discontent and distress

Table 1.1. Opinion Survey on Citizens' Daily Lives (Selected Questionnaire)

Q 1. Has the quality of life in your household improved recently, compared to this time last year?	It has improved (7.2%) It has not changed (47.3%) It has worsened (41.9%) Do not know (3.6 %)
Q 2. How do you think the quality of life in society will change from now on?	It will improve (10.0%) It will not change (24.8%) It will worsen (40.2%) Do not know (25%)
Q 3. How about the quality of life in your household?	It will improve (11.9%) It will not change (39.5%) It will worsen (30.9%) Do not know (17%)
Q 13. In which of the three categories of clothing, food, and housing are you in most difficulty or need?	Food (28.7%) Clothing (24.0%) Housing (11.5%) All of them (13.3%) None of them (17.6%) Do not know (4.9%)

Poll of three thousand people between twenty and fifty-nine years of age in Japan, conducted by the Prime Minister's Office in February 1955. Based on data provided by the Cabinet Office (https://survey.gov-online.go.jp/index-ko.html).

among the masses regarding the quality of their lives and that changes to growth and prosperity were taking place only slowly.

It is a coincidence that Kawashima's *Susaki Paradise* was released in the same month of the same year as the publication of this white paper, but I see it as what we may call an inevitable coincidence in that they are two among many different discourses engendered by and responding to the same socioeconomic milieu of Japan at that historical moment, even if their forms, focuses, and concerns may seem to differ. This inevitable coincidence offers an intriguing reference point from which to better appreciate the historical significances of *Susaki Paradise*. Juxtaposing the film and the white paper allows us to recognize that the former participated in the national debate generated by the latter about the state of the Japanese economy, especially how to interpret its reconstruction a decade after defeat in war. The film portrayed those very aspects of the Japanese economy that the white paper occluded and about which its critics were concerned, illuminating the uneven development that was becoming apparent in contemporary Japanese society.

Legacies of the War, Delayed Reconstruction

Susaki Paradise starts with the couple Yoshiji and Tsutae on Kachidoki Bridge, which spans the Sumida River, wondering about lodging for that night. A small travel bag is all they carry. They have no jobs and no one to rely on. After buying a packet of cigarettes, they are left with only 60 yen—not enough for even a simple meal (we later see, for example, curry rice costing 80 yen; fried rice, 80 yen; and an omelet, 70 yen). Tsutae criticizes Yoshiji, who cannot come up with any reasonable solution to their financial problem. Irritated by his indecision, Tsutae boards a bus, and Yoshiji follows her. When the conductor announces "Susaki Bentenchō" as the next stop, she stands up and disembarks. Again, Yoshiji follows her. The couple come right up to Susaki Bridge, with its tall neon sign reading "Susaki Paradise." Tsutae used to work as a prostitute in the licensed quarter that lies just beyond and thinks that she can earn some money there again if there are no other options. They do not cross the bridge, however. Tsutae notices a flyer seeking a live-in maid at a bar located right by the bridge and asks the owner to hire her. The owner, a plump and kind-looking middle-aged woman named O-toku (Todoroki Yukiko) hesitates to hire Tsutae, worried that such a pretty young woman will leave the bar as soon as she finds a better-paid job "beyond the bridge" (*hashi no mukō*), in Susaki Paradise. Tsutae laughs and reassures O-toku that her concern is unnecessary since she is burdened with a man. Tsutae begins working at the bar the same night, and O-toku promises to look for a job for Yoshiji, too.

Both Shibaki's novella and Kawashima's film make only brief reference to how the two have ended up penniless and homeless. In the novella, Yoshiji lost his job at a storage company because he embezzled money from it. Tsutae, the second of seven siblings, left her hometown in Ibaraki Prefecture and came to Tokyo to find work through a broker. Her father and brother are sick and unable to work, and she has to send money home to support them. We are left to speculate that Yoshiji embezzled the money to help Tsutae. In the film, too, Yoshiji's embezzlement, Tsutae's impoverished family back home, and her need to send money to them are mentioned. In both cases, their financial hardship appears at first to be a personal affair.

However, it is important for us to be mindful of the age and generation of these two in the context of mid-1950s Japan and to appreciate correctly what their unspoken backstories communicated to the audience. In Shibaki's novella, Yoshiji is twenty-five years old. In the film, we do not know exactly how old he is, but the appearance of the actor Mihashi Tatsuya gives us the impression that he is around the same age as the actor himself is, or at most in his early thirties. This suggests that Yoshiji was born roughly between 1925 and 1930, when Japan was hit first by the Shōwa Financial Crisis and then by the Great Depression. As the parliamentary democracy that had been institutionalized during the Taishō era was unable to offer effective solutions to the country's economic impasse, a series of right-wing terrorist attacks incited political instability, enabling the growing influence of the military in the political arena. Meanwhile, Japan's imperialism reached a new stage: the Kwantung Army invaded Manchuria in 1931 and established the puppet state of Manchukuo the next year. In 1937, the Second Sino-Japanese War broke out, and, accordingly, the ruling elite—both military and civilian leaders—organized a total mobilization system for the optimal employment of all available human and material resources.

It is possible that men in this generation were too young to be conscripted during the Pacific War. But many of them had to spend their early youth experiencing US air raids, starvation, and the death of family members, just like the authors Nosaka Akiyuki and Kaikō Takeshi, who were born in 1930, grew up in Kobe and Osaka respectively, and later identified themselves as "the faction of the ruins and black market," or *yakeato yamiichi-ha* (Kaikō and Nosaka 1968). Or, it is also possible that they were sent to the battlefield if they had reached the conscription age by the end of the war (which had been lowered to nineteen in 1944), like the actor Mihashi Tatsuya himself (born in 1923), who was detained in Siberia and could not repatriate until 1947.[10] In either case, men (and women, of course) in this generation were immersed within militaristic and nationalistic education during the sensitive years of their youth and then, after defeat, forced to undergo a thorough transformation of values in the name of peace and democracy. For them, therefore, defeat in the war signified not only material deprivation and physical exhaustion but also emotional and spiritual confusion. According to Tsutae, Yoshiji habitually mentions death. He is nihilistic, lazy, tired of working, and lacks a fundamental desire for life. This annoys the tough and practical Tsutae, who believes that one should do anything necessary to survive. She scolds him: "You always talk about dying, but people have to live until the day they die" ("Futakotome ni wa shinu shinu-tte. Ningen shinu toki made ikinakya nan'nain desu kara ne"). If we consider Yoshiji's jaded attitude toward life in the light of his generational experience, we may perceive it to be a prolonged effect of the disillusion and exhaustion brought about by the war and defeat.

The film also hints at Tsutae's age and generation. In the novella, when O-toku reminisces about the candies that were popular from the late Taishō era to early Shōwa, Tsutae has no idea about them because she had not yet been born (Shibaki [1955] 1994, 31). This suggests that she was born in the early 1930s at the earliest and was in her early to mid teens when the war ended. We know that Tsutae came to Tokyo to find work through the mediation of a broker—a detail that raises the issue of *miuri*, that is, the selling of children by their impoverished parents. It is well known that *miuri* was a serious social problem in agrarian villages during the 1930s as the Great Depression hit Japan, but this problem reemerged in the early postwar period, triggered by food shortages and a sharp increase in population in the countryside due to repatriation from the former colonies as well as the absorption of the urban unemployed during the Doge Plan recession. While the Labor Standards Act of 1947 prohibited an employer from "offsetting wages against advances of money or advances of other credit as a condition for work" (article 17), in reality many young children were forced to work under harsh conditions until they repaid their parents' debt. For girls, brothels were a common destination. According to an investigation conducted by the Ministry of Labor for one year between July 1950 and June 1951, 55 percent of those subjected to *miuri*, including one nine-year-old girl, were sold into prostitution, while others became factory workers, nannies, and maids ("Mata fueta miuri" 1951). Alarmed by this trend, the 1951 labor yearbook published by the Ōhara Institute for Social Research identified this phenomenon as a form of human trafficking and spent one section discussing it as a symptom of the economic misery of agrarian villages (Ōhara Shakai Mondai Kenkyūjo 1951, 139). It is reasonable to view Tsutae as one of those many girls who were sold into prostitution or had to subject themselves to it, just like those women in Mizoguchi's *Street of Shame*, and to understand her economic situation not simply as a personal issue but also as a societal one.

How, then, does the film represent the neighborhood at which this couple arrives, the neighborhood "outside the bridge" (*hashi no soto*)? The location shooting that Kawashima conducted in the neighborhood of Susaki establishes the prominence of small, family-owned businesses. The densely populated eastern neighborhoods of the city of Tokyo, including Susaki-Bentenchō, had been burnt to ashes by the US fire-bombing on March 10, 1945, which killed more than 100,000 people in one night (Saotome 1971; Tōkyō Kyōshokuin Kumiai Kōtō Shibu 1987, 148–49). In the film, the neighborhood is filled with small wooden buildings that appear to have been constructed in an impromptu manner in the immediate postwar period. These include bars, sushi restaurants, a coffee shop, a noodle shop, and a *horumon* (beef and pork organ meat) restaurant, all of which attest that this place provided regular working people with an opportunity for casual and affordable dining.

In this neighborhood, Chigusa, where Tsutae gets a job, is a typical bar in appearance and size (see figure 1.1). It can accommodate only five or six customers at most. There are no tables, only a counter and stools. Until Tsutae's arrival, O-toku has been running the bar by herself. In order to earn some extra cash, she also rents boats for visitors to take out on the river that flows under the bridge. The bar is part of O-toku's house, which also has a kitchen (or at least a small area with a sink), one room where she and her two sons sleep, and an attic, where Tsutae and Yoshiji stay. The walls, windows, and doors are all flimsy and crumbling, and rain leaks through the ceiling. This neighborhood reminds us of not so much the Japanese economy that was supposedly taking off as the slow pace of reconstruction

Figure 1.1. *Susaki Paradise Red Light* (1956). Chigusa, to which Yoshiji and Tsutae end up drifting, is a small, rickety bar located just by the bridge that leads to Susaki Paradise.

from wartime damage, the daily struggle of ordinary people, and the instability of household economies, which critics of the white paper underscored.

Another feature of this neighborhood is that its economy is tightly linked to—or, more correctly, dependent upon—the economy beyond the bridge, that is, of Susaki Paradise. Helpful here is Maeda Ai's memorable discussion of Higuchi Ichiyō's ([1894–96] 2003) short story *Growing Up* (*Takekurabe*), which details the complex affects of the children in their early adolescent years in the neighborhood of Daionjimae in Tokyo. Examining Ichiyō's descriptions of this neighborhood, located right next to Yoshiwara, Maeda points out its convoluted relationship to the licensed quarter dictated by the money it brings and by built-up resentment, its "existential duality" in which it was "isolated from the Yoshiwara's prosperity yet firmly under its control" (Maeda [1982] 2004, 119–20; Maeda 1982, 290). Kawashima's film finds similar qualities in the economic relationship between the neighborhood by the bridge and Susaki Paradise. Most people who visit the neighborhood are involved with the licensed quarter beyond the bridge in one way or another. Customers at Chigusa include prostitutes who work in Susaki Paradise and men who want a few drinks before visiting the brothels. O-toku does feel disdain and disgust for those women who sell their bodies as sexual commodities and for those men who pay for them while their families wait at home. These feelings are fueled by the fact that her own husband ran away with a woman working in Susaki Paradise, but she also recognizes that she and her family cannot survive without this licensed quarter. To borrow Maeda's expression, this neighborhood's "parasitic dependence" upon Susaki Paradise is apparent (Maeda [1982] 2004, 120; Maeda 1982, 290).

Maeda has also argued that in Daionjimae not only adults but also children find themselves under Yoshiwara's domination. They play and socialize as residents subject to the money that Yoshiwara generates and come to understand their positions in the economic structure that Daionjimae and the licensed quarter constitute. Similarly, *Susaki Paradise* depicts the socialization of children in a neighborhood that is economically inseparable from the world beyond the bridge. Early in the film, the two sons at Chigusa are laying out their futon while their mother is still working in the bar. When Toshio, who appears to be in first or second grade, farts, Kazuo, his older brother, tells him to open the window. From the wide-open window, Toshio, who is still learning to read, sees the large neon sign over the bridge and reads the word aloud, slowly and tentatively: "pa-ra-da-i-su." Then, he and Kazuo have the following conversation:

> TOSHIO: Brother, what does "paradise" [*paradaisu*] mean?
>
> KAZUO: That means heaven [*tengoku*].
>
> TOSHIO: What's heaven?
>
> KAZUO: Heaven is just heaven.

Clearly, there is a gap in the two brothers' understanding of Susaki Paradise. Still innocent, Toshio does not know what the word *paradise* means, let alone what it refers to in this case. What is not so clear from the conversation is how much Kazuo, who is probably in fourth or fifth grade, knows. He can explain the word's literal meaning, but we do not know whether he recognizes the crude nature of Susaki Paradise and refrains from sharing it with his brother because he is still too young or whether he is genuinely unaware of that nature. Yet we can easily imagine how, in this neighborhood, the large neon sign reading "paradise" stimulates young boys' and girls' constant curiosity, inciting conversations similar to the one above at various stages of their childhood.

Shortly after this, there follows a scene in which Toshio plays with a condom that he appears to have found on the street with his friends, making a balloon out of it. His mother, horrified to see them engaged in such play, tells him to throw the condom away immediately. For O-toku, condoms are a symbol of the sexual services that prostitutes offer beyond the bridge, and it was one of those prostitutes who stole her husband, destroyed her marriage, and placed her in the current economic plight. Therefore, she cannot hide her anger at her son, who is innocently playing with a condom. For Toshio (and other children of his age), condoms have different connotations. He has already heard the term *paradise*. He is now having direct contact with a condom. Sooner or later, older children, perhaps his own older brother, will tell him what condoms are used for, which will function almost as an initiation into adulthood. Through this, he will learn about the kinds of activities that make the place beyond the bridge a "paradise" for certain men but inspire resentment among certain women like O-toku.

Unlike Daionjimae in the Meiji era, however, the neighborhood by the bridge in the mid-1950s did not have hope for further growth. The Anti-Prostitution Law had already passed the Diet in May 1956. Those *tokuingai* districts were to be closed upon the enforcement of the law in 1958 (and Susaki Paradise was indeed closed, although some other districts, like Yoshiwara and Tobita in Osaka, managed to continue their business by finding legal loopholes). Although ignorant about the details, O-toku is aware that a law has passed that might change her life and business fundamentally. One of her customers, Ochiai, whom I will discuss in next section, consoles her, saying that the owners of brothels are "clever" (*rikō*) and therefore she need not worry, but she cannot suppress her anxiety. Thus, *Susaki Paradise*, while made as the national economy was entering the stage of high-speed growth, represents the neighborhood by the bridge as an urban space marked by the legacies of the war and delayed reconstruction whose possibility of growth has been severed.

Tensions of Uneven Development

Now, I want to shift attention to the two other places represented in the film (one directly shown in the film and the other only implied) to articulate the position of this neighborhood within the economy of the nation and the metropolis. The concept of uneven development is useful for a better understanding of the nature of interactions between the neighborhood by the bridge and these places. Uneven development is inevitably produced by capitalist expansion because capital, by its nature, seeks greater profits by identifying promising and lucrative industries for investment, and this leads to a heavy concentration of wealth in certain industries that enjoy the most up-to-date technologies and high productivity and the sacrifice of other industries deemed lacking growth potential and unworthy of investment. As Neil Smith ([1984] 2008) emphasizes, one conspicuous way that uneven development manifests itself is spatially, for capitalism has the endogenous tendency to incessantly (re)territorialize new and old spaces under its domination (i.e., equalization) but at the same time imposes particular patterns of labor, production, and consumption on each space and assigns to it particular roles within the larger economic structure—the city, the state, or the globe (i.e., differentiation). The 1956 white paper mentioned above focused primarily on the success of the national economy enabled by the growth of large companies with little reference to uneven development.[11] *Susaki Paradise*, on the contrary, by showing the interactions and negotiations between the neighborhood by the bridge and these other two places, permits us to explore the tension of uneven development that had been building up in the city since the end of the war.

The first place that I want to mention is the artificial island that was being constructed beyond Susaki Paradise. This island does not appear in the film but is implied by the constant presence of the dump trucks that run through the neighborhood. Those trucks cross the bridge on their way into Susaki Paradise loaded with piles of stones and return empty. From the beginning of the film, these trucks are so prominent that they cannot help catching the audience's attention.

When asked by Tsutae about these dump trucks, O-toku responds that they are for landfill, which immediately associates them with a landfill project that was in fact proceeding south of Susaki Paradise at that time. The Tokyo metropolitan government had actively pursued landfill in this eastern quarter of the city since the Tokugawa era, and, as mentioned above, Susaki Paradise itself was located on an artificial island built in the Meiji era. In the postwar era, economic development, accompanied by the rapid growth of heavy and chemical industries and a sharp population increase, entailed further land development in the metropolitan area. The central and local governments accelerated the landfill project in the 1950s. Tokyo quickly expanded its territory beyond Susaki Paradise to the south, into Tokyo Bay. Because of intense landfill, the size of the Kōtō ward of metropolitan Tokyo, which included Susaki and its surrounding neighborhoods, had more than doubled by 1950 to 9.9 square miles, compared to the middle of the Meiji era (in 1882; Kōtō Kuyakusho 1967, 1255).[12] The speed of landfill would be accelerated around the time of the 1964 Tokyo Summer Olympics.

Large corporations, driven by their growing production power and in need of new space for further investment, built factories, distribution centers, and storage facilities on new landfill, giving this part of Tokyo a reputation as a hub of production and logistics (Tōkyō Kyōshokuin Kumiai Kōtō Shibu 1987, 176–77). In the mid-1950s, therefore, these landfill areas conspicuously symbolized the nascent era of economic growth.[13] The fast-moving trucks mobilized for landfill in the film crudely demonstrate the inexorable speed of capitalist expansion and the rapid conversion of nature into quantifiable space whose primary purpose is to create surplus value. Furthermore, these trucks simply passing through the neighborhood by the bridge serves as a constant reminder of the fact that capital flows also passed this neighborhood by, as Japan's high-speed economic growth left it behind.[14] Given that these scenes of the trucks were a new addition when Shibaki's novella was adapted for film, we can observe therein Kawashima's conscious attempt to highlight unevenness in reconstruction through the contrast of these two places at the exact historical moment of the mid-1950s.

The second place I want to highlight that figures in the film is Akihabara (see map 1.1), a neighborhood in central Tokyo, only four miles from Susaki to the northwest, newly emerging as a center for electronics. This is the hometown of the man named Ochiai, whom Tsutae, tired of Yoshiji, takes as a lover after moving to the neighborhood by the bridge. In the prewar era, there were only a few dealers of electronic appliances in this area. Just like many other neighborhoods of Tokyo including Susaki, Akihabara was destroyed during the war. After Japan's defeat, people hungry for entertainment and information began gathering in this neighborhood to sell spare radio parts. Those who owned army-surplus radios distributed them to retailers, accelerating the specialization and professionalization of this business. In September 1951, the US occupation forces ordered the dissolution of these street vendors and their reconsolidation in a market right below the train tracks at the National Railways' Akihabara Station. After that, Akihabara rapidly became what we know today as the largest "electric town," or *denkigai*, in Japan. As of July 1956—the year Kawashima's film was released—33 percent of wholesale electronic-appliance dealers, 37 percent of employees in this industry, and 40 percent of monthly sales turnover in Tokyo's twenty-three wards were concentrated in Chiyoda Ward, which includes Akihabara (Chiyodaku 1960, 708, 714–18).

Kawashima conducted location shooting in Akihabara and vividly recorded the urban space that was materializing there. Such spatial advantages as proximity to major stations, including Tokyo, Ochanomizu, and Kanda, contributed to its prompt recovery from wartime devastation, and this marked a sharp contrast with the neighborhood by the bridge in Susaki. If the latter is characterized by the legacies of war and delayed reconstruction, the former symbolizes the future and rapid growth. The neighborhood around Akihabara Station is vibrant and ebullient, filled with shops and customers, many of whom are well-dressed businessmen and students. We see large signs for such companies as Mitsubishi, National (now Panasonic), and Toshiba. Among the numerous retailers of radios, washing machines, and other appliances are some selling televisions, which attract many people curious about this new luxury item. Television broadcasts had started in Japan in 1953, but Japan's first mass-produced television device, sold by Sharp, cost 175,000 yen, when the first monthly salary for a public employee with a high school diploma was only 5,400 yen (Sharp Kabushiki-gaisha 1992, 20). In the mid-1950s, therefore, this prohibitively expensive device had not been adopted by regular households (this situation would change quite dramatically in the next ten years or so; it will be discussed in detail in chapter 3). Akihabara provided a space where people could enjoy a tangible experience of this most up-to-date technology.

Two men in the film travel between the neighborhood by the bridge and Akihabara, and their movements underscore the tensions of uneven development between the two urban spaces. First, let us consider Tsutae's lover, Ochiai. This wealthy and generous middle-aged man, who runs a radio shop in Akihabara, stops at Chigusa for drinks on his way to Susaki Paradise and there meets Tsutae for the first time. He quickly develops feelings for her, admiring the charm of a nonprofessional woman (she conceals the fact that she was once a prostitute "beyond the bridge"). Tsutae, too, immediately feels attracted to him, since he embodies everything Yoshiji lacks: cheerfulness, confidence, and decisiveness. Ochiai is also financially comfortable; this is demonstrated by his thick wallet and generous spending at Chigusa and beyond the bridge. He rides a scooter, increasingly popular by the mid-1950s, and Tsutae effusively admires it, asking how much it cost and commenting on how "fine-looking" (*rippa*) and "shiny" (*pikapika*) it is. The two men are completely different in physical appearance, too. Yoshiji, played by Mihashi Tatsuya, is scrawny and shabbily dressed, while Ochiai, played by Kawazu Seizaburō, is stocky, well fed, and prosperous looking.

Interestingly, in the process of adaptation for film, the business that Ochiai owns was changed from a medical-devices store to a radio store. What does this change tell us? It is worth considering the position that radios occupied within the Japanese economy at the early stage of high-speed growth. When *Susaki Paradise* was made in the mid-1950s, tube radios were still dominant (in fact, the broken radio at Chigusa that Ochiai repairs is a tube radio), but major electronics makers such as Sony were already developing transistor radios. The miniaturization of radios would advance rapidly, contributing to a change in the use of radios, from household possessions to individual possessions. Moreover, while Japan's main export in the early postwar years was textiles, an industry with a long history beginning in the Meiji era, the export of transistor radios increased sharply from the late 1950s, supported by growing demand in the US market (Keizai Kikakuchō 1960, 9, 39–41, 77–82). Already in the mid-1950s, radios were products with high potential for growth in both the domestic and international markets. The name of Ochiai's store—Nichibei Denka Rūmu ("Japan-US Electronics Room")—indicates his strategic intention to highlight this potential and stimulate customers' growing desire for entertainment within the rising postwar consumer culture enabled and bolstered by the US-Japan alliance.

Throughout the film, the two main female characters—O-toku and Tsutae—treat Ochiai with extra care. O-toku speaks to him using the polite sentence-ending forms *desu* and *masu*, while Ochiai does not reciprocate. She is careful not to counter him when he states his opinions. Tsutae acts in an extremely feminine and coquettish way (which she never shows to Yoshiji), emphasizing her docility and gentleness. One way to interpret Ochiai's relationship with O-toku and Tsutae is, of course, to acknowledge the gender-based power dynamic between a male client and female service provider. But it is equally important to recognize that their relationship is a reflection at the personal level of the unequal distribution of wealth between the two places at the social level. Financial comfort and status as the owner of a prosperous electronics shop in Akihabara give Ochiai an aura of self-assurance and pride (and I must add that actor Kawazu Seizaburō does a brilliant job creating this aura). He takes it for granted that he is treated with respect. The two women in the neighborhood by the bridge faithfully conform to this expectation. In the middle of the film, Ochiai, charmed by Tsutae and convinced that she is an innocent, nonprofessional woman, finds an apartment for her on a "hill along the Kanda River" ("Kanda-gawa ni sotta takadai"), and she leaves the bar without telling Yoshiji and settles in as Ochiai's lover (see figure 1.2). This can be read as the rescue of a woman in the declining neighborhood from her economic plight by a man in Akihabara or Tsutae's pragmatic use of Ochiai for upward social mobility. In either case, the unevenness between the two places is one crucial factor that mediates and consolidates their relation as lovers.

Yoshiji is the other character who travels between the two places, but, contrary to Ochiai, he travels from Susaki to Akihabara. He goes there to talk to Ochiai, who has taken Tsutae away from him. This character, who fits comfortably within the landscape of Susaki, appears incongruent amid the prosperity of Akihabara. In a sweaty, worn-out jacket and muddy old shoes, he searches in vain for Ochiai among the countless radio shops (see figure 1.3). The only information Yoshiji has is Ochiai's surname. He is exhausted, helpless, and disoriented, and these senses are heightened by the jarring Latin music. While Ochiai from Akihabara is welcomed and enjoys his free time in Susaki, Yoshiji from Susaki is not welcomed by anyone in Akihabara. After

Figure 1.2. *Susaki Paradise Red Light* (1956). Attracted by Ochiai's money, Tsutae decides to move into an apartment that he has found for her.

Figure 1.3. *Susaki Paradise Red Light* (1956). Yoshiji wanders through Akihabara to find Ochiai and get Tsutae back. Exhausted and dehydrated, he is about to collapse.

walking for a long time under the strong summer sun, he finally loses consciousness and collapses, as if the town has rejected him as an inappropriate outsider and is urging him to return to his familiar territory in Susaki.

Yoshiji is saved by road construction workers who, judging by their appearance, are day laborers. When he wakes up, one woman among them offers him a cup of water or tea, and a man offers his half-eaten rice ball. Because this man speaks rather slowly in an intonation not common in Tokyo, we suspect that he is not a Tokyo native but from the countryside (though it is difficult to determine exactly where he is from, given that he speaks only briefly). If we interpret this scene together with the historical fact that a massive number of people from the countryside were migrating to major metropolitan areas for job opportunities during the high-speed growth era (which will be discussed in detail in chapter 2), this is an excellent reminder that the affluence of such urban spaces, not only Akihabara but also other neighborhoods in central Tokyo under rapid reconstruction, was made possible by the labor of those cheaply paid workers displaced from their hometowns. It is also suggestive that, among the countless people in that town, construction workers were the ones to help Yoshiji. The intimacy that develops between Yoshiji and these workers, however brief and transient, indicates their class affinity—that they all belong to the bottom of the hierarchical socioeconomic structure engendered by uneven development.

Liminal Space: *Muen*, or "No Ties"

The discussion so far has demonstrated that the neighborhood by the bridge relies parasitically on Susaki Paradise for its economic survival and that future growth is not an option since the closure of the licensed quarter has already been determined. What was it, then, that attracted drifters like Yoshiji and Tsutae to this neighborhood? In this section, I argue that this neighborhood is represented as a liminal space located between Susaki Paradise and the broader outside world, or what in Japanese is commonly called the world of *katagi*—that is, respectable life and work as opposed to the world of yakuza, gambling, and/or entertainment businesses. As such, this neighborhood loosens or partially suspends the social constraints of both worlds.[15]

First, we must recognize that both Susaki Paradise and the outside world of *katagi* are ruled by their own laws. In the world of *katagi*, workers sign a contract with their employers and receive compensation by selling their labor power as a commodity. The reason that Yoshiji and Tsutae had to leave this world was that Yoshiji, perhaps encouraged by Tsutae, embezzled his company's money. He took money without providing his labor power to his employer, as agreed in the contract, or going through the proper procedure to establish a creditor-debtor relation with his employer. He violated a basic rule that governs modern capitalist society. On the other hand, Susaki Paradise has its own law, too. Within this licensed quarter, many women work to pay back the debt that they or their families have incurred. Until they pay it back completely, their physical freedom is strictly limited. They are practically indentured laborers. While these two worlds may operate under different laws, it is also true that they are both contract-based worlds in which people are bound by the obligations stipulated in the legal documents they have signed, whether voluntarily or involuntarily.

The neighborhood by the bridge, located between the world of *katagi* and Susaki Paradise, attracts people who have trouble with highly organized life in both worlds and offers them a temporary refuge. For example, O-toku casually hires Tsutae as a live-in maid without establishing a formal contractual relationship. The next day, she even goes out to find a job for Yoshiji and recommends him to nearby soba restaurant Damasare-ya as a deliveryman. The owner of Damasare-ya, too, hires him immediately after casting a quick glance over him. Both O-toku and the owner of the soba restaurant are probably aware that Tsutae and Yoshiji have come to this neighborhood for a reason that they cannot easily share, but these shop owners do not seem to care much. Similarly, the other young workers at Damasare-ya—funny and frivolous Sankichi (Ozawa Shōichi) and caring Tamako (Ashikawa Izumi)—seem to have their own unique pasts, which led them to this neighborhood. Meanwhile, some prostitutes from Susaki Paradise go to Chigusa for help or simple commiseration. One young prostitute did not know that the work she was hired for was prostitution. She and her boyfriend, a driver of one of the trucks that run through the neighborhood, ask O-toku to find a job for her so that she can get out of the licensed quarter. Another prostitute, middle-aged and drunk, complains to O-toku about how difficult it is for an aging woman like herself to compete with younger prostitutes in Susaki Paradise.

The notion of *muen* (無縁), or "no ties," helps us understand the film's representations of this liminality. Amino Yoshihiko ([1978] 1996), one of the most distinguished historians of Japan, has demonstrated that there were sacred places in medieval Japan where residents and visitors were liberated from the secular relations that would otherwise have bound them to a particular social status and identity, such as husband-wife, master-subordinate, or creditor-debtor. Authorities generally respected their autonomy and refrained from intervening in the management of these places. The examples that Amino gives include certain temples, marketplaces, and port cities. He portrays these as places of *muen* (and, indeed, contemporary documents did use this expression to refer to such places). Although this Buddhist term has mostly negative and undesirable implications in present-day Japan, such as the absence of family, friends, and acquaintances and seclusion and alienation from society, Amino avers that it used to indicate the principle of treating all people without prejudice, and it is in this sense that the historian identifies the nature of peace and freedom in medieval Japan as *muen*.

As the Tokugawa leadership unified Japan and consolidated its power, many of these places of *muen* lost autonomy. But Jinnai Hidenobu (1985, 1995), a historian of architecture, maintains that Amino's discussion of the places of *muen*—especially the notion that water and places linked to water, such as bridges and riversides, were often regarded as possessing the attribute of *muen*—permits us to appreciate the development of the city of Edo in the Tokugawa era, too. He points out that large entertainment districts commonly existed in open spaces located by bridges, often at the city limits, and attracted a number of people looking for brief escape from everyday life under the rigid status system while evading strict regulation by the ruling elite. Through this example, Jinnai claims that the principle of *muen* survived in these places even in the Tokugawa era.[16]

If we incorporate these two scholars' arguments into our analysis of the neighborhood by the bridge, we realize that the film represents the liminality of this neighborhood in such a way as to evoke the sense of *muen* that had long been recognized among common people in Japan. First of all, this has to do with the fact that this neighborhood is located by the water, at the foot of a bridge—a space whose *muen* nature was believed to relax existing relations and constraints. Indeed, we are reminded of the neighborhood's vicinity to the water over and over through numerous visual images, such as the sparkling surface of the river reflecting the neon sign of Susaki Paradise; the houses, including Chigusa, that look like old ships floating on the river when seen from the bridge; Yoshiji, in a musing mood, leaning against the rail of the bridge and smoking; Tsutae looking over the rainy river from the attic of Chigusa and realizing that she is back in Susaki; people—a young couple, prostitutes from Susaki Paradise, and so on—rowing rental boats from Chigusa (see figure 1.4). These images carefully embedded throughout the film contribute to shaping our perception of this neighborhood as a concrete and discrete place linked to water. Second, Tsutae, who has drawn Yoshiji to this neighborhood, explicitly expresses her craving for water. During a conversation at Chigusa, Ochiai mentions that he was born near Kanda River, which runs through the central part of the city. Tsutae replies that she is from an island on Tone River, the second-largest river in Japan, in the northern Kanto region.[17] Then she says, "I love rivers. They make me feel so relieved" ("Kawa-tte daisuki sa.

Figure 1.4. *Susaki Paradise Red Light* (1956). Visual images of water and verbal references to it are prominent throughout the film.

Seisei suru"). So it is not only the possibility of a job but also the location itself and the power of water that have led Tsutae back to this neighborhood in Susaki.

Two more details further establish the neighborhood by the bridge as a liminal space of *muen*. First, near the beginning of the film, O-toku's two sons, who have been off playing, come home for supper shouting "Engacho! Engacho!" This is a brief but extremely intriguing scene. *Engacho* is a ludic term that small children used to use nationwide until a few decades ago. When they saw a friend come in contact with something dirty or impure (e.g., stepping on a dog's stool), they would shout this term while crossing their index and middle fingers (though there were many variations in both the term and the way of crossing fingers throughout Japan). By doing so, they believed that they could establish immunity to that dirtiness or impurity. Even if that friend touched them, they would not be infected by it. Thus, the use of the term *engacho* was meant to detach oneself from the common everyday-life environment and to create a sacred space protected from undesirable outside influence.[18] Although the exact origin of this term is unknown, Amino, in the same book where he discusses *muen*, explains that the "en" of *engacho* indeed refers to *en* (縁), which means "ties" or "bond," and that *engacho* means the cutting of all ties ([1978] 1996, 13–20). Interestingly, when the two boys come home shouting this term, we see no particular object from which they are trying to protect themselves nor anyone who has had contact with such an object. This gives us the impression that they are shouting it for the sake of their entire house or even neighborhood, detaching it from both Susaki Paradise and the outside world and declaring its immunity and inviolability.

Second, the repeated appearance of a traveling troupe of actors, or *tabiyakusha*, also reinforces the image of *muen* in the neighborhood. We first see a poster for the traveling troupe, headed by Shizu Kan'ichirō, at Chigusa. Later, we see actors from the troupe walking the main street in their Tokugawa-era costumes while playing music to promote their performance. Finally, Tsutae and Ochiai go to watch the troupe in an old wooden theater, which stood just outside Susaki Paradise, at its northwest corner, next to Susaki Shrine (see figure 1.5). This form of theater by traveling actors—so-called *taishū engeki*, which literally means "theater for the masses"—was widely popular in Japan during this period as it offered reasonable and accessible amusement when many working people still had little disposable

Figure 1.5. *Susaki Paradise Red Light* (1956). The film effectively uses the historical image of traveling troupes to accentuate the *muen* nature of the neighborhood by the bridge.

money for such pastimes. These traveling troupes often consisted of family members including small children and visited small theaters in urban working-class neighborhoods and hot-spring resort towns alike.[19] This practice has its historical origin in the premodern era. Because the ruling warrior class in Tokugawa Japan regarded actors as a marginal group outside the four-status system, they did not (or were not allowed to) belong to particular local communities based on territorial and occupational ties but wandered from one place to another to make a living through performance. As Jinnai as well as others (e.g., Okiura 2006) note, these wandering actors were an essential feature of those waterside entertainment districts. When we watch the traveling actors in *Susaki Paradise* with this historical knowledge in mind, it becomes evident that the film uses them to highlight the eccentricity of the neighborhood by the bridge and to point to the uprooted and floating nature of people living and working there, like Tsutae and Yoshiji, in a society where settlement is normalized as the most standard form of living.

In this way, water, *engacho*, and the traveling troupe can be all seen to make the audience perceive the neighborhood by the bridge as a liminal space of *muen*. In fact, *muen* can be a key concept for better appreciating some of Kawashima's other films made around the same time. Take, for example, *The Sun in the Last Days of the Shogunate* (*Bakumatsu taiyōden*, 1957), probably the best-known Kawashima film in English-speaking countries, which he directed the year after *Susaki Paradise*. A brilliant comedy set in a Shinagawa brothel several years before the Meiji Restoration, it stars Frankie Sakai as Saheiji, who ends up working there because of the extravagant party that he threw there with no means to pay for it. In this film, Kawashima imagined this brothel, facing the Tokyo Bay, as a space that enabled the encounters of people of diverse social backgrounds, such as prostitutes, warriors, and merchants—a rare space within a Tokugawa society ruled by a strict status system. *Room for Rent* (*Kashima ari*, 1959), adapted from Ibuse Masuji's novel, depicted the comical interactions among the residents of an "apartment mansion" (*apāto yashiki*)—a large old house converted into apartments—in contemporary Yūhigaoka, near Tennōji in Osaka (switched from Ogikubo, in Tokyo, in Ibuse's original). All the residents in this mansion—Frankie Sakai, Awashima Chikage, Naniwa Chieko, Otowa Nobuko, Sazanka Kyū, and so on—somehow deviate from mainstream corporate life. They include an inventor, a ceramics artist, a smuggler of foreign liquors, a junk shop owner, and a mistress with three patrons. Though the mansion is not near the water, it is physically separated from the rest of the world, standing atop a hill from which one can overlook the southern part of the city, including the Tsūtenkaku tower. At the beginning of the film, one of the residents, a jolly konjak maker played by Katsura Kokinji, urinates (!) from the edge of the hill toward Tsūtenkaku as if he were demarcating the apartment mansion's discrete territory. Just as in the neighborhood by the bridge in *Susaki Paradise*, at both the Shinagawa brothel and the Yūhigaoka apartment mansion, people comfortably (but sometimes uneasily) mingle with one another while tolerating ways of living that would be dismissed or even castigated in the world outside these places. It seems safe to argue that Kawashima thought fondly of these kinds of *muen* places in urban settings, which exist as extensions of everyday life but are also somewhat separated and estranged from it.

Then, what is the implication of representing the places of *muen* like the neighborhood by the bridge within the larger social context of mid-1950s Japan? It seems like a subtle but critical reference to the state's and society's growing efforts at the beginning of the high-speed growth era to produce cooperative workers and citizens. In the year before the film was released, corporate leaders and the Japanese government had established the Japan Productivity Center with funds from the United States in order to raise the productivity of workers through the promotion of harmonious relations between management and labor. They expected the raised standard of living for workers to attenuate the militant unionism that had been dominant in Japanese society since the end of the war (Gordon 1993, 1998). Simultaneously, the so-called New Life campaign (*shin-seikatsu undō*) was evolving at the national level. In the same year that the Productivity Center was inaugurated, the Japanese government funded the launch of the New Life Campaign Association. The association aimed for the rationalization of household economies and daily customs as well as the elevation of public morals and spirits. The campaign involved a wide range of public- and private-sector agents. It enlisted support from various ministries, including the Ministry of Health and Welfare, while encouraging collaboration from youth, women's, and neighborhood associations (Garon 1999; Unoki 2012). The Japanese state was aware that the improvement of workplace productivity, or more precisely the productivity of male workers, must be accompanied by the fundamental reform of the private sphere, for which wives and mothers were supposed to be responsible.

This impulse for productivity, rationality, and morality in the workplace and at home makes more sense when we take into account the fact that the idea of the welfare state was also consolidating in this period. In its 1955 platform, the LDP—the party that would maintain uninterrupted power until 1993—declared its support for the welfare state (Jiyū Minshutō 1966, 22). Facing the Cold War in the international arena and growing popular support for the Socialist Party at home, the LDP aimed for full employment and reinforced social security and strove to advance the social integration of the masses through such provisions as universal health care and a national pension. The state became the "guarantor of progress" (Donzelot 1991, 173), taking an active role in mediating social relations and improving the people's living and working conditions. Naturally, in a welfare state, the people cannot remain passive subjects but must make their own efforts to become worthy of state support. According to Nikolas Rose

(1999, 253–56), "welfare citizenship" not only recognizes the people's economic and social rights but also asks each person to fulfill "certain obligations of responsibility, prudence, self-reliance, and civic duty." We can reasonably regard the movements for productivity, rationality, and morality as an attempt to confirm reciprocal relations between the state and the people for the effective management of the forthcoming welfare state.

The neighborhood by the bridge is filled with the kind of people who do not abide by the ways of life endorsed by the movements mentioned above. Yoshiji is by no means an industrious worker. He is moody, reckless, and mainly concerned about how to get by each day. He even steals money from his soba restaurant (although he returns it before the owner finds out). After Tsutae leaves him, he does try to live more seriously as a man of *katagi* with the help of Tamako. When Tsutae returns, however, he easily gives up such a stable life. Meanwhile, Tsutae lacks prescribed middle-class sexual morals. While trying to settle in the neighborhood by the bridge with Yoshiji, she flirts with Ochiai at Chigusa and, after the second meeting, sleeps with him and makes him buy her an expensive kimono. Soon after, she moves into an apartment he has rented for her. Then, becoming bored with the quiet life of a kept woman, she goes back to Yoshiji. O-toku and her husband are also far from middle-class domesticity. When her husband, who ran away with a prostitute from Susaki Paradise, returns to Chigusa after four years of absence, O-toku accepts him without accusing him at all. The husband has no job, however. All he can do is to help his wife at Chigusa and take care of the two sons. Conventional gender roles are reversed. At the end, he is murdered by his former lover, which takes O-toku back to her old life as a single working mother.

It is not my aim to read this as a resistance to the disciplined social atmosphere of the time. Rather, my point is that the film's representation of the neighborhood by the bridge as a liminal space of *muen* draws attention to the obvious fact that modern life inevitably generates those who refuse or fail to comply with the disciplining forces of productivity, rationality, and morality and necessitates and creates urban spaces where these disciplining forces do not always pervade. To put it another way, at a moment in Japanese history when the quality of a person was increasingly measured against the criterion of how much they could contribute to the nation's economic growth, this film, by borrowing an image of *muen* that had existed long before the rise of modern capitalist society, elucidated an urban space where people were not exclusively held to such a criterion and implied a subtle discomfort with concerted efforts to build a corporate-centered cooperative society (we will come back to this question of a corporate society in chapter 3).

Thus, although Kawashima's 1956 film has often been dismissed as a simple *fūzoku* film, a careful historical contextualization enables us to recognize it as a critical commentary on the high-speed economic growth that was just launching at that time. While the Japanese state highlighted the nation's swift recovery from wartime damage and sought to galvanize the people for continued growth, *Susaki Paradise* exposed the tensions of uneven development and the presence of an urban space that served as a refuge from highly organized everyday life, thereby disquieting the linear narrative of growth and success that was then prevailing in Japanese society.

2

A Girl from Izu

Labor Migration and Modern Subjectivity in Masumura Yasuzō's *Blue-Sky Girl* (1957)

No one turns this way
The spring of my first year, I am standing alone
People walking on the street chase their days
Hoping today, at least, will be a secure day
I look up to the sky that appears fleetingly after the rain
Putting on a smile, I ask how I look

—"I Am Well" ("Genki desu"),
sung by Yoshida Takurō, 1980

If I could have my wish now, I would like wings
Put on my back; white wings like a bird's
Spreading my wings, I want to fly in this big sky
Flapping my wings, I want to go to a world of freedom and
  no sorrow

—"Give Me Wings" ("Tsubasa o kudasai"),
sung by Akai Tori, 1971

One of the most dramatic and longest-lasting consequences of high-speed growth was the dismantling of rural communities throughout Japan. Lured by the possibility of greater opportunities, higher wages, and economic success, tens of thousands of young people left their hometowns and set out for the major cities year after year. In 1955, when high-speed growth was just beginning, 41 percent of the total labor force worked in primary industries.[1] By 1975, two years after the oil crisis brought an end to high-speed growth, Japan had metamorphosed into a highly industrialized society whose population was concentrated in the metropolitan regions along the Pacific Ocean and Inland Sea, from Tokyo-Yokohama to Nagoya and on to Osaka-Kobe. Those working in primary industries had dropped to 13.8 percent of the total labor force.[2] Over the course of twenty years or so, high-speed growth had drastically altered Japan's demographic and geographical landscape.

In this chapter, I examine cinematic representations of the exodus of young workers to cities through an analysis of Masumura Yasuzō's *Blue-Sky Girl* (*Aozora musume*), released in 1957. This is the second film that Masumura directed, after *Kisses* (*Kuchizuke*, 1957), and the first on which he collaborated with Wakao Ayako, the actress who would play unforgettable heroines in a number of his films until the end of the 1960s. Based on Genji Keita's ([1957] 1980) novel of the same title, *Blue-Sky Girl* centers on Yūko, played by Wakao, a girl from a small fishing town in Izu in Shizuoka Prefecture, who moves to Tokyo and faces mistreatment by her stepmother and half-sister, but never lets herself down, and ultimately reunites with her biological mother and meets a man who truly loves her. It is a postwar Japanese version of "Cinderella" or of *The Tale of Ochikubo* (*Ochikubo monogatari*), a Heian-period story with a plot very similar to that of "Cinderella."[3] While the plot submits her to all sorts of melodramatic trials, such as separation from her mother, recurring family-related troubles, and a loneliness in the city, Yūko's strong will to improve her life through her own effort, Wakao's upbeat acting, and the colorful, rhythmic, and fast-paced cinematography all prevent melodramatic pathos from dominating the film. *Blue-Sky Girl* is a heartening film that leaves a pleasant and comforting impression on the audience.

Satō Tadao (2012, 37), a well-known film critic, has commented that *Blue-Sky Girl* is a "trivial, B-grade work" ("taai no nai bī-kyū sakuhin"), and that, as such, it has been almost forgotten. To be clear, the critic did not make this comment to disparage the film. On the contrary, his point was to emphasize the outstanding talent and charm of Wakao Ayako, which shines even in such a film (and I certainly agree with Satō in this regard). But it is also true that by labeling the film as "trivial" and "B-grade," we may risk suggesting that the film does not deserve serious and thorough analysis. It is this kind of dismissive treatment of *Blue-Sky Girl* (and the other films discussed in this book) that I want to resist. This chapter demonstrates how the historical contextualization of *Blue-Sky Girl* enables us to read it as an allusion to the large-scale migration of young workers from the countryside to cities in the late 1950s. Representing the protagonist Yūko as a working girl in Tokyo, the film illuminates the arduous and lonely lives of those numerous young workers displaced from their hometowns, who bolstered Japan's high-speed growth as a cheap, disposable labor force but are often dismissed in the narrative of the "economic miracle." If *Susaki Paradise* points to the uneven distribution of wealth within the city of Tokyo, *Blue-Sky Girl* deals with the uneven distribution of wealth within the nation-state and the migration of workers that was both a cause and a consequence of this unevenness.

In order to provide a context of rapid industrialization and urbanization for the analysis of *Blue-Sky Girl*, I start with a discussion of Genji Keita, the author of the novel Masumura adapted for the film, and the genre of "salaryman" novels in which he worked. Then, I examine the representations of Yūko as a maid who comes from Izu to work in Tokyo and explain how the film mobilizes the positive image of this luxurious resort town and the intertextual image of the actress, Wakao, as a cheerful girl next door to demonstrate sympathy and support for the many working-class girls and boys who had to endure alienation and economic difficulty in Tokyo. After this, I address the question of subjectivity. Director Masumura mercilessly criticized those characters represented in Japanese films as feudal and repressed and strove to create modern, liberated characters with a strong sense of an autonomous self. For this young director, Yūko in *Blue-Sky Girl* was the embodiment of a subjectivity that possessed these qualities. While this positive-minded heroine certainly signaled the advent of the new era of freedom, democracy, and growth, I want to offer a more complex reading. Instead of looking at her subjectivity simply in terms of liberation, I examine it in terms of discipline and calculation, as a product of a historically specific ideology. I detail how Yūko seeks to achieve economic success in Tokyo and effectively uses her body for this purpose in the Japanese society of the 1950s, when options for (particularly working-class) women's independence, success, and even survival were extremely limited.

Genji Keita and the "Salaryman" Genre

Genji Keita, the author of *Blue-Sky Girl*, began drawing popular attention as a novelist in the immediate postwar era and rose to become a bestselling author during the era of high-speed economic growth, in the 1960s. Drawing on his own experiences as a businessman in Osaka in the 1930s, he authored numerous novels depicting with humor and wit the struggles, sorrows, and aspirations of urban white-collar workers, who were also his target readership. His style was straightforward, his plots simple, and his endings never tragic, disturbing, nor surprising, all of which was meant to suit the needs of harried businessmen with limited time for pleasure reading. The reader could enjoy his books casually on commuter trains, for example, with a great sense of security and comfort. As an author of "popular literature" (*taishū bungaku*), as opposed to more serious "pure literature" (*jun-bungaku*), Genji is now seldom treated as an object of scholarly analysis, but we should note that he was massively popular in his time and that not only readers but also film production companies seeking opportunities for adaptation hungrily awaited his next novel.

One of Genji's best-known stories is *Third-Rate Executives* (*Santō jūyaku*), first serialized in the weekly magazine *Sandē Mainichi* between 1951 and 1952 (Genji [1951] 1979). It tells of an ordinary businessman with no particular talent or skill who has accidently been made president of a company because the former president was purged by the US occupation forces as a war collaborator. Tōhō immediately adapted the novel into a film starring Kawamura Reikichi as the company president and Morishige Hisaya as the head of the personnel office. The commercial success of this film prompted Tōhō to produce two sequels in 1952 and 1953. Tōhō further capitalized on Morishige's popularity as a multitalented actor and comedian by producing a spin-off film, *Company President with a Secret Stash* (*Hesokuri shachō*, 1956), in which he played a company president who lacked authority and feared his wife. The film was serialized, and the resulting "Company President" (*Shachō*) series enjoyed extraordinary longevity: more than thirty installments, all starring Morishige, were made between 1956 and 1970.⁴

The genres that Genji helped establish, known as *sararīman shōsetsu* (salaryman novels) and *sararīman eiga* (salaryman films), were closely interrelated, as major film production companies often adapted popular novels into films, and the favorable acceptance of these films in the market encouraged the authors to write sequels or similar stories in turn. For example, in 1954, Nakamura Takeshi, an employee at Japan National Railways, published *Salaryman Mejiro Sanpei: A Novel* (*Sararīman Mejiro Sanpei: Shōsetsu*), and Tōei made a film adaptation the next year, featuring Ryū Chishū as Mejiro and Mochizuki Yūko as his wife. Over the next two decades, Nakamura published numerous stories in the same series. Yamaguchi Hitomi's *The Elegant Life of Mr. Everyman* (*Eburi Man-shi no yūga na seikatsu*; [1963] 2009) first appeared in the monthly journal *Fujin gahō* between 1961 and 1962. This was a collection of short stories that comically depict the trivial everyday life of ordinary businessman Mr. Eburi. In 1963, Okamoto Kihachi from Tōhō turned these short stories into a feature-length film by the same title, with Kobayashi Keiju, a regular for the *Shachō* series, and Aratama Michiyo (who played Tsutae in *Susaki Paradise Red Light*). The same year, Yamaguchi published a sequel entitled *The Splendid Life of Mr. Every Man* (*Eburi Man-shi no karei na seikatsu*; [1963] 1996) and would continue writing broadly about the life of the urban "salaryman."⁵

The proliferation of these genres reflects a change in the structure of the economy that was taking place in Japanese society—namely, the growth in the number of white-collar workers. These workers had emerged as a new social class in the interwar years and received a great deal of media attention for embodying the most up-to-date modern life (e.g., living in suburban houses, commuting by train, giving their children a good education), as we see in Shōchiku's *shōshimin* or petit-bourgeois films such as Ozu Yasujirō's *I Was Born, But . . .* (*Umarete wa mita keredo*, 1932) and Shimazu Yasujirō's *Our Neighbor, Miss Yae* (*Tonari no Yae-chan*, 1934). Back then, however, this was strictly an urban phenomenon, as such workers still constituted a small minority of the overall working population in the country; a large number of workers remained engaged in primary industries.⁶ In the postwar era, the number of white-collar workers sharply increased, in response to and influenced by such factors as the rapid growth of secondary and tertiary industries and the increase in the high school and college advancement rates. In postwar society, they were no longer considered an urban elite with cultural and intellectual sophistication. This changing status of white-collar workers can be clearly observed in the common representations of this social class in these novels and films—average and unexceptional in their talent and desire, apolitical, and concerned mostly about quotidian issues in the private sphere.

Although written by Genji Keita, *Blue-Sky Girl* is not one of these "salaryman novels." It features a young female protagonist and details her romance and search for her mother. Genji released it first in *Myōjō* as a serialized novel between the July 1956 and November 1957 issues. *Myōjō* is a monthly entertainment magazine that Shūeisha launched in 1952, targeting mainly young readers in their teens and early twenties, to compete with *Heibon*, published by Bonjinsha. Both *Heibon* and *Myōjō* specialized in content about show-business celebrities with numerous pictures, offering young readers a momentary escape from their busy working lives. Genji carefully designed this novel to suit the interests of the magazine's target audience. The protagonist Yūko is a working woman who has just graduated from high school and moved to Tokyo. Just like many of the magazine's readers, she is occupied with personal struggles, but she proactively seeks happiness and is eventually redeemed by a handsome and wealthy boyfriend. Initially, this novel gives an impression quite different from that of Genji's usual novels. Like those salaryman novels, however, *Blue-Sky Girl* concerns the quickly changing structure of the Japanese economy in the 1950s. If Genji's salaryman novels depicted the recovery and growth of the middle class constituted by urban white-collar workers and their families, *Blue-Sky Girl* drew attention to the formation of the urban working class constituted by young wage laborers who left their hometowns in rural Japan. These were two different aspects of the same phenomenon, the expansion of urbanization and industrialization in the 1950s, the seeds of which had already been planted in the interwar years and would mature over the next few decades. Indeed, it is within this broader context of the 1950s economy that I want to analyze the film version of *Blue-Sky Girl*, paying particular attention to the deployment of the labor force within the nation-state, the flow of workers to cities, and the specific subjectivity entailed for this transformation.

The Migration of Young Workers: "Going up to the Capital"

Blue-Sky Girl starts with a scene in which Yūko is taking photos with her two friends on their high school graduation day. They are standing on a cliff facing the Pacific, beneath a deep blue sky. While Yūko's father, mother, sister, and brothers live in Tokyo, she lives in a small fishing town in Izu with her grandmother because, according to her grandmother, she has been physically weak since childhood (although she has no recollection of being sick). But now that she has graduated from high school, she is supposed to move to Tokyo to live with her own parents and siblings. As she shares with her friends her anxiety about moving to a place she has never been to, their art teacher, Mr. Futami, or Futami-sensei (Sugawara Kenji), arrives by bike to tell Yūko that her grandmother has collapsed. She rushes home. Aware that her life is close to its end, her grandmother makes a surprising confession. The woman in Tokyo who Yūko has believed is her mother is actually not her biological mother. Her father had an affair with a secretary working at his company, named Mimura Machiko, and she is Yūko's biological mother. After Machiko gave birth to Yūko, her grandmother decided to raise Yūko on her own and asked Machiko to give up Yūko and never contact them again. Her grandmother knows that Machiko got married and moved to Manchuria with her husband, but nothing more.

Her grandmother dies soon after, and Yūko, now alone in Izu, is ready to move to Tokyo. While worried about her new life with her stepmother and half-siblings, she learns that Mr. Futami is also moving to Tokyo for a new job at a public relations company, and this alleviates her anxiety. Standing on the cliff together, the two of them say a fond farewell to the familiar sky of Izu (see figure 2.1). Then, the title sequence begins with the deep-blue Izu sky as the backdrop. It cuts to a scene of a Kokutetsu (National Railways) train bound for Tokyo, the bird's eye view indicating that Yūko is merely one of many people making this journey. The sentimental, wordless vocalizing by a women's chorus that accompanies this sequence accentuates the mixed sense of disquiet and hope felt by not only Yūko but also the many others who have left their rural hometowns for the city. At the end of the title sequence, the train arrives at Tokyo terminal station, a splendid red-brick building reconstructed about ten years earlier, after its destruction in the war.

Figure 2.1. *Blue-Sky Girl* (1957). Yūko and her high school teacher Futami-sensei bid farewell to the blue sky of Izu before moving to Tokyo.

From its beginning, *Blue-Sky Girl* presents itself to the audience as a story of "going up to the capital," or *jōkyō*. Since the Meiji era, Tokyo, the capital of the unified nation-state and one of its concentrations of material wealth and information, has stimulated many people's desire for economic success, political achievement, intellectual sophistication, cultural snobbery, and personal freedom.[7] The motifs of people from the countryside "going up" to Tokyo, living in Tokyo, and missing their hometowns have become extremely familiar as they are represented frequently and saliently in literature, cinema, and popular music; we see these motifs, for instance, in Natsumei Sōseki's novel *Sanshirō* ([1908] 2011), Muroo Saisei's poems in *Short Lyrical Songs* (*Jojō shōkyokushū*; [1918] 1995), Tanizaki Jun'ichirō's novel *Naomi* (*Chijin no ai*; [1924] 1985), Futamura Teiichi's hit song "A Fancy Man" ("Share otoko," 1930, an adaptation of the popular American song "A Gay Caballero"), Ozu Yasujirō's film *The Only Son* (*Hitori musuko*, 1936), and Kirishima Noboru's hit song "Who Wouldn't Think of Their Hometown?" ("Dare ka kokyō o omowazaru," 1940).[8]

With economic reconstruction and the launch of high-speed growth in the 1950s, representations of Tokyo burgeoned as never before. These representations are excellent indicators of changing perceptions of Tokyo and changing relations between the city and the countryside within the context of ever-expanding capitalism. For example, Ozu's *Tokyo Story* (1953), made eight years after defeat in the war and slightly before high-speed growth took off, portrays an elderly married couple's journey from Onomichi in Hiroshima Prefecture to Tokyo to visit their grown-up children. Through the eyes of the couple (Ryū Chishū and Higashiyama Chieko), the audience observes the postwar reconstruction of the middle-class families that had migrated to Tokyo in the prewar era. At the same time, it shows the growing and almost unamendable disconnection between generations, which also manifests as the spatial and cultural disconnection between the countryside, symbolized by the parents, who speak the Onomichi dialect, and the city, symbolized by the grown-up children, who speak perfect "standard" Japanese.

Imamura Shōhei's *The Insect Woman* (*Nippon konchūki*, 1963), released ten years after *Tokyo Story*, depicts a woman named Tome (Hidari Sachiko), from a poor farming family in the Tohoku region, who moves to Tokyo during the Korean War and works as a maid for the household of an American soldier and his Japanese lover, who used to be a street prostitute, or *pan-pan*. To escape poverty, Tome ends up becoming a prostitute herself and then the manager of a prostitution organization, only to be arrested for violating the Anti-Prostitution Law, and falls into economic misery once again. While made amid the Ikeda cabinet's "income doubling plan," which was one of the major symbolic events of the high-speed growth era, the film brutally shatters the illusion that economic benefits were expanding widely throughout the nation and highlights the unevenness of wealth distribution. It reveals the violence of capital, especially against working-class women in a society where the constitution recognizes both gender equality and the state's responsibility for the people's welfare but where neither was properly put into practice. In this film, Tokyo is represented as a place of survival for lonely, uprooted women like Tome, with no money, education, or familial and communal support.

How, then, should we understand the motif of going up to Tokyo in *Blue-Sky Girl*, taking into consideration the fact that it was made in 1957, between *Tokyo Story* and *The Insect Woman*, at the very beginning of high-speed growth? We must read it as an allusion to the large-scale migration of teenage girls and boys from farming and fishing communities to metropolitan cities. Attracted by greater opportunities for economic success in cities and distressed by the shortage thereof in the countryside, they left their hometowns, became wage laborers in cities, worked under precarious conditions without much job security (e.g., in small factories and mom-and-pop stores), and often settled and formed families there. This movement had just begun around the time the film was released and would last throughout the high-speed growth era. As of 1955, the populations of Tokyo, Osaka, and Aichi Prefectures were about 8 million, 4.6 million, and 3.8 million respectively. In 1975, after the end of high-speed growth, their populations had grown to 11.7 million, 8.3 million, and 5.9 million respectively, whereas the populations of rural prefectures in such regions as Tohoku, Shikoku, and Kyushu remained relatively stable or decreased despite rapid population growth at the national level (Sōrifu Tōkeikyoku 1977a, 6–9; see tables 2.1 and 2.2). Massive industrialization and urbanization during the high-speed growth era were enabled by this flow of cheap, abundant labor from the countryside.

Table 2.1. Populations of selected prefectures with major cities

Region	Prefecture	Population (1955)	Population (1975)
Kanto	Tokyo	8,037,084	11,673,554
Kanto	Kanagawa (including Yokohama)	2,919,497	5,397,748
Kanto	Chiba	2,205,060	4,149,147
Kanto	Saitama	2,262,623	4,821,340
Chubu	Aichi (including Nagoya)	3,769,209	5,923,569
Kinki	Osaka	4,618,308	8,278,925
Kinki	Hyogo (including Kobe)	3,620,947	4,992,140
Kinki	Kyoto	1,935,161	2,424,856

Source: Sōrifu Tōkeikyoku (1977a, 6–9).

Table 2.2. Populations of Selected Rural Prefectures

Region	Prefecture	Population (1955)	Population (1975)
Tōhoku	Aomori	1,382,523	1,484,646
Tōhoku	Akita	1,348,871	1,232,481
Tōhoku	Fukushima	2,095,237	1,970,616
Hokuriku	Toyama	1,021,121	1,070,791
San'in	Tottori	614,259	581,311
Chūgoku	Yamaguchi	1,609,839	1,555,218
Shikoku	Kagawa	943,823	961,292
Shikoku	Kōchi	882,683	808,397
Kyushu	Miyazaki	1,139,384	1,085,055
Kyushu	Kagoshima	2,044,212	1,723,902

Source: Sōrifu Tōkeikyoku (1977a, 6–9).

Many of those young workers moved to cities under the system called *shūdan shūshoku*, or "mass employment." As Japanese capitalism entered a phase of rapid growth, urban employers in such metropolitan areas as Tokyo/Yokohama, Osaka/Kobe, and Nagoya, especially small- and medium-sized business owners, became concerned about labor shortages and looked to middle school graduates in rural regions such as Tōhoku, northern Kanto, Shikoku, and Kyushu as a solution to this problem. They had a hard time recruiting young workers in cities since they could not compete with large companies in salaries, benefits, and reputation, so they extended their search to those rural regions. From the standpoint of agrarian and fishing communities in rural Japan, this was one way of addressing the problem of a large relative surplus population, which was becoming increasingly difficult to resolve at the local level. The public sector—the Ministry of Labor, the employment security offices, and the prefectural governments—served as mediators between urban employers and rural communities and job seekers. As Yamaguchi Satoshi (2016), a geographer who has written extensively on this topic, points out, this was postwar Japan's attempt to (re)construct a national labor market in the aftermath of the collapse of empire by effectively transferring a young labor force to those areas of labor shortage.[9]

It was around the time of the release of *Blue-Sky Girl* that the movement of teenage workers across the archipelago began to receive intense media attention every March, at the end of the academic year. For example, the *Asahi* newspaper of March 20, 1957, informs us that 1,050 middle school graduates from Miyagi Prefecture in the Tōhoku region had arrived at Ueno Station to take up work at small factories and stores across Tokyo—the first group to migrate to the city that spring ("Ashidori mo karuku" 1957). The *Asahi* on March 23 published another article on the topic, showing that groups of middle school graduates, many from the Tōhoku prefectures of Fukushima, Aomori, Yamagata, and Akita, were arriving in Tokyo one after another. The article estimated the total number of middle school graduates who would settle in Tokyo that spring to be about twelve thousand, an increase of three thousand over the previous year ("Shūdan shūshoku tsuzuite nyūkyō" 1957). Throughout the high-speed growth era, the arrival of rural young workers at major cities would become a seasonal event covered by the national and local media every spring. This large-scale migration lasted until the 1970s, resulting in the rapid expansion of metropolitan areas, fueling young people's dreams of urban middle-class life, and exacerbating not only the economic gap but also the cultural gap between urban and provincial Japan.

Within this context, Yūko's experience of going up to the capital speaks for those ordinary, nameless young girls and boys who had to leave their families and hometowns to become wage laborers in cities. Just like those young workers, Yūko is confused and disoriented when she arrives in Tokyo and desperate for help. Once the title sequence is over, we see Yūko exiting Tokyo Station, to be greeted immediately by urban bustle and speed. Not knowing how to get to her father's house in Aoyama, an affluent neighborhood in the southwestern part of Tokyo's twenty-three wards (about three miles west of Tokyo Station), she asks a businessman the way. Preoccupied, this businessman does not pay much attention to her and just shouts, "Streetcar! Streetcar! If not, the subway!" ("Toden da yo, toden. Janakattara chikatetsu da ne") in a perfunctory manner. Next, Yūko asks a young woman the same question. She does not hide her annoyance at being stopped by a stranger and angrily replies, "There!" ("Atchi!"), pointing vaguely and probably inaccurately, with no intention of helping Yūko (see figure 2.2). Then, the woman's friend, a man wearing makeup and earrings, shows up, and the two quickly disappear as if they never saw Yūko. Immediately after this, Yūko gets caught by a male college

Figure 2.2. *Blue-Sky Girl* (1957). Just outside Tokyo Station, Yūko asks a woman the way to Aoyama, but people in Tokyo are not as kind as those in her hometown.

student, who fanatically tries to convince her of the imminent possibility of a nuclear war. Within the first few minutes of her arrival in Tokyo, Yūko encounters three representative types of urban creatures hardly seen in her hometown: the busy businessman; the young adult unbound by middle-class, nuclear-family values; and the intellectual but neurotic student.

The maid, Yae (Miyako Chōchō), finally finds Yūko and takes her to her father's gorgeous house in Aoyama. There, she realizes that none of her half-siblings welcome her. Hiroshi, her younger half-brother, calls her a maid and tells her to call him *botchan*, or "young master." Her stepmother, Tatsuko (Sawamura Sadako), abhors Yūko since she is a living reminder of the infidelity that her husband indulged in when they were still newlyweds. Tatsuko, like her biological children, treats Yūko as a maid and tells her to help Yae with daily chores because there are many guests at their house and Yae is currently the only maid. Yae tries to protest, but Yūko, not wanting to cause unnecessary trouble between them, stops her and agrees to work as a maid. The room she is assigned is a small, dark, and dusty storage space beneath the stairs. The next morning, she gets up earlier than anyone else in the house and starts working with Yae, taking care of the dog, preparing breakfast for the family, and cleaning the house.

Again, this was a situation familiar to many female workers at that time; it was common for girls from rural Japan to work as live-in maids for upper- and middle-class families in the city. According to the 1955 national census, there were more than 300,000 women working as maids in Japan, and nearly two-thirds of them were young women between fifteen and twenty-four years old (Sōrifu Tōkeikyoku 1959, 238, 374). Back then, before high-speed growth raised labor costs and before home electric appliances enabled a sharp reduction of time spent on housework, it was far more common than now for an upper- to middle-class household with decent disposable income in urban Japan to keep one or more live-in maids.[10] The conditions for young workers from the countryside were far less desirable than those of their urban counterparts, due to their lower wages and longer hours, and even among those from the countryside, the girls who became maids had to endure some of the worst working conditions. Their work time was hardly distinguished from their free time. It was not uncommon for them to work for more than twelve hours a day. Two days off a month was considered normal. The 1947 Labor Standards Act excluded maids from its purview, which meant that they could not seek collective action as organized workers to improve their conditions and that many of them indeed had to deal with arbitrary treatment by their employers without effective legal recourse. For these reasons, this occupation began losing its attraction quickly for young women in the postwar era when workers became increasingly conscious of their economic and social rights (Shimizu Michiko 2004).

Many contemporary accounts corroborate the sense of frustration and loneliness that these atomized workers shared while facing class-based discrimination. Kimura Masayo, a seventeen-year-old maid who left her hometown in southern Hokkaido in a "mass employment" campaign to work for a family in Shinjuku in Tokyo, confesses that she hates to be called a maid. She is of course aware that she is a maid, but when the fifth-grade son of the family shouts "Hey, Maid! Maid!" ("Korā, jochū, jochū!"), she becomes immersed in a sad feeling that she "does not know how to express with words" ("nan to kotoba ni ii arawashite yoi no ka wakaranai"). When she is alone, she likes fantasizing about her future, such as the kind of house and the number of children she wants to have. But when the boy calls her, this pleasurable moment of fantasy dissipates quickly "as if it were snatched away by a great wind" ("ōkaze ni demo sarawareta yō ni"), and she has to reply with a smile ("Shūdan shūshoku shita nenshō rōdōsha" 1958, 18). Similarly, Watanabe Mitsuyo, who moved to Tokyo yearning for urban life, says that she senses the air of contempt when people use the term *jochū* (maid) and realizes that there are ranks in occupations. She insists that she is also a "respectable human being" ("rippa na ningen") ("Jochū-san no kai" 1955, 38).

Like these young women, Yūko in *Blue-Sky Girl* feels dismayed when her younger half-brother Hiroshi, who also looks like a fifth-grade boy, addresses her with *omae* (a rude form of second-person pronoun, which a child would never use for an adult in ordinary circumstances) and calls her *jochū*, showing obvious disdain for her and her occupation. Here, she is disturbed by the realization that she is placed nearly at the bottom of the social hierarchy and denied dignity as an individual person in the very place to which she came in hopes of a new life with her own family. This leads her, just like the girl from Hokkaido above, to the world of fantasy. Whenever facing difficulty, she dreams of flying freely anywhere she likes (the question of "fantasy" will be discussed in detail later in this chapter). Thus, Yūko's life in Tokyo is represented in such a way as to echo the working lives of young maids in cities and to suggest the absurd reality in highly stratified class society—that urban employers treat maids without courtesy, perceiving their occupation in close association with the social class to which they belong as well as the rural Japan from which they come.

A Special Maid from Izu

The representations of Yūko as a maid, however, are by no means realistic. Although she faces maltreatment by her stepmother and half-sister, we do not see the crude reality of the life of a typical maid, including severe poverty, deterioration of health due to long work hours, sexual exploitation by a man of the household, and so on. The trouble that Yūko faces functions at most to add some thrill to a plot that eventually resolves in a happy ending (i.e., Yūko's finding her biological mother and her future husband). Yūko as a maid is represented in a rather idealized manner, and, through this, the film intends to construct an affirmative image of her occupation, which was underappreciated in contemporary Japanese society even among those in occupations commonly associated with working-class women. To examine this point, we can compare her situation with that of typical working girls in Tokyo—where in the nation-state they came from and what cultural meanings people in the capital attributed to those places during the era of high-speed growth. In other words, we need to consider the politics of the images of places within the nation-state and how *Blue-Sky Girl*, in order to develop the character of the female protagonist, capitalizes on an image specific to her place of origin.

First, at the national level, there were clear patterns in labor migration in the 1950s, and this resulted in the consolidation of several discrete region-based labor markets (which were by no means independent from one another). That is, because of geographical proximity, Tokyo attracted young workers mainly from northern Japan; Osaka absorbed those mainly from western and southern Japan; and Aichi, located in between Tokyo and Osaka and a center of manufacturing with such large companies as Toyota, recruited workers from both the north and south (Yamaguchi Sataoshi 2016, 59–77). This means that around the time of the release of *Blue-Sky Girl* many working girls (and boys) in Tokyo, including maids, came from the Tohoku region.

In fact, there are a fair number of literary and cinematic representations of maids from Tohoku in the 1950s, and these help us understand the widespread images of Tohoku maids that the Tokyo-centered media fashioned. For instance, *Maid's Boy* (*Jochūkko*) is a novel that Yuki Shigeko ([1955] 1968) first published in *Shōsetsu Shinchō* in 1954; the next year, Nikkatsu director Tasaka Tomotaka adapted it for film with the same title. The protagonist, Hatsu (Hidari Sachiko), is a maid from Akita (in the novel, she is from Yamagata, another Tohoku prefecture) and works for an upper-middle-class family in Setagaya Ward—a wealthy, mostly residential ward located in the westernmost part of Tokyo's twenty-three wards. She speaks a heavy Tohoku dialect, which the family ridicules. She wears *monpe*—loose work pants worn by women in farming communities, which had been popularized during the war but were becoming extremely rare, if not extinct, in cities in the 1950s. She is mesmerized by modern and sophisticated urban life, such as bright light bulbs, a gas space heater, and the Western-style room with books that is assigned to her as a "maid's room." While being treated fairly decently by the family, Hatsu is at the end blamed for a theft committed by Katsumi—the younger son of the family. Because of her class-based inferiority, lack of education, and devotion to Katsumi, she is unable to deny the charge and is fired. Right before taking the train back to Akita, she stops by the elementary school that Katsumi attends. Unaware that this is his last time to see her and embarrassed to be seen with a maid (or to be called "a maid's boy" by his friends), he treats her in a perfunctory manner. Saddened by this, she leaves Tokyo quietly.

A Young Miss (*Ojōsan*, 1961) is another interesting example. This is a film adaptation of Mishima Yukio's ([1960] 2010) novel of the same title, directed by Yuge Tarō, a young Daiei director. It is a light romantic comedy, representative of this film studio in that era, starring Wakao Ayako as the daughter of a bourgeois family in Tokyo and depicting her romance with a handsome playboy (Kawaguchi Hiroshi). This family employs a maid named Yoshii, played by Miyakawa Kazuko. Her role in the film is minor, and the audience has no opportunity to learn exactly where she is from. But the film uses the exaggerated images of Tohoku maids that were circulating by that time in order to help the audience identify the maid's regional origin. This maid, like Hatsu in *Maid's Boy*, speaks a heavy Tohoku dialect, for which the mistress of the household occasionally scolds her. She wears unrefined clothes (but not *monpe*) and hairstyle, which contrasts sharply with the other female characters' fashionable urban appearance, especially Wakao's. Both of these films attest to the Tokyo media's condescending, almost derisive representation of maids from Tohoku as simple, ignorant, and unsophisticated, as if they needed to be enlightened by the capital's advanced culture. Moreover, these representations of maids are part of the larger discourse of the Tohoku region itself as a savage peripheral land resistant to national unification and left behind by modernization—a discourse that the capital and the nation-state have reproduced since the Meiji era (Kawanishi 2001, 2007).[11]

What, then, of Yūko in *Blue-Sky Girl*? She is not from Tohoku and is therefore free from the saturated meanings given to maids from this region. Genji Keita's original novel set Yūko's home in a rural town along the Inland Sea in western Japan. Although it is not explicitly identified, if we consider the fact that she goes to Tokyo through Osaka and stops at Osaka on the way back to her hometown, we can speculate that it is somewhere in Okayama, Hiroshima, or Yamaguchi Prefecture in the San'yo region, well-known for its warm and sunny weather and beautiful coasts, right next to the Kansai region with its three major cities: Osaka, Kobe, and Kyoto. For Genji, who lived and worked in Osaka for a long time, it was only natural to set his young heroine's hometown in this region (as many young workers from this region moved to Osaka and Kobe during the high-speed growth era).

In Masumura's film, however, Yūko's hometown has been switched to a fishing village on the Izu peninsula in Shizuoka Prefecture. Location shooting was conducted in Itō, a city located in the eastern part of the Izu peninsula, along the Pacific. The high cliff standing in the blue sky and overlooking the ocean appears several times in the film, including the beginning and the end, constituting some of the most memorable scenes, each of which marks an important phase of Yūko's journey to find her own happiness in Tokyo. For this director, who was born in Yamanashi and attended Tokyo University, the San'yo region in western Japan was so far away that it probably did not carry much significance. Also, it was probably the case that Shizuoka's proximity to Tokyo was attractive for location shooting. But I also want to point out that the film cleverly capitalizes on the beautiful and upscale image of Izu that had been well established in Japan to counter the negative perceptions of maids from rural Japan.

During the Tokugawa era, this area—known as Izu-no-kuni, or Izu Province—functioned as a key traffic site, since it was located right on the Tōkaidō, the highway connecting Edo and Kyō, hosting its tenth to twelfth stations: Hakone, Mishima, and Numazu. In the Meiji era, as industrialization generated urban problems common to any emerging capitalist state, such as overcrowding and air pollution, upper-class Tokyoites rediscovered Izu as a scenic resort town with a mild climate, easily accessible from the capital. Itō and Atami (just north of Itō on the same peninsula) gained fame for their hot springs and pristine, beautiful beaches. Further north, beyond the peninsula, at the foot of Mount Fuji, a cool, dry climate made Gotenba an ideal summer resort. A number of wealthy urbanites, including Tanizaki

Jun'ichirō, Shiga Naoya, and Tokutomi Sohō, built vacation or year-round houses in this region. There is no shortage of well-known cultural representations of Izu, including, in literature, Ozaki Kōyō's *Golden Demon* (*Konjiki yasha*; [1898–1903] 1969), Kikuchi Kan's *Madame Pearl* (*Shinju-fujin*; [1920] 2002), Kawabata Yasunari's *The Izu Dancer* (*Izu no odoriko*; [1927] 2003), Dazai Osamu's *The Setting Sun* (*Shayō*; [1947] 2003), and Mishima Yukio's *Death in Midsummer* (*Manatsu no shi*; [1953] 1970); and, in cinema, Mizoguchi Kenji's *Portrait of Madame Yuki* (*Yuki-fujin ezu*, 1950) and Ozu Yasujirō's *Tokyo Story* (1953), not to mention the many film adaptations of *The Izu Dancer* that have been made since the 1930s. Izu is probably one of the most heavily represented, frequently cited, and richly imagined rural places in modern Japan.

However, Yūko's hometown in *Blue-Sky Girl* is a small fishing village with humble-looking houses. Nothing in the film suggests that it is part of the affluent resort loved and frequented by the urban rich. But this is where intertextuality matters. By this time, numerous cultural representations had consolidated the image of Izu stated above nationwide. Anyone who engaged with literature, film, monthly and weekly journals, or radio broadcasting at even a minimal level would have been familiar with this popular image and would have understood Yūko's hometown in relation to it. In this regard, an interesting article appeared in *Myōjō*—the magazine in which Genji first published *Blue-Sky Girl* as a serialized novel—around the time of the release of the film ("Aozora-musume roke hōkoku" 1957). This article reported on how the film was being shot on the Jōgasaki coast, a famous tourist site in Itō (see figure 2.3). It praised the deep-blue sky on the horizon and featured several photos of the smiling stars between takes, including Wakao, Sugawara Kenji, and Kawasaki Keizō, who played Yūko's boyfriend and future husband, Mr. Hirooka. The article clearly builds upon the widely circulated bright, positive image of Izu and entices readers to mobilize their intertextual knowledge of this scenic, prosperous resort town. When we perceive Yūko and her occupation with this knowledge, she is not simply a maid from any rural town in Japan, desperate for a job in Tokyo, apologetic for her unsophistication, and waiting to be enlightened by the capital's culture, but a special maid from a privileged rural Japan that even Tokyoites aspire to visit.

Figure 2.3. *Blue-Sky Girl* (1957). Location shooting was conducted on the Jōgasaki coast, a scenic part of Izu.

The Intertextuality of Wakao Ayako

If we are to read *Blue-Sky Girl* as speaking on behalf of countless working-class girls in Tokyo displaced from their hometowns, we need to consider not only the ways that the occupation of maid is represented but also the meanings of the actress playing that maid: Wakao Ayako, one of Daiei's most profitable stars and a symbol of the golden age of Japanese cinema, who, in her early career, was an object of enthusiastic admiration among teenage girls.

Today, Wakao is remembered most vividly for the passionate and almost obsessive heroines that she played in Masumura's later films, such as *A Wife Confesses* (*Tsuma wa kokuhaku suru*, 1961), *The Husband Witnessed* (*Otto ga mita*, 1964), *Seisaku's Wife* (*Seisaku no tsuma*, 1965), and *Red Angel* (*Akai tenshi*, 1966). While the plots and settings of these films differ, the heroines share a strong desire for love and a determination to pursue the men they love despite various obstacles and/or the punishment of society.[12] Some fans (including myself) may recollect the savvy, less emotional, slightly eccentric, and somewhat comical heroines that she played in three of Kawashima Yūzō's films: *A Woman Is Born Twice* (*Onna wa nido umareru*, 1961), *Temple of the Wild Geese* (*Gan no tera*, 1962), and *Elegant Beast* (*Shitoyaka na kedamono*, 1962). As Irene González points out in her essay on Wakao's star persona, however, in the beginning of her career in the late 1950s, the media and fans identified "charming sweetness" and "ordinariness" as the most representative features of Wakao the actress (González 2014, 41). She was seen primarily as a girl-next-door type with the kind of beauty that could be found even among ordinary girls outside show business, as opposed to those actresses with extraordinary, unobtainable beauty, such as Kyō Machiko (of international fame) and Yamamoto Fujiko (the 1950 Miss Nippon), both of whom were in Wakao's cohort at Daiei. The president of Daiei, Nagata Masaichi, characterized her as "a flower of humble height" (*hikune no hana*), punning on the well-known Japanese expression "a flower of lofty height" (*takane no hana*), meaning someone or something special and difficult to obtain (Satō Tadao 2012, 32).

In a 1956 article for *Kinema junpō*, the social psychologist Minami Hiroshi and two other researchers analyzed the contents of the 2,955 fan letters that Wakao received over one month of 1955 (Minami et al. 1956). The article uses such terms as *heibon* (ordinary), *shominteki* (like ordinary people), *junjō* (pure), and *akarui* (cheerful) multiple times to describe her appeal. It points out that most of her fans are women in their teens and twenties with working-class backgrounds who are not very satisfied with their lives and that Wakao's approachability allowed them to write to her casually and share their concerns as though talking to their own sister. As this article indicates, Mizoguchi Kenji's 1953 *A Geisha* (*Gion bayashi*), ranked ninth by *Kinema junpō* for the year, was one of the films through which the actress solidified her approachable, girl-next-door appeal to young female fans. In this film, she plays the young heroine Eiko, who has become a geisha because she had no one to rely on. Eiko is not yet tainted by the world of money, sex, and games and refuses to be consumed by men as a commodity. While Omocha and Kimichō, the unforgettable heroines played brilliantly by Yamada Isuzu in Mizoguchi's prewar *Sisters of Gion* (*Gion no kyōdai*, 1936) and by Kyō Machiko in Yoshimura Kōzaburō's early postwar *Clothes of Deception* (*Itsuwareru seisō*, 1951), respectively, unapologetically capitalize on and manipulate male carnal desire for their own advantage (and get punished precisely for this), Eiko in *A Geisha* remains fairly innocent throughout the film, without falling into professional cunning, calculation, or greed. Unlike Omocha and Kimichō, who seem comfortable playing in the role of geisha, Eiko is just a regular girl who happens to be a geisha because of her unfortunate living circumstances.[13] The star image of Wakao thus created suited the new era of postwar democracy, in which the power of the masses had so grown that cultural industries felt increasingly compelled to appeal to this emerging social group through the promotion of stars who did not differ greatly from those masses (or who pretended not to differ from them).

When we consider this star image of Wakao Ayako, it makes sense that Masumura's *Blue-Sky Girl* featured her as its heroine. Published in *Myōjō*, Genji Keita's original novel was intended as a story that would enlist empathy and support from teenage girls, featuring the kind of heroine with whom those young readers could identify. It is not hard to imagine that, when the idea of a film adaptation arose, Masumura and Daiei chose Wakao from among the many actresses contracted to the company because of her specific fan demographic and the star image that had developed around her. Her approachability and unpretentiousness were perfect qualifications for the heroine of *Blue-Sky Girl*, who was expected to communicate with, cheer up, and speak for those young fans by depicting a regular working girl just like them.[14]

In his book on stardom, Richard Dyer (2004, 16) examines stars as the "embodiments of the social categories in which people are placed and through which they have to make sense of their lives, and indeed through which we make our lives—categories of class, gender, ethnicity, religion, sexual orientation, and so on" and maintains that they show us ways of discerning or crafting the meanings of our material experiences in a tangible manner. If we agree with Dyer, one critical implication of Wakao as a star constructed around the star image detailed above is that she indicated to young working-class fans the possibility of achieving economic success in capitalist society. Although we who live in neoliberal capitalist societies in the twenty-first century often try to convince ourselves or are taught to believe that individual effort is a major source of economic success (despite the presence of indisputable counterevidence), it was not easy to endorse this kind of rhetoric in 1950s Japan. What economists call the "dual structure" of the economy—the coexistence of profitable and stable large companies with large capital and precarious medium-sized and small companies that depended on the former for survival—kept the labor market divided (Nakamura Takafusa 1993, 1995; Kurihara 1989). Educational level, geographical origin, family origin, inherited wealth, connections, and gender served as critical factors in determining one's place in society, and therefore it was extremely difficult for those young workers from rural Japan, many of them with only a middle school education, to gain entry into the upper part of this structure (e.g., by becoming a white-collar worker at Sony, Panasonic, or Toyota in Tokyo, Osaka, or Nagoya). For them, competing in the market was often an agonizing experience filled with frustration and despair. Cut off from communal relations with their hometowns and atomized as individual workers in cities, they were made to realize time and again that, apart from their individual effort, many other things over which they had no control had already placed them in a disadvantageous position compared to their urban middle-class counterparts.[15] Playing the kind of roles that young female workers could identify with, Wakao presented one interpretation of their work lives—that the hardship and loneliness they were enduring might someday be rewarded with upward social mobility, as long as they remained diligent, cheerful, and, above all, positive.

In this regard, I want to mention one more film. In 1958, the year after *Blue-Sky Girl* was released, established Daiei director Yoshimura Kōzaburō made *A Grain of Wheat* (*Hitotsubu no mugi*). Unlike *Blue-Sky Girl*, this film deals directly with the issues of mass employment and class- and region-based discrimination. A group of young workers who have moved to Tokyo from a small town in Fukushima Prefecture in Tohoku are the protagonists of this dark-toned film, and their struggle, poverty, and alienation in the city are its main themes. It features both Sugawara Kenji and Wakao Ayako, the couple from *Blue-Sky Girl*. Sugawara, Mr. Futami in *Blue-Sky Girl*, plays a passionate teacher at the middle school that the young workers attend in Fukushima. In this film, Wakao does not play a young worker but Sugawara's caring colleague and, later, wife. Both worry incessantly about their former students' lives in Tokyo. Their hearts get broken whenever these former students meet with misfortune—not getting paid by their employer, losing a job due to the company's bankruptcy, returning to their hometown due to illness, and so forth.

On August 30, 1958, two weeks before its official release, *A Grain of Wheat* was screened at an event for young workers who had moved to Tokyo from the countryside under mass employment. The Ministry of Labor, together with Daiei and the Asahi Shimbun Social Welfare Organization, co-organized this event to recognize these young workers' hard work, which, while making significant contributions to the country's economy, was hardly given sufficient and appropriate attention by Japanese society. This event was attended by Wakao and Sugawara. Prior to the screening, they threw signed balls to the young audience to lighten the atmosphere and build rapport. The other important attendees included the vice-minister of labor and the president of Daiei. The former, in his opening speech, bolstered young workers' morale and encouraged them not to be defeated by hardship in the workplace. The latter, Nagata Masaichi, explaining the intention of the film, emphasized the importance of workers' patience and cooperative relations between employers and employees while admonishing workers against making unreasonable demands of their employers ("Shūdan shūshoku shita wakōdo" 1958). These people who belonged to the ruling elite in postwar society viewed the purpose of the film as keeping those young workers, who were likely to be discontent and might easily have inclined toward leftist and radical ideology, in their place within the existing economic system. In their understanding, the film's primary message was that there was no other solution to economic hardship but enduring it in good spirits. It was especially important to them to confirm this point explicitly in the late 1950s, when the organized labor movement was growing rapidly (note that the famous Miike struggle in Kyushu, one of the largest labor disputes in postwar Japan, would start the following year).

When we take the intertextual effect of Wakao Ayako into consideration, however, a quite different reading is possible. With her star image constructed through the performance of outgoing heroines in such films as *Blue-Sky Girl*, this actress adds a slight degree of hope and optimism to this unsentimental, realist film, which again and again underscores the powerlessness of young rural workers in the face of greedy and inhumane capitalist forces. Although the teacher that Wakao plays in *A Grain of Wheat*—Ichiko-sensei, or Ms. Ichiko—is a fairly conventional and docile character who accepts her own fate and that of her students as more or less inevitable, we can superimpose on this character the intertextual image of Wakao as an actress who has repeatedly played regular but strong-willed women who seek to find happiness on their own. It then becomes possible for us to interpret the film not only as an unemotional portrayal of the predicament of young workers from Tohoku but also as a demonstration of solidarity with them, reassuring them of the possibility of redemption in a manner similar to *Blue-Sky Girl* (or providing them with some fantasy of a bright future), and thereby helping them to make some sense of the quite unbearable harshness of life in the city as wage laborers.

Individualism as a Critique of Japanese Society

The strong-willed heroine not easily defeated by hardship is one of the main factors that make *Blue-Sky Girl* irresistible. Masumura Yasuzō consciously created this type of heroine in the numerous films on which he collaborated with Wakao, beginning with *Blue-Sky Girl*. This section will locate the significance of this heroine type within the specific intellectual context of the early postwar years and examine it as the embodiment of a subjectivity that the director felt urged to promote through film in a society he believed was feudal and backward.

Masumura was a passionate advocate of individualism and a relentless critic of contemporary Japanese society.[16] His critique derived from his experience in the wartime era, when he was still a high school student. Witnessing the democratic atmosphere of the Taishō era quickly replaced by Shōwa totalitarianism, he reached one realization about humans: they were an "extremely ephemeral existence that weakly yields to massive power" ("kyodai na kenryoku no mae ni wa moroku mo kuppuku suru kiwamete hakanai sonzai"). Even after this realization, however, he still clung to a slight hope for humans and wondered about their exact nature. But neither fascism nor emperor-centered spiritualism offered him a convincing answer. He was drafted near the end of the war and spent three months as a private in a state of resignation, feeling that he might have to die for his country (Masumura [1967] 2014, 31–34).

Masumura states that the American occupation did not fundamentally alter his conclusion about humans. The US occupation forces, which "imposed" (*oshitsuke*) American-style democracy on Japan, were as authoritarian as the wartime government. The occupation forces' last-minute ban of the February 1 general strike in 1947 (through which the American occupiers clearly indicated that democratic reforms would be tolerated only within the existing economic system) further reinforced Masumura's disillusionment with powerless humans (34–35). Then, the moment of change came. After earning two degrees from Tokyo University and working for Daiei as a part-time assistant director for four years, Masumura won a prestigious scholarship to study at the Centro Sperimentale di Cinematografia in Italy. He spent two years there, beginning in 1952. Travel abroad was not liberalized in postwar Japan until 1964, which made it extremely difficult, if not impossible, for ordinary citizens to travel as far as Europe. Masumura's stay in Italy was therefore a privileged opportunity allowed only to those with an elite education, sufficient money and time, and extensive connections.

In Italy, Masumura encountered humans living freely and cheerfully—the kind that he thought had already perished in Japan. This greatly surprised him because Italy, like Japan, had been destroyed by the war, and therefore he had expected Italian society to be "dark and desperate" ("kuraku zetsubōteki"). In reality, however, humans in Italy seemed fearless and proud of themselves and knew how to enjoy life without being deflated by defeat in the war. Masumura located the basis of this pride in the civilization that the Italians had advanced for centuries. This, in his opinion, nurtured their unshakeable confidence in humans' "intellect and beauty" ("chisei to bi"), which would not easily be altered or extinguished by changes in political regimes. This, in turn, made him realize why humans in Japan, a country that had copied foreign ideas without producing its own civilization, were so susceptible to greater powers and organizations (35–38).

In Masumura's search for strong and independent humans, it is not hard to observe the profound influence of Enlightenment thought, which privileged the individual as the most basic unit in society and endorsed autonomy and freedom from external forces. While the notion of the free and autonomous individual emerged out of a specific historical context of modern Europe, Masumura seems to have believed that it could be used to gauge the extent of the maturity of civil society in Japan and lamented the gap between his ideal and the situation in which he perceived Japan and the Japanese to be at that time.

This disconsolate perception of Japan was by no means unusual within the intellectual community of early postwar Japan. Heavily influenced by the prewar Kōza school of Marxists, which, when evaluating the state of Japanese capitalism, had insisted on the backwardness of post-Restoration Japanese society by pointing out "feudal remnants" in the emperor system (that is, in their understanding, an absolute monarchy), modernists in post-defeat Japan were convinced that national reconstruction would entail the complete overthrow of feudalism and the building of a bourgeois democratic society. While coming from various disciplines with various ideological backgrounds, they generally agreed that this new society could not be simply about change in political institutions but must be accompanied by a fundamental internal transformation of the people themselves.[17]

For example, the political scientist Maruyama Masao ([1946] 1995), concerned about Japanese society's acquiescence to the militarized state during World War II, identified the absence of the free subject as the fundamental cause of what he thought of as a pathological deviation from the normative path to democracy. Where there were no free subjects with a firm consciousness of the self clearly demarcated from the external world, he believed, each person simply submitted irresponsibly and blindly to a higher authority, which was ultimately linked to the emperor—the embodiment of the highest value. Similarly, the legal scholar Kawashima Takeyoshi ([1948] 2000) criticized the family system, which, according to him, required members to demonstrate unconditional obedience to authority (i.e., father and husband) and familial order, thereby preventing them from thinking and acting independently. He saw the family as the epitome of oppressive Japanese society and maintained that the pseudofamilial relations of *oyabun* (boss) and *kobun* (henchmen) dictated all social relations. While their objects of study were different, both Maruyama and Kawashima accused Japanese society of privileging the collective over the individual; for them, the pursuit of bourgeois democracy was almost synonymous with the recognition of individualism.[18]

Just as Maruyama and Kawashima used their own writings to enlighten the public about the need for individualism, Masumura regarded film as a critical medium for achieving the same goal. While still in Rome, he made a promise to himself:

> If I had an opportunity to make a film someday, I thought, I would depict the "individual," which did not exist in Japan. I thought I would bring up not humans who would give

way, compromise, and yield within the "relations" called husband-wife, family, company, society, and the state, but those who would fight against those "relations," resist, and insist on themselves. (Masumura [1967] 2014, 39)

Once he started to make films as a Daiei director, Masumura urgently highlighted the novelty of his own works while criticizing the world of Japanese cinematic tradition. He was particularly unsympathetic to the family dramas of the Shōchiku Company's Ōfuna studio—a genre that had enjoyed great popularity since the 1930s that depicted the everyday lives of the urban petit-bourgeoisie with humor and pathos. It appeared to Masumura that the characters in these films were pathetic creatures confined in a small "bird cage" (*torikago*) and consumed by trivial day-to-day concerns without knowing the world that exists beyond their immediate life space. To a European audience with strong individual consciousness, he thought, these films would be simply boring. Such an audience would be more interested in people who "fight against society" ("shakai to tatakai") and "advance society" ("shakai o zenshin sasete") for the sake of "humanity" ("ningen-sei"; Masumura [1958] 2014a, 32–33).

Masumura presented his work as a critical response to the tradition of Japanese cinema. His goal was to create characters faithful to their own desire and determined to change their surroundings through their own effort—the kind of characters he did not believe had ever existed in Japanese cinema. The first thing he had to do for this was to affirm and embrace human emotions as the driving force that would evoke discord in the seemingly harmonious society. He stated:

> I want to express human emotions—delight, anger, sorrow, and pleasure—as freely as possible. I want to blow out powerfully the social constraints in which the Japanese have been locked and create the ways in which they laugh, cry, and sing freely. . . . I want to shout the songs that the Japanese have concealed deep in their mind and have never talked about, on a full screen, noisily in a loud voice; it's OK even if it looks crazy. (Masumura [1958] 2014c, 44–45)

The implication of this statement is that individuals are essentially oppositional to society, as the former have the tendency to act according to emotions and instincts, while the latter incessantly monitors conduct to keep individuals in place, thereby maintaining order. In other words, Masumura indicates that one's subjectivity as an individual must be constructed through confrontation with, resistance to, and above all liberation from society's regulating and standardizing forces. As typical examples of characters who embody this type of subjectivity, he points to the young couple played by Kawaguchi Hiroshi and Nozoe Hitomi in *Kisses*, who first meet when they visit the prison where their fathers are both jailed and fall passionately in love; Ishiwata Gin in *Warm Current* (*Danryū*, 1957), played by Hidari Sachiko, who unabashedly shouts at Tokyo Station to the man she loves that she can become his mistress and wait for him forever, while knowing that he loves another woman; and of course Yūko in *Blue-Sky Girl* (Masumura [1958] 2014c, 45; [1958] 2014b, 38).

Ideology and Subjectivity

On the one hand, it appears that the promotion of this type of female subjectivity suited the social atmosphere of early postwar Japan, in which women, after a long struggle since the prewar era, finally obtained political citizenship (i.e., freedom of association, suffrage, and the right to hold office) and legal equality with men (set forth in articles 14 and 24 of the constitution). What is interesting to me, however, is that despite Masumura's commitment to presenting the free individual who bravely confronts society to unleash the repressed self, *Blue-Sky Girl* paradoxically shows us how one's subjectivity is actually a historical product of relations of power and how one gets constructed as a proper member of society through its dominant ideology. That is, subjectivity must be seen not as self-sufficient consciousness that exists independently from society but as that which requires mediation by society for its very emergence and reproduction.

We can delve into this point by examining the meanings of *aozora*, or "blue sky," mentioned again and again throughout the film, and how it leads Yūko to the construction of a historically specific subjectivity. Mr. Futami is the one who introduces Yūko to *aozora*. When she realizes at the beginning of the film that the woman who is waiting for her in Tokyo is not her biological mother but her stepmother, she becomes anxious about her move. Futami, standing next to Yūko on the hill facing the Pacific, tells her, "Each of us has a blue sky over our head" ("Minna no atama no ue ni aozora wa hitotsu zutsu aru"). He continues that if only she sticks her chest out and juts her chin forward, she can see *aozora* even with her eyes closed. As he makes this statement, she closes her eyes. He asks her whether she can see *aozora*. She responds "yes." *Aozora* in the film, therefore, appears not only as actual physical space but as a fantasy. Throughout the film, both Yūko and Futami frequently reference this fantasy. Yūko starts her first morning in Tokyo by greeting *aozora*. When Futami calls Yūko after moving to Tokyo shortly after Yūko does, he asks whether she is happy. She replies that she is "very unhappy" ("taihen fushiawase") but "can see *aozora* very well" ("aozora ga miemasu, tottemo yoku"), even though she is speaking on the phone inside the house with no visual access to the sky. When Futami meets up with Yūko for the first time in Tokyo, he encourages her not to forget about *aozora*.

Neither Futami nor Yūko articulates what *aozora* as a fantasy refers to, but observing their social environment gives us a fairly clear idea. In Tokyo, both Yūko and Futami experience many troubles and hardships. As we already know, Yūko is maltreated by her stepmother and half-sister and has to resign herself to serving as a maid in her own father's house. Futami's job as a commercial poster designer is hectic. His apartment is old and small and is located in Higashi-Nakano, an inexpensive neighborhood west of Shinjuku. The contrast with Aoyama, where Yūko's family lives, is made clear in glimpses of the National Railways' Higashi-Nakano Station, constructed of wood, and the surrounding neighborhood. Futami constantly mentions financial pressures. According to him, he cannot feed himself unless he draws many posters ("Posutā o mori mori kakanto meshi ga kuen!"), and neither can he have a girlfriend in Tokyo because of his low salary. At the fundamental level, their struggles are about socioeconomic inequality in a class-based society.

For Yūko and Futami, *aozora* signifies a perfect world that they believe will be realized after they overcome the adversity that they are facing, and it provides them with the patience, strength, and optimism they need to continue enduring such adversity. That is, the *aozora* that they fantasize about works as an ideology in that it offers them a way of understanding the present and envisaging the future. A common understanding of ideology that derives from conventional Marxism may posit that it instills in people a false consciousness about the true nature of social relations and thereby legitimizes and perpetuates the existing bourgeois domination of society. But a crucial point about ideology in modern capitalist societies, especially those operating with liberal democracy as their governing principle, is that it does not necessarily impose specific thinking and behavior on us but resorts to recognition, persuasion, and encouragement for its reinforcement. As Louis Althusser ([1970] 2001) has maintained, ideology "interpellates" us and constitutes us as subjects who can take an active part in bolstering and reproducing the system. It is not a veil that one can consciously lift to reveal reality; rather, it is deeply embedded in, or indissoluble from, our being as subjects with multiple roles and responsibilities in various social relations.

In *Blue-Sky Girl*, we can observe how *aozora* interpellates Yūko and how she constructs herself as a subject committed to improving her own life. She is convinced that ceaseless effort and great optimism will in the end secure her happiness, or, more concretely, economic success in the bourgeois society in which she is living. Indeed, economic success is a key to making sense of the ways that Yūko acts and interacts with other people in the two main plots of the film: first, her pursuit of romantic love, and second, her search for her biological mother. In both cases, her conduct is driven primarily by desire to achieve economic success—that is, a financially secure life—in the specific historical context of 1950s Japan; it is not spontaneous nor instinctive but appears rather calculating and ingenious.

First, let us examine her pursuit of romantic love. Two men are romantically interested in her: Mr. Futami and Mr. Hirooka, a handsome businessman from a wealthy Tokyo family and the heir to the prosperous Nittō Corporation. It is obvious from the beginning that Yūko admires Futami and that he cares for Yūko not only as one of his many students but also as a woman. He explains that he has decided to move to Tokyo for a new job, but it is natural to suspect that Yūko's move to Tokyo also motivated this decision. Yūko first meets Hirooka at her father's house in Aoyama. He is one of the many male friends with whom her half-sister Teruko (Hodaka Noriko) hangs out, and she is hoping to build a relationship with him and marry him in the near future. But Hirooka does not reciprocate Teruko's attentions. Seeing Yūko working hard as a maid, he immediately becomes entranced by her. He soon learns that she is not just a maid but a daughter of Mr. Ono and begins approaching her aggressively. When he meets her for the second time, he proposes to Yūko. But she responds that there is someone else she likes, that is, Futami. The realization that Futami is just her former high school teacher convinces Hirooka that Yūko's special feeling for him is like "measles" (*hashika*), a crush that will pass when she finds true love.

As Hirooka has predicted, Yūko's heart gradually drifts away from Futami. The decisive moment comes when she visits his apartment in Higashi-Nakano. Because of her trouble with her half-sister, she has had to leave her house in Aoyama. With no money and nowhere else to go, she asks Futami for help. Futami, about to leave for Osaka for a business trip, gives her some money and tells her to stay at his apartment while he is away—and keep looking up at *aozora*, of course. Right after he leaves, however, a woman who claims to be Futami's girlfriend—a self-identified model who does not seem to be in high demand—comes in, looks at Yūko suspiciously, and talks to her rudely. Yūko gives her the money that she borrowed from Futami, asking her to return it to him, and then leaves his apartment. Next, she calls Hirooka, who works in Marunouchi (a business district near Tokyo Station), meets him, and borrows money from him. After this, the distance between the two quickly shrinks as Yūko begins accepting Hirooka as her boyfriend and considering him seriously as a prospective husband.

The conventional reading of the swift dissipation of Yūko's feeling for Futami would be that it was in fact like "measles," a passing fancy that many unexperienced, immature teenage girls and boys undergo before finding true love as adults. But another reading, which aligns with the ideology of *aozora*, is that Yūko, propelled by the idea of success, brings socioeconomic factors into the selection of her future husband. She grows apart from Futami not only because she finds out that he has a girlfriend but also because she realizes that her high school teacher, who looked confident and reliable back in her rural town in Izu, is just a financially struggling man living in a small apartment in a working-class neighborhood in Tokyo with little possibility of future success. Then, she chooses Hirooka, despite her half-sister's determination to pursue him, precisely because of his family's wealth and his status as a successful businessman in central Tokyo.

In Japan in the 1950s (and throughout the high-speed-economic-growth era, and even now), gender-based economic inequality in the workplace was an essential part of the management of society. As the economy was normalized and as white-collar workers began to account for a large part of the workforce in this period, the corporate world and the LDP government promoted the nuclear family with a breadwinning husband and a stay-at-home wife as the ideal model of the middle-class family, curtailing the possibility for women of building professional careers in the workplace. Most jobs available to women were temporary and part-time. Even if they had full-time jobs, women were expected to retire upon marriage. In fact, many private companies, whether officially or not, had the retirement age for female workers set younger than male workers.[19] The 1961 revision of the Income Tax Act would introduce a generous spousal deduction for households with housewives with no or limited income, establishing a legal arrangement that would systematically relegate women to the private sphere and encourage them to serve as caretakers for their "corporate warrior" husbands and devote themselves to unpaid reproductive work at home (Sugino and Yonemura 2000).[20]

Within this context, Yūko's decision to give up Futami and marry Hirooka makes perfect sense. It was extremely difficult, if not impossible, for a woman like her, who had come from rural Japan but lost her own father's patriarchal protection and could no longer count on his assets and connections, to become self-sustaining through her own effort and talent. Subjecting herself to another patriarchal order by marrying into a wealthy family was one of the few paths available to her for upward social mobility. While the film may give us the impression that Yūko develops a romantic relationship with Hirooka because she is genuinely attracted to his personality and passion, it is more natural to assume that she employs marriage in a utilitarian way, as what Pierre Bourdieu (1986) has called social capital—a network of relationships and connections that one can assemble to achieve success in society. The film also permits us to discern the contradictory nature of modern capitalist society, which places foremost importance on individual freedom and consent (that is, romantic love) but simultaneously uses this freedom and consent to channel women's desire and emotions toward the acceptance of a particular form of gender relations (that is, patriarchy).[21]

Yūko's desire for economic success also helps us make sense of the other major plot—her search for her biological mother, Machiko (Miyake Kuniko). Facing daily her stepmother's and half-sister's hostility, Yūko comes to believe that she will never be happy unless she finds Machiko and reunites with her. In the film, Machiko appears as a woman who transgressed bourgeois respectability in her sexual conduct. While working as a secretary for Yūko's father, who was already married with children, Machiko began an affair with him and became pregnant (judging by Yūko's age, all this took place around 1940). This transgression brought severe punishment. Her lover's mother (that is, Yūko's grandmother on her father's side) took her baby, Yūko, away from her and asked her never to contact them again. Probably in deep despair, Machiko married another man and moved to Manchuria. Yūko's grandmother lost contact with Machiko and worried what happened to her as the war devastated this de facto colony of Japan. Yūko does not know any of this until her grandmother confesses it to her on the day of her high school graduation.

In popular media of the early postwar years, Manchuria was often represented as a remote place to which those women were relegated who had committed sexual misconduct or were otherwise on the periphery of the middle-class nuclear-family system. For example, Naruse Mikio's *Late Chrysanthemums* (*Bangiku*, 1954), loosely based on Hayashi Fumiko's ([1948–49] 1992) novellas *Late Chrysanthemums*, *Narcissus* (*Suisen*), and *Egret* (*Shirasagi*), is about four middle-aged women in Tokyo, one of whom, Tomi (Mochizuki Yūko), spent some time in Manchuria as a geisha and had many adventurous experiences with men. According to her, she had a "jumble" (*champon*) of drinks and men, from Japanese to Russian to Manchurian, and used to ride on men's backs while drunk. Now that the war is over and she has returned to Tokyo, Tomi is having difficulty reconstructing a financially responsible life. Her income as a cleaning woman is modest. She likes drinking and spends money as she earns it. She does not have her own apartment, so she stays at her friend's. She is unmaternal and even begs money from her own daughter (Arima Ineko). In Ozu Yasujirō's *Tokyo Twilight* (*Tōkyō boshoku*, 1957), released the same year as *Blue-Sky Girl,* Kikuko (Yamada Isuzu) has a backstory as follows: She fell in love with a man in Tokyo while her husband was away in Keijō (the name given to Seoul under Japanese colonial rule) for work. She abandoned her husband and children and then ran away to Manchuria with him. After Japan's defeat, her lover was detained in Siberia by the Soviets and died there. She came back to Tokyo with another man she had met in Manchuria. In the film, she and this man—now her husband—earn a modest income running a mah-jongg parlor. Although she finds out that her two daughters (Hara Setsuko and Arima Ineko) live not far from her, neither forgives her sexual misconduct. At the end of the film, she and her husband move to Hokkaido—the land seen as the last frontier within Japan after the country lost all its overseas territories, including Manchuria, after the war.

Yūko's mother, Machiko, is similar to the women in these films by Naruse and Ozu in that her drifting to Manchuria marks her moral collapse and continues to define her socioeconomic status in postwar society. In the middle of the movie, it turns out that she is back in Tokyo, but her husband has already died. She is an impoverished widow working as a cleaning woman (just like Tomi in *Late Chrysanthemums*) and living alone in a small, run-down apartment. Almost twenty years later, Machiko still endures the consequences of an extramarital relationship and an illegitimate child. In this light-toned film, where all other characters are outgoing, vocal, and oriented to the future, she is the only person who directly reminds us of the defeat in war, the fall of empire, and the political and economic befuddlement in the immediate postwar years, as Tsutae and Yoshiji do in *Susaki Paradise*.

Unlike Tomi and Kikuko, however, Machiko is ultimately redeemed, and it is her own daughter Yūko who accomplishes this task. Yūko is determined to postpone her pursuit of romance with Hirooka until she finds Machiko. She tells him that she does not want to be happy alone, thereby enlisting (or demanding) help from her future husband. Right after this, Futami realizes that the cleaning woman working in his office building is the same woman as the one in the photo that Yūko carries with her. Futami shares this information with Hirooka. With this as a clue, Hirooka locates her apartment and arranges a reunion between mother and daughter. By mobilizing her wealthy boyfriend's disposable time, money, and sexual desire effectively, Yūko manages to save her mother from an economic quagmire and moral punishment. She can now marry Hirooka and bring Machiko into the bourgeois household that she and Hirooka are about to establish, which she can enjoy only with the enormous wealth of Hirooka's family and his corporation. Thus, Yūko had to give up Futami and develop a romance with Hirooka for her own upward social mobility and for the recuperation of her mother.

The Reflexive Body

The discussion to this point has made it clear that Yūko's subjectivity must be understood in relation to the particular historical context of 1950s Japan, where working women had very few options for economic autonomy. In this final section, I want to shift attention to issues of the body, since Yūko's vigorous bodily movement shown in full shot is one of the main attractions of *Blue-Sky Girl*. One way of appreciating the meaning of her active, moving body is to find in it Masumura's yearning to introduce to the Japanese audience the free individual true to their desire and unconstrained by social norms. Masumura ([1958] 2014c, 41–44) vehemently criticized Japanese films' heavy use of close-ups, which, according to him, were appropriate only for conveying the intricacy and nuance of one's repressed emotions. The director presented the incessant movement of Yūko's body as an antithesis to this cinematic tradition. I argue, however, that just like her subjectivity, Yūko's body is a corollary of the relations of power and that we need to link her bodily movement to her aspiration for economic success in 1950s Japan. What her body reveals is not uninhibited freedom but the discipline and control that she employs to achieve this goal. If she uses marriage as social capital, we can argue that the body for her is crucial physical capital (Shilling 2018) that helps her turn a world full of hardship and hostility to her own advantage.

Yūko's young, healthy, and active body cannot help catching the audience's attention from the beginning. The film starts with a scene in which Yūko, on the day of her high school graduation, is posing in front of a camera with two of her friends. While taking photos, these high school graduates comment on the good health that Yūko has enjoyed since childhood. She has never been sick, she was a track-and-field athlete at school, her arms and legs are "sprightly" (*pin-pin*), and her cheeks are "cherry-colored" (*sakura-iro*). The sunny sky and deep-blue ocean in Izu reinforce this wholesome image of the heroine. Throughout the film, Yūko is dressed in the 1950s classic fit and flare style—shirts that show her fleshy arms and skirts that highlight her narrow waist and add healthy volume to her lower body. She appears buoyant and graceful as she walks in this clothing, as if she could start skipping at any moment. As mentioned earlier, in Masumura's later films, Wakao would often be represented as an embodiment of female sexual desire, but *Blue-Sky Girl* emphasizes the innocence of an inexperienced young woman.

Throughout the film, Yūko repeatedly demonstrates her physical mobility. As a maid, she moves industriously inside and outside the house, vacuuming, cooking, ironing, cutting the grass, feeding the dog, serving house guests, and running errands. After moving out of her father's house, she works at a cabaret, washing dishes and doing other chores in the kitchen. Her body moves efficiently and tirelessly as she performs this physical labor. Borrowing an expression of Hirooka's mother (Higashiyama Chieko), who admires her industriousness and strongly endorses her as her son's future wife, Yūko bustles around like a *komanezumi*, or a "little mouse."

We can observe her physical mobility most clearly in the following three scenes. The first is a fight with her half-brother Hiroshi. Shortly after Yūko starts working at her father's house, Hiroshi tells her to do his homework because she is a maid and has graduated from high school. Yūko refuses this order. Hiroshi gets upset, and a fight begins. During this wrestling-like fight, which she ultimately wins, Yūko's body exhibits dynamic and energetic motion (see figure 2.4). The second exemplary scene is of Yūko's Ping-Pong match with Hirooka. This match occurs at a gathering that her half-sister, Teruko, organizes at the house. Teruko intends this gathering as an opportunity to narrow her pool of suitors and is interested particularly in Hirooka. When Hirooka sees Yūko serving as a maid, his attention is drawn to her healthy legs, and he immediately recognizes her athletic talent. Despite Teruko's opposition, he draws Yūko into a game of Ping-Pong. Although she is at first reluctant to socialize with Teruko's prospective husband, Yūko soon becomes serious and plays the game with Hirooka in earnest, defeating him (see figure 2.5). The third scene is Yūko's dance with her father (Shin Kinzō). Feeling sorry for Yūko's maltreatment as a maid, her father sends the driver from his company to pick her up at the house so that they can spend an evening together without the other family members' interference. The two go out to Ginza. Her father buys her fashionable clothes and shoes—the kind that she could never afford herself—and takes her to dinner at an expensive restaurant. Their dance takes place there after dinner. Although this is her first time in this upscale neighborhood in central Tokyo, she comfortably joins the affluent crowd at the restaurant, dancing elegantly and confidently (see

Figure 2.4. *Blue-Sky Girl* (1957). Yūko turns her fight with her half-brother Hiroshi into a recreational activity for bonding.

Figure 2.5. *Blue-Sky Girl* (1957). Yūko demonstrates her athletic ability in a Ping-Pong match at the gathering her half-sister has organized.

Figure 2.6. *Blue-Sky Girl* (1957). Yūko dances with her father and impresses him, just as her mother did.

figure 2.6).

Most importantly, all three physical activities mentioned above have a performative nature. They are by no means extemporaneous and instinctive movements that derive from one's physiological necessity or desire but entail a set of rules and goals, self-conscious learning, and devoted and repetitive practice. This is clear enough in the case of sports (Ping-Pong) and dancing, but some might wonder about the fight scene since it seems more like a spontaneous act. In fact, the fight between them does start spontaneously when Hiroshi, furious at Yūko, who refused to do his math homework for him, tries to punch her. While Yūko first attempts to reason with him, he does not abandon his belligerent attitude. His bourgeois class consciousness does not permit him to question his own ability to force a maid into submission. Then, Yūko gets ready to fight but quickly turns it into a ludic activity through the following conversation:

Hiroshi: You, looks like you're ready to go.

Yūko: What if I am?

HIROSHI: Great!

YŪKO: But if you are a man, don't whine in the middle. We'll do it till one of us surrenders. Come on!

She sets a rule and fights in compliance with this rule. She has no intention of causing Hiroshi any physical harm. She does not lose her temper but remains calm and keeps her smile throughout the fight. Instead of defeating her half-brother, she seeks to establish a bond with him. Their fight is recreational and fun, close to what Elias and Dunning (1986, 59), discussing the civilizing process in modern Europe, have termed "mimetic battles," activities that could bring about bodily excitement and pleasure but with a minimized possibility of physical harm.

The notion of reflexivity helps us better understand the performative nature of these three activities in *Blue-Sky Girl*. Anthony Giddens (1991) argues that building self-identity is a reflexive project in which one constantly contemplates, analyzes, monitors, and alters oneself based on newly acquired knowledge and information. For Giddens, this is one of the most fundamental aspects of modern institutions, in which tradition (or historically accumulated practices) alone no longer provides legitimate and sufficient reference for individual conduct, but people are expected to make conscious decisions for continual improvement. In modernity, even the body, which seems like a biological given, becomes an object of endless reflexive processes, intertwined with one's desire about how to understand oneself in a coherent manner and how to present oneself within a given society. Giddens writes, "Regularized control of the body is a fundamental means whereby a biography of self-identity is maintained; yet at the same time the self is also more or less constantly 'on display' to others in terms of its embodiment" (57–58). By pointing out the centrality of reflexivity, he is not simply embracing the greater rationalization that the modern world seems to have ensured but indicating the growing importance of self-control and self-correction as prerequisites for success in social life.

Yūko's three performative activities all attest to the reflexive body. She seems highly cognizant of her physical abilities and attraction. She cleverly and effectively mobilizes her own body to charm the three men involved in these activities, all of whom have or may have an immense impact on her life: her half-brother Hiroshi, a potential ally in a household whose members are either hostile to or dismissive of her; Hirooka, her potential boyfriend and husband with money and status; and her father, the guardian on whom she financially depends. Consequently, the existing power relations between her and these men shift in her favor.

First, through her victory in the fight, she successfully tames Hiroshi and wins his respect. Soon after, this half-brother acknowledges her as his sister and begins calling her *onē-san*, or "big sister," instead of "you maid." Second, Yūko's victory in the Ping-Pong match makes Hirooka fall in love with her. Her strength and unpretentiousness contrast with her half-sister's neediness and coquettishness. Hirooka finds in Yūko traits uncommon among girls of his social class and thus becomes intrigued by her and begins chasing her (we can also argue that Hirooka has become attracted to Yūko precisely because of the potential that she shows as a healthy and hardworking wife and mother). Third, Yūko impresses her father with her dancing skills, just as her mother did, and this leads him to care for her even more than before. While dancing, she confesses to him that she plans to leave his house to search for her mother, but he begs her to stay because his current marriage is loveless and Yūko is reminiscent of the woman he truly loved. Sorry for her lonely father, she decides to postpone her departure. She has now metamorphosed from a beneficiary of sympathy from her father into a benefactor, offering sympathy to him, which marks her psychological independence from him. At the very end of the film, after securing economic independence by uniting with Hirooka, she visits her father, scolds him for his ambiguous attitude toward both her mother and stepmother, and says a permanent farewell to him, although he is seriously ill.

In this way, the body serves as physical capital by which Yūko seeks to achieve economic success. Therefore, we must resist our instinctive desire to read her body simply in terms of liberation from confines and repressions. What we should see in her body is the degree of discipline that this protagonist—displaced from her hometown, alienated in the city, and unable to realize a self-sustaining life on her own—exhibits for upward social mobility and personal happiness within the specific gender order constructed by Japan's capitalist economy in the 1950s. Despite the upbeat first impression that it may give and despite its seemingly straightforward Cinderella-story-like plot, *Blue-Sky Girl* allows us to engage in a far more complex reading. It points to the plight of young workers in Tokyo and their struggle for survival at the beginning of high-speed growth, when the unprecedented level of labor migration was rapidly changing postwar Japan's urban landscape.

3

Osaka, City of Spies

The Powerless Worker in Industrial Society in Inoue Akira's *Black Weapon* (1964)

> At 7:30 every morning
> I get up with my depressed mind
> I leave for work while suppressing my own soul
>
> —"Saturday Night and Sunday Morning" ("Doyō no yoru to nichiyō no asa"), sung by Hamada Shōgo (1981)
>
> At dusk, the bell at the end of work
> Frees my imprisoned mind and body
> In the homeward crowd, I take off my tie
> I don't know why, but I sometimes feel like shouting in anger
>
> —"J. Boy," sung by Hamada Shōgo (1986)

❈

MANY PEOPLE IN JAPAN remember the year 1964 proudly. In the midst of high-speed economic growth, the country hosted Asia's first Summer Olympics in Tokyo. The Shinkansen, the world's first high-speed train, started service between Tokyo and

Shin-Osaka, reducing travel time between these two metropolises (approximately 310 miles) from six and half hours to just four (the next year it would be further reduced to three hours and ten minutes). Overseas tourism, which the government had restricted since the occupation in an effort to retain foreign currency reserves, was finally liberalized and began fueling the desire of the Japanese middle class for consumption and novel experiences. Japan also moved toward the liberalization of international trade by accepting the obligations stipulated in article 8 of the Articles of Agreement of the International Monetary Fund, under which it was no longer possible to control foreign exchange for the purpose of stabilizing its balance of payment. At the same time, it joined the Organisation for Economic Co-operation and Development (OECD), transforming from a country that required economic assistance into one that would provide it to developing countries. About twenty years after defeat in war, people in Japan began sensing the country's affluence in comparison with those industrialized countries in North America and Western Europe that had been the models for its state-led modernizing project since the Meiji era. In the conventional narrative of postwar Japanese history, the mid-1960s is considered the height of high-speed economic growth.

In June 1964, a few months before the Tokyo Olympics, Daiei released a film entitled *Black Weapon* (*Kuro no kyōki*), directed by Inoue Akira. This film was part of the *Kuro* ("Black") series that Daiei produced between 1962 and 1964. Seven directors, including Masumura Yasuzō, were involved in the making of a total of eleven films. Each film had an independent story. There was no connection in characters or settings among these films, but almost all shed light on the downsides of the economic prosperity that Japan was supposedly enjoying at that time, including espionage, intrigue, corruption, counterfeiting, murder, and other clandestine, illegal, and criminal activities in, for instance, the automobile, banking, pharmaceutical, consumer appliance, and sports industries. With a few exceptions, the films in this series were gloomy and unsettling. Above all, the titles of all these films started with "black," which clearly meant to draw the audience's attention to secrecy and greed operating behind the scenes within the corporate world.

Black Weapon was the ninth of the "Black" series. The film is set in contemporary Osaka and represents this hyperindustrialized metropolis as a place where spies play a major role in the competition among corporations for the most up-to-date technology and greater profits. This noir film stars Tamiya Jirō, one of the Daiei's most profitable box-office stars, whose dandyish and strikingly handsome but somehow icy and unemotional appearance won him a number of picaresque roles. In *Black Weapon*, he plays a lonely and angry industrial spy committed to retaliating against the people who cajoled him into stealing top-secret information from his own company, thereby destroying his professional career and his personal dream of marrying his girlfriend and pleasing his mother. In his study on British spy thrillers, Michael Denning has argued that thrillers since the early twentieth century have been "cover stories" for the culture of the English-speaking world, "paralleling reality" and "telling the 'History of Contemporary Society.'" Spy thrillers are often inspired by "the cover stories of the daily news," and thrillers thus serve to translate "the political and cultural transformations of the twentieth century into the intrigues of a shadow world of secret agents" (Denning 1987, 1–2). *Black Weapon* demonstrates the applicability of this argument to the postwar Japanese context.

If, as Denning (1987, 101–13) suggests, Ian Fleming's James Bond stories tell us about critical elements of consumer and spectacle culture in post–World War II Britain, such as tourism (through Bond's adventures in the decolonizing world) and pornography (through his sexual encounters with women), what can *Black Weapon* tell us about contemporary Japanese society, and how can we understand the fact that the film was produced in 1964, when Japanese capitalism had completed its reconstruction from the wartime and was enjoying an unprecedented level of prosperity?[1] While *Black Weapon* may not have been the most commercially successful nor the most critically acclaimed of the eleven "Black" films, my intention is to read this film, through historical contextualization such as I have performed in the previous two chapters, as expressing the discontent with the rapid growth of corporation-dominated life in 1960s Japan.

I first discuss Kajiyama Toshiyuki, the author of *Shadow Weapon* (*Kage no kyōki*), the novel from which *Black Weapon* was adapted, and how his works responded to contemporary Japanese society's search for stimulation and spectacle as the economy stabilized and as people were increasingly integrated into highly organized corporate life. Then, I examine the ways that *Black Weapon* sheds light on the brutality of corporate espionage warfare and the powerlessness of individual workers and argue that industrial spies were imagined as heroic figures who could uncover the secrecy and intrigue of the corporate world. Lastly, I move on to a discussion of the representations of Osaka, especially two places within it: Senri New Town and Uehonmachi Station. I explain how the film uses visual images of the former place—a newly constructed, large-scale suburb—to underscore the standardization and uniformity of everyday life in industrial society, while the other—an old train terminal in a historical neighborhood in the central part of the city—appears as a symptom of desire for an organic place not yet mapped by industrial society's homogenizing and standardizing forces.

Kajiyama Toshiyuki, "Business Novels," and the "Black" Series

Kajiyama Toshiyuki was one of the cultural icons who most prominently embodied the sensibilities of high-speed economic growth in the 1960s. As a novelist, he always kept abreast of trends in society (or *fūzoku*, as discussed in chapter 1). He found topics for his novels in the kind of events that filled the front page of the newspaper (or "cover stories," to use Michael Denning's expression), such as the building of the Shinkansen, the Tokyo Olympics, and the 1973 oil crisis, and dramatized them with eccentric characters in thrilling settings. He enjoyed massive commercial success during the 1960s and early 1970s, appearing consistently in the annual list of people with highest declared income (sadly, he passed away in 1975 at the age of forty-five, the same as the age at which Kawashima Yūzō died). In fact, in 1969, he ranked first on that list in the category of writers, topping such established novelists as Matsumoto Seichō (second), Shiba Ryōtarō (fourth), and Kawabata Yasunari (eighth).

Kajiyama's sensitivity to contemporary events may be explained by his career before he turned to novels. He had started his writing career in the 1950s as a journalist for weekly magazines. As high-speed growth launched and as urbanization advanced in this decade, establishment publishers found in this new medium the potential to attract busy, urban white-collar workers. The Diamond inaugurated its weekly magazine in 1955, Shinchō did the next year, and other publishers followed them. These weekly magazines consisted of many photos and a variety of short articles on current politics, economy, sports, and entertainment, including scandals of politicians and show-business people, intending to both enlighten the reader with up-to-date information and entertain them with language much more candid, crude, and sensational than newspapers offered.

Kajiyama first stood out as a writer for *Shūkan Myōjō*, inaugurated in 1958. He did so by writing a scoop article on the romance of the crown prince (the current emperor emeritus) and Shōda Michiko (empress emerita)—the first fiancée of a crown prince to come from a nonaristocratic family—for the November 23 issue the same year. Although newspaper publishers had voluntarily entered an agreement not to report this news until the Imperial Household Agency gave the green light and other magazine publishers also respected this agreement, *Myōjō* broke it with Kajiyama's article, thereby catching a great deal of attention (Kajiyama 1958).[2] This issue sold out in three days. Kajiyama then involved himself in the 1959 launch of *Shūkan Bunshun*, published by the respected literary press Bungei Shunjū. He and his team produced a number of articles based on intensive field research and interviews, for which he soon earned the nickname *toppu-ya*, or "top shop," since his articles often made the headline of the magazine (Kajiyama Toshiyuki Kinen Jigyō Jikkō Iinkai 2007, 51). In addition to weekly magazines, he also wrote actively for monthly magazines and radio dramas.

In 1962, after working as a *toppu-ya* for a few years, he published his first novel, *Black Test Car* (*Kuro no shisōsha*), which dealt with a bruising espionage war in the automobile industry. This novel was immediately adapted for film by Masumura Yasuzō of Daiei and released in 1962 as the first of the "Black" series, and probably the best-known and most critically acclaimed entry in the series. Kajiyama's novel and Masumura's film greatly contributed to the popularization of the term "industrial spy," or *sangyō supai*, and ignited a spy boom, prompting publications on this topic as well as revealing the presence of spies in the real corporate world (which I will discuss in detail later). That same year and the next, he published the two-volume novel *Red Diamond* (*Akai daiya*), about an ambitious broker who intends to make a fortune through futures contracts in the adzuki bean market. A film version was directed by Konishi Michio and released by Tōei with the same title in 1964. *Dream Super-Express* (*Yume no chōtokkyū*), another well-known novel by Kajiyama published in 1963, depicted corruption in land acquisition for the building of Shinkansen tracks in Osaka and Yokohama. As of 1963, the Tōkaidō Shinkansen tracks between Tokyo and Shin-Osaka were still under construction. The service started in October the following year; the film adaptation of this novel, directed by Masumura, was released that same month as *Black Super-Express* (*Kuro no chōtokkyū*)—the last film of the "Black" series. It was in this year that Kajiyama also published *Shadow Weapon*, which was immediately adapted into another "Black" film.

Because of his numerous novels dealing with the corporate world, Kajiyama is considered one of the pioneers of the so-called business novel, or *keizai shōsetsu*, which earned full recognition as a discrete genre in the 1960s and has maintained its popularity to this day.[3] Other authors in this genre in this decade include Shiroyama Saburō, who won the Naoki Prize in 1959 for *Kinjō the Corporate Bouncer* (*Sōkaiya Kinjō*; [1959] 1963); Kunimitsu Shirō, whose *Top Secret* (*Shagai gokuhi*; [1962] 1985) was nominated for the Naoki Prize; and Yamasaki Toyoko, whose *The White Tower* (*Shiroi kyotō*; 1965, 1969) and *Splendid Family* (*Karei naru ichizoku*; 1973), for example, have been adapted into numerous films and TV dramas.

In the last chapter, I discussed "salaryman novels" by Genji Keita, who began publishing vigorously in the early 1950s. Salaryman novels attested to the economic recovery from wartime, and the reconstruction and growth of the urban middle class. The general tone of salaryman novels was light and humorous, corresponding to the eventless and mundane but peaceful nature of the lives of white-collar businessmen, particularly those working for large-capital companies, whose stable monthly salaries, steady promotion, and security until retirement were more or less guaranteed. The relation between individuals and organizations was often represented as one of mutual dependence—the company provides economic well-being for their workers, while workers demonstrate loyalty or at least conformity to the company.

In the 1960s, as the complex bureaucratization of corporate management further advanced, as corporate competition intensified, and as employers increasingly expected workers to devote their entire lives to work, it was becoming hard to maintain this type of optimistic view of corporate life. "Business novels" paid great attention to the uneven distribution of power, resources, and information between individuals and organizations and the confrontation between them.

Works by Kajiyama, Shiroyama, and other authors in this genre represented corporations (or bureaucracy) as cruel institutions that lightly sacrifice individuals to the good of the whole. Protagonists often find themselves at the margin of an organization (or already excluded from it), witness its ugly and inhumane side, and have to challenge it for their own survival. These business novels made a sharp contrast with salaryman novels in that they disseminated a view of work life in a highly industrialized society like postwar Japan as one that entailed incessant calculation, precise foresight, and extra physical and mental strength, making the reader think about fundamental questions of human existence in modern society: What do humans work for, why do they belong to organizations, and will organizations truly protect members when they encounter trouble?

Daiei's "Black" series capitalized on and further contributed to the popularity of business novels and Japanese society's fascination with the secrecy surrounding the corporate world. Within a brief period between July 1962 and October 1964, Daiei released eleven films in this series. In addition to Inoue Akira and Masumura Yasuzō, young Daiei directors early in their careers, including Yuge Tarō, Murayama Mitsuo, Mizuho Shunkai, Tomimoto Sōkichi, and Inoue Umetsugu, took part in the making of these films. Six of the eleven films featured Tamiya Jirō; three featured Utsui Ken, a young actor who had just moved from Shin-Tōhō to Daiei after the former's bankruptcy; one featured Kawasaki Keizō, who played Mr. Hirooka in *Blue-Sky Girl*; and one, both Tamiya and Utsui (see table 3.1).

Among these eleven "Black" films, I have chosen to examine Inoue Akira's *Black Weapon* in detail for several reasons. First, this film not only deals with the issues of industrial spies directly but also forces us to look into their economic and social context extensively, such as raging corporate competition and the corporate domination and control of workers in the 1960s, and in this sense it is a representative work of the numerous industrial spy films made around that time. Second, *Black Weapon* offers much more intricate and multifaceted representations of industrial spies than other such films. On the one hand, industrial spies in *Black Weapon* are victims of the economic system that privileges productivity and profit and aims to reproduce docile workers. On the other hand, they invoke the audience's longing for free and flexible lifestyles uninhibited by corporate norms, which will

Table 3.1. Daiei's "Black" series

Title	Year	Studio	Director	Starring Actor	Theme
Black Test Car (*Kuro no tesutokā*)	1962	Tokyo	Masumura Yasuzō	Tamiya Jirō	Espionage in the automobile industry
Black Report (*Kuro no hōkokusho*)	1963	Tokyo	Masumura Yasuzō	Utusi Ken	Corruption in the legal community
Black Bills (*Kuro no satsutaba*)	1963	Tokyo	Murayama Mitsuo	Kawasaki Keizō	Counterfeiting
Black Hit-by-Pitch (*Kuro no shikyū*)	1963	Tokyo	Mizuho Shunkai	Utusi Ken	Murder related to baseball scouting
Black Trademark (*Kuro no torēdo māku*)	1963	Tokyo	Yuge Tarō	Utsui Ken	Murder related to a fake trademark
Black Parking (*Kuro no chūshajō*)	1963	Tokyo	Yuge Tarō	Tamiya Jirō	Murder and espionage in the pharmaceutical industry
Black Runaway (*Kuro no bakusō*)	1964	Tokyo	Tomimoto Sōkichi	Tamiya Jirō	Police investigation of a traffic accident
Black Challenger (*Kuro no chōsensha*)	1964	Kyoto	Murayama Mitsuo	Tamiya Jirō	Murder related to a secret party for the rich
Black Weapon (*Kuro no kyōki*)	1964	Kyoto	Inoue Akira	Tamiya Jirō	Espionage in the home-appliances industry
Black Trump Card (*Kuro no kirifuda*)	1964	Tokyo	Inoue Umetsugu	Tamiya Jirō / Utsui Ken	Corruption and lawlessness within the business community
Black Super-Express (*Kuro no chōtokkyū*)	1964	Tokyo	Masumura Yasuzō	Tamiya Jirō	Corruption related to the purchase of land for the Shinkansen

help us appreciate how spies were imagined in contemporary Japanese society. Lastly, within the "Black" series, *Black Weapon* is one of only two films made not at Daiei's Tokyo studio but at its Kyoto studio, and it was shot almost entirely in Osaka (located just west of Kyoto). Therefore, I find this film valuable for the purpose of diversifying the narratives of high-speed growth and calling attention to this historical event not only as a national event but also as the amalgamation of various local experiences. My aim is to articulate how the film subverts the existing historical image of this old merchant city and represents it as an unmarked modern industrial city that symbolizes standardization aggravated by postwar Japan's rapid economic growth.

War of Home Appliances

The film opens with the image of a cracked mirror and the sound of an unsettling jazzy melody, setting a gloomy tone and foreshadowing the destruction of the protagonist's life. During the title sequence, a large television factory is shown in bird's-eye view. This quickly switches to images of the inside of the quiet factory filled with brand-new cathode-ray tubes waiting to be installed, highlighting the mass production system of this new electronic device, which had advanced at an astonishing speed in the past decade. This title sequence is accompanied by the following narration from the protagonist—an industrious factory worker named Katayanagi (Tamiya Jirō)—who informs the audience of how he lost his peaceful work life and ended up an industrial spy:

> At that time, every electric maker was accelerating the production of televisions. About sixty thousand televisions a month and 2,500 a day, that is—don't be surprised—one television born every twelve seconds. In order to win this hyper-competition, each maker had to either increase or reduce the size of televisions or aim for the distribution of color televisions. In any case, they had to do something new.

The film thus sets a context for Katayanagi's fall into the clandestine world of espionage, that is, fierce corporate rivalry within the growing home-appliances industry in the 1960s. Throughout the film, two major electric-appliance companies—Dai-Nihon Denki (Greater Japan Electric), for which Katayanagi works, and Taiyō Denki (Sun Electric), which is Dai-Nihon's rival—engage in merciless competition to develop appealing products with the latest technology to gain a better share of the market. To win this competition, both sides are willing to take the risk of using industrial spies to steal top-secret information.

Dai-Nihon and Taiyō battle over three home appliances. As Katayanagi's introductory narration suggests, the first is the television. One night, at a bar he visits with his colleagues after work, he meets a beautiful young bar waitress named Reiko (Hamada Yūko) and falls in love with her. He soon learns that Reiko enjoys an unusually affluent life for a bar waitress. She tells him that she makes money off stocks and advises him that the value of Dai-Nihon's stocks will probably rise because of the new television that they are developing, namely the RV-17. But she wants to have more concrete information on this product to determine whether to buy the company's stocks or not and asks Katayanagi to help her. Blinded by love, he finds nothing suspicious in her request. He goes to the incinerator attached to the company's research facility, finds what seems like a fragment of the RV-17's cathode-ray tube, and gives it to Reiko. Soon after, Katayanagi is called by his boss during lunch hour and told that he will be laid off. The boss informs him that Reiko is an industrial spy for Taiyō. Without realizing it, Katayanagi has provided Dai-Nihon's rival company with a part from his own company's most up-to-date product. Meanwhile, based on this fragment, Taiyō manages to discover that Dai-Nihon is developing a new micro television. Katayanagi searches for Reiko, but she has already disappeared. Heartbroken, unemployed, and furious, Katayanagi decides to become an industrial spy himself in order to retaliate against Taiyō, Dai-Nihon, and Reiko.

Next comes a battle over the electric kettle. This part of the story is set three years after Katayanagi's dismissal from Dai-Nihon. An employee from Dai-Nihon named Takasugi is traveling from Osaka to Nagoya in a Kintetsu express train. He needs to attend a conference to discuss the company's latest electric kettle and is carrying the blueprint of this product in his briefcase. An industrial spy hired by Taiyō comes in from Yokkaichi Station, posing as a Dai-Nihon employee dispatched from a branch office. Heading to the buffet car with his lover, Takasugi asks this man to watch the briefcase. Before Takasugi comes back, the Taiyō spy gets off the train with the blueprint at Kuwana Station. At the platform, however, he is stopped by Katayanagi, who has now metamorphosed into a trained industrial spy. Katayanagi snatches the blueprint from the Taiyō spy. Katayanagi is not an industrial spy for Dai-Nihon, but he hopes to sell this blueprint back to Dai-Nihon and, by demonstrating his talent and ability, persuade them to hire him as their spy so he can revenge himself against Taiyō.

In the third and last battle, Katayanagi, now employed by Dai-Nihon as an industrial spy, vows to steal information on a refrigerator that Taiyō is developing. He stages the fake kidnapping of the son of Kuronuma, Taiyō's executive director (the son is actually on vacation at Shirahama beach in Wakayama with Mariko, the woman whom Katayanagi sent to Kuronuma's house as a maid so that she could spy on his private life at home). As the condition for the release of his son, Katayanagi asks Kuronuma to surrender the information on their refrigerator. Instead of receiving the information in person, he demands that it be broadcasted over a UHF channel. The Taiyō side accepts this demand, but, at the same time, they pursue Katayanagi and his Dai-Nihon supporters, who are driving around, searching for a flat place free of obstruction from which to receive the broadcast. Katayanagi, however, manages to escape Taiyō's aggressive chase and successfully secures the data, thereby completing his revenge on the company that ruined his life. This car chase comes near the end of the film and constitutes the highlight of the battle between the two companies.

This corporate war over home appliances was clearly inspired by the actual situation surrounding this industry in contemporary Japan. The dissemination of home appliances had started in the mid-1950s, when the urban upper-middle and middle classes began demonstrating their interest in improvement of their everyday lives beyond subsistence. In the second half of the 1950s, the media stimulated people's desire for consumption and affluence by referring to the black-and-white television, electric washing machine, and electric refrigerator as "three sacred treasures" (*sanshu no jingi*), comparing them to the mythical treasures allegedly possessed by the imperial line. By the early 1960s, the mass production system for these home appliances had been established, and this resulted in a steady decline in prices and their further dissemination among regular households. As of 1958, the penetration rates of the black-and-white television, electric washing machine, and electric refrigerator among households in Japan were 10.4 percent, 24.6 percent, and 3.2 percent, respectively. By 1964, these rates had risen to 87.8 percent, 61.4 percent, and 38.2 percent (see table 3.2).

Technological innovation in the 1960s was quite impressive. In 1960, NHK and four private companies started color-television broadcasting in Tokyo and Osaka, and, accordingly, home-appliances companies like Hitachi and Sharp began to sell color televisions. The first color televisions sold by these companies in 1960 cost 500,000 yen, still prohibitively expensive given the starting monthly salary for a public employee was only 10,800 yen. But prices dropped sharply. In 1964, right before the Tokyo Summer Olympics, Hitachi made its device available for less than 200,000 yen (Sharp Kabushiki-gaisha 1992, 28; Hitachi Seisakusho 2010, 70). Around the same time, sales of vacuum cleaners, air conditioners, home stereo systems, and video cameras were also gradually growing. By the time of the release of *Black Weapon*, home appliances, at least those basic ones like black-and-white televisions and washing machines, had ceased to be "sacred treasures." They were no longer symbols of the wealth that only the privileged could possess but had become essentials for regular households. Home appliances could no longer sell solely based on their novelty. Consumers were becoming increasingly enlightened and exacting, which threw companies into a bruising and endless competition for greater surplus value.

Comparing the meanings of home appliances in *Black Weapon* to those in the other films that we have examined so far in this book

Table 3.2. Penetration rates of appliances in the household (%)

Appliance	1958	1961	1964	1967	1970
Black-and-white television	10.4	62.5	87.8	96.2	90.2
Washing machine	24.6	50.2	61.4	79.8	91.4
Refrigerator	3.2	17.2	38.2	69.7	89.1
Vacuum cleaner	0	15.4	26.8	47.2	68.3
Air conditioner	0	0.4	1.7	2.8	5.9
Color television	0	0	0	1.6	26.3

Based on data provided by the Cabinet Office (https://www.esri.cao.go.jp/jp/stat/shouhi/shouhi.html).

allows us to understand the rapidly changing place they occupied in postwar society. As discussed in chapter 1, *Susaki Paradise*, released in 1956, includes a memorable scene of television broadcasting in Akihabara. Yoshiji visits this lively neighborhood in central Tokyo to search for his girlfriend Tsutae, who has run away with her lover, Ochiai. A number of curious and excited people are gathering in front of an appliance store to watch a program aired through this latest technology. Made at the onset of high-speed economic growth, *Susaki Paradise* used television as a symbol of recovery from the war and the vibrancy of the urban space of Akihabara. In *Blue-Sky Girl*, released in 1957, when our protagonist, Yūko, works as a maid for her father's house, she uses a vacuum cleaner, a washing machine, an electric refrigerator, and a blender. The ownership of these appliances signals the material wealth of her family in their upscale neighborhood of Aoyama in Tokyo. Home appliances in these films were still seen positively, as something that one could aim to earn as part of upward social mobility and an urban lifestyle, something favorable that would provide entertainment and reduce the amount of time spent at chores.

This kind of straightforward optimism about home appliances is absent in *Black Weapon*. Shedding light on the inside of the industry, the film reveals two points that complicate our understanding of home appliances as a symbol of high-speed growth. First is technological innovation as "a fetish object of capitalist desire" (Harvey 2014, 95). The corporate elite of both Dai-Nihon and Taiyō in *Black Weapon* are driven by an obsessive compulsion to develop new technology faster than the other or to keep the other from developing a new technology, and yet we hardly hear them talk about consumers' needs and satisfaction or see customers' faces. Victory in the corporate war is represented not as a way of providing consumers with better products (which is what most corporations would claim to be doing) but as an ultimate goal in itself. Technology is fetishized as a major source of profit when in reality it is social relations (i.e., how a given society organizes the distribution of wealth between capital and labor) that produce profit, and technological innovation is one means of transforming these relations, mainly in capital's favor (Harvey 2003a). The result of this fetishism, as we see in the film, is that technology, though created by humans themselves, has acquired the power to enthrall, manipulate, and even madden humans and to subject them to itself, as if it possessed its own agency independent from human will.

This leads us to the second point, that is, the specific psyche that inheres within capitalism. As Todd McGowan puts it, "capitalism commands accumulation as an end that the subject can never reach, and this command holds in all aspects of the capitalist system," incessantly creating new desire for new goods, services, and information (2016, 21). Companies compelled to engage permanently in technological innovation, like Dai-Nihon and Taiyō, must continue to sell products with the latest technology, one after another. People must continue buying until they feel fully satisfied with what they have—a moment that never comes. But people's desire for consumption does not arise autonomously. They need to be trained and socialized as proper consumers who do not question the goal of keeping up with the lifestyles promoted by corporations and eagerly spend money on those lifestyles while fetishizing technology just as corporations do. What *Black Weapon* implies, then, is the presence of the bourgeoning advertising and public relations industry, commissioned to galvanize people to keep buying new products, whether televisions, washing machines, or air conditioners, by providing them with concrete images of the improved quality of life enabled by those products. In fact, starting in the late 1950s, corporations' spending on advertisement grew precipitously as commercial television broadcasting (from four stations in 1956 to forty-eight stations in 1964 throughout Japan) established itself as a major mass means for this purpose (Enomoto and Matsuda 2012).[4] Thus, while it would not be wrong to view the rapid diffusion of home appliances as a symptom of the affluence that was prevailing in postwar society, we also need to bear in mind that this society, just like many other capitalist societies since the nineteenth century, was (and still is) founded upon and dictated by the never-ending course of technological innovation, artificially created desire for consumption, and the unquestioned assumption that these are natural and integral parts of the course of human history.

Advent of an Industrial Society

The mushrooming of corporate power and the spread of the corporate value of permanent growth in the 1960s were not the results of the effort of the business community alone; the state played a critical role. After the massive protest against revision of the Security Treaty with the United States in 1960, the LDP had to rework the authoritarian and confrontational approach that Prime Minister Kishi had adopted to suppress the protest and mend the deep ideological division that it had created within Japanese society. Ikeda Hayato, who became the prime minister shortly after this protest, set aside the pursuit of controversial political agenda items, especially the revision of the constitution, under the spirit of "tolerance and patience" (*kan'yō to nintai*), and sought to direct the people's attention to economic affairs by accelerating the economic growth that had already been taking place over the past several years. In his "income doubling plan," Ikeda and his cabinet, in collaboration with the business community, bureaucrats, and pundits, implemented a variety of policies in order to double the country's GNP in ten years. The numerous resulting large-scale public works projects contributed not only to infrastructure but also to full employment, which Ikeda, a student of Keynesian economics, believed crucial for economic growth. The lowering of income and corporate taxes as well as the interest rate stimulated the private sector's investment in technological innovation. Generous government investment and loans for heavy and chemical industries raised the Japanese economy's international competitiveness. The enhancement of social security through the introduction of universal health care and a national pension fostered workers' loyalty to their employers and their general confidence in the society run by the coalition between the LDP and corporations, detaching them from the leftist parties and political radicalism.[5]

Social scientists wondered how best to interpret this ongoing historical change, how to narrate it, and how to place it within the broad current of world history. Marxism offered an important line of analysis. The renowned economist Ōuchi Tsutomu (1970), son of Ōuchi Hyōe and student of Uno Kōzō, identified the system that postwar Japan was developing as state monopoly capitalism and vigorously published on this topic throughout the 1960s. Expanding on studies by Marx (his crisis theory in *Capital*; [1894] 1991), Lenin (his theory of imperialism and monopoly capitalism; [1917] 1987), and other Marxist theorists, Ōuchi argued that this was a new form of capitalism that many states adopted for survival during the Great Depression, advanced through imperialist expansion before and during World War II, and perfected in the postwar era. Under this system, the state actively intervenes in the market through fiscal and monetary policies, thereby solidifying its interdependence with big-capital corporations and reinforcing control over workers. It also assists in the reproduction of labor power through various social policies aimed at workers' welfare and the enhancement of their purchasing power. In so doing, it plays a critical role in maintaining the proper balance between demand and supply in the market, preventing the overproduction of capital—a problem immanent to capitalism and the main cause of economic crisis. By insisting on this, Ōuchi critiqued the welfare state, which the LDP had been attempting to establish since the 1950s, as fostering the regimentation of workers' lives. For him, postwar Japan, no matter how prosperous and peaceful it looked, was a fragile and unstable society roiled beneath the surface by the unresolvable contradictions of capital—necessitating labor for expansion but unable to control it entirely—and threatened by the possibility that class conflict prompted by these contradictions would explode.[6]

But in the Japanese society of the 1960s, when high-speed growth seemed to guarantee an unprecedented level of prosperity, this kind of class-based analysis—grim and pessimistic—was not widely accepted. American-born modernization theory, propounded by such economists as W. W. Rostow ([1960] 1971), was gaining influence as a new way of conceptualizing growth, glorifying mass consumption as the highest stage of development and inspiring Japanese pride in the performance of the national economy even in comparison to the Western countries that Japan had admired as models since the nineteenth century. Around the same time, the theory of "industrial society," or *sangyō shakai*, was emerging to complement modernization theory by explaining (and warranting to some degree) the new social configurations materializing within Japanese society. Of course, in a strict sense, an industrial society had already been taking shape in Japan since the industrial revolution at the end of the nineteenth century. But changes in the postwar era, including the striking growth of heavy and chemical industries, complex bureaucratization and specialization in the workplace, the abundance of consumer goods in the market, massive urbanization, growing interest in education, and rapid dismantling of rural communities, all indicated that industrialization in Japanese society had entered a new phase, entailing a new theory for the accurate understanding of these changes.

Scholars of industrial society from the field of sociology, such as Odaka Kunio (1958), Tominaga Ken'ichi (1965), and Shimizu Ikutarō

([1966] 1993), engaged closely with related literature from the United States and Europe and sought to explicate how people's lives were affected and transformed by the highly industrialized, bureaucratized, and corporatized social structure.[7] Their most basic belief was that industrialization would help to realize an affluent society where all members could explore economic and educational opportunities and achieve greater happiness at both work and home. They regarded their studies—the description and analysis of various aspects of society, such as the management styles of companies, capital-labor relations, and the prominence of small and medium-sized companies—not as critiques of the fundamentals of the social structure itself but rather as ways of strengthening and improving it for optimal operation. For them, capitalism was the basic context out of which industrialization advanced and therefore did not seem to entail any radical changes, and this was one of the major differences from Marxist analysis. Because of this affirmative nature, the theory of industrial society was welcomed by the ruling elite. It was expected to provide the scientific basis on which to develop the nation's economic planning and to foster the kind of workforce that could contribute voluntarily to high-speed growth. For example, the Japan Association of Corporate Executives (Keizai Dōyūkai) was involved in the production of Tominaga's *New Industrial Society* (*Atarashii sangyō shakai*, 1965). Economist Nakayama Ichirō, who had studied with Joseph Schumpeter and consolidated the field of "modern economics" as opposed to Marxist economics in Japanese academia, was a member of the Personnel Branch within the Economic Council, an advisory body to the prime minister, and actively spoke about the talent and personality necessitated by industrial society and the centrality of school education in the cultivation of such talent and personality (Nakayama and Ōhara 1962).

Black Weapon certainly references the advent of an industrial society in postwar Japan. The Dai-Nihon factory at which Katayanagi works is immense, modern, and equipped with a research center for technological innovation. Hundreds of workers there wear clean uniforms, work industriously, and seem like a well-trained, disciplined, and standardized workforce. Although Katayanagi is a factory worker (and as such probably receives an hourly wage), he is hoping to earn full-time-worker status as an engineer (and thereby receive a monthly salary). For this, he must pass an exam, and he is taking evening classes at college to prepare. If he becomes a full-time worker, according to him, his income will double, which will please his mother, with whom he lives in a modest apartment. Dai-Nihon does have a labor union, but Katayanagi does not seem to be an active member or to support a particular political party or ideology. He has no major complaints about the stable work conditions guaranteed by his employer but is a firm believer in meritocracy and is moderately ambitious. What we can observe here is the ideal landscape of industrial society that the Japanese state and the corporate world had striven to establish since the 1950s, in which economic growth was supposedly enabled by collaboration between highly capitalized modern corporations and diligent and apolitical workers.

But the reciprocal relationship between the management (Dai-Nihon) and the worker (Katayanagi) lasts for only the first fifteen minutes of the film. It quickly collapses, and Katayanagi realizes its illusionary nature. As explained earlier in this chapter, he provides Reiko, the bar waitress he loves, with information on Dai-Nihon's new television without knowing she is a spy from Taiyō. Upon learning of this incident, Dai-Nihon's management immediately informs him that he will be fired. He is not given an opportunity to prove that he never intended to engage in espionage. Dai-Nihon's labor union supports the management's decision to fire him. Without the union's help, he is powerless. He loses his only source of income and organizational backing. Not only that; his modest dreams of marrying Reiko and acquiring a middle-class life collapse, and his mother, shocked and disappointed, falls ill and dies.

In this way, in *Black Weapon*, the protagonist is not rewarded at all for being an industrious and loyal worker. The Taiyō elite easily tricks him into stealing his own company's top-secret information because he is so innocent that he has never dreamt of industrial society's ugly clandestine intrigues. The management at Dai-Nihon takes advantage of his docility and quickly fires him with little protest from him. Most of the film is spent depicting how power is unequally distributed between management and workers in industrial society and how management manipulates workers and disposes of them when they are no longer useful. In fact, not only *Black Weapon* but also many other Daiei films dealing with corporate and organizational battles in the 1960s explored this issue repeatedly. For example, in Tomimoto Sōkichi's *Midday Trap* (*Mahiru no wana*, 1962), Tamiya Jirō's character, Fuji, an elite businessman, is set up for the murder that his boss committed over a land purchase and thereby gets thrown from the career ladder. In Yuge Tarō's *Ninja in a Suit* (*Sebiro no ninja*, 1963), a regular worker, Hinuma (yes, played by Tamiya again!), encounters the ugly reality of the corporate battle concerning the development of a new portable television while investigating the suspicious death of his boss. When he says "entire corporations are trying to advance by trampling over humans for their selfish games" ("kigyō zentai ga jibun katte na kakehiki no tame ni ningen nanka fumitsubushite ikō to shite irunda"), this statement succinctly epitomizes the industrial relation that these films sought to underwrite. The experiences of Tamiya's characters in these films remind us not so much of the self-motivated and self-realizing worker in the theory of industrial society as of the powerless "sand-like masses" ("suna no yō na taishū"), which Maruyama Masao ([1952] 1995, 188) had identified already in the early 1950s when he warned against passivity and the loss of critical awareness caused by mass production and mass consumption, and the "one-dimensional man" named by Herbert Marcuse (1964), who in the same year as the release of *Black Weapon* pointed out how industrial society's rationality backed by science and technology imposes standardized ways of thinking and behavior, thereby curtailing the possibilities of resistance.

Spies as Cosmopolitan Urbanites

There is a three-year blank in the film between the expulsion of Katayanagi from the corporate world and his return. When he comes back to the corporate world, he is no longer an innocuous and docile worker but an outsider—fearless, a bit arrogant, and confident of his ability to compete with the greedy corporate elite. He claims he has had three years of training to become a professional industrial spy, though we never learn where he ended up after being fired, who trained him, or whether he belongs to any intelligence agency or not.[8] All we know is that he is motivated by personal rancor and fully committed to retaliating against those who destroyed his life—both Dai-Nihon and Taiyō Electric.

Once back in Osaka as an industrial spy, Katayanagi successfully challenges the authority of the corporate elite. He acquires the blueprint for Dai-Nihon's electric kettle, which was stolen by Taiyō agents, and sells it back to Dai-Nihon for 3.5 million yen (an amount far higher than a corporate executive's annual salary). Then, he convinces Dai-Nihon management to hire him as their exclusive spy for five million yen. Within three years, he has splendidly transformed from a wage laborer whose survival relied entirely on his employer to a self-made entrepreneur. Moreover, he demonstrates not only intelligence and cunning but also physical capabilities. He beats up thugs sent by Dai-Nihon and engages in a hazardous car chase with Taiyō employees (and of course, we, the audience, have to wonder again and again what kind of amazing training he has received in the past three years!). In that his intelligence and physical capabilities are far superior to those of the corporate elite and their entourage and that he is not scared or threatened by corporate power but seeks to appropriate and undermine it, Katayanagi as an industrial spy is an antithesis to what industrial society expects of its workers.

Katayanagi as an industrial spy is also culturally sophisticated and cosmopolitan. The film communicates this through his distinctive appearance and stylish lifestyle (see figure 3.1). His 1960s-style slim, three-button suit with narrow lapels and a skinny tie perfectly fit the six-foot-tall, thin, and strikingly handsome actor, who portrayed this type of shadowy and nihilistic character in numerous Daiei films and television dramas. He drives a Mercedes-Benz. His lover Reiko, who tricks him into stealing confidential information from Dai-Nihon but later helps him by working as a mole, complements the protagonist's image created through these items. She is dressed in Chanel-inspired but slightly more casual well-fitted dresses. Her long hair is piled up in the so-called beehive hairstyle that enjoyed great popularity in the 1960s. Her car is a Ford Thunderbird (see figure 3.2). Her apartment, where the two meet, is small but tasteful: some combination of chic mid-century modern and decorative Hollywood Regency. Ōtsuka Zenshō, an Osakan jazz composer and musician, was in charge of the soundtrack; the major scenes featuring the lovers, including their love scenes, are accompanied by his cool jazz. The spies in *Black Weapon* emanate the mysterious aura of stylish urbanites who can appreciate and afford the most up-to-date material life widely craved in contemporary advanced capitalist states—the life that ordinary middle-class families on corporate salaries in contemporary Japan could not easily attain back then.

Figure 3.1. *Black Weapon* (1964). Katayanagi is represented as a stylish and culturally sophisticated industrial spy.

Figure 3.2. *Black Weapon* (1964). Reiko, an industrial spy who trapped Katayanagi, drives a Ford Thunderbird.

What should we read into these representations of industrial spies? What did these representations mean to the audience in mid-1960s Japan? First, I want to point out that Japanese society at that time was obsessed with industrial spies and their clandestine activities in the real world. Starting in the early 1960s, journalists began reporting on the pervasiveness of industrial spies. The so-called Nippon Gakki spy incident of 1961 was one of the earliest incidents to alert the Japanese population to the presence of spies and their severe competition in the corporate world. In this incident, the well-known musical instruments company Nippon Gakki (now the Yamaha Corporation) hired George Terentyev, a Russian agent living in Japan and believed to have worked for the US Army's Counter Intelligence Corps, to disturb the sales network of newly emerging Kawai in the same industry. Terentyev hired several Japanese agents and had them infiltrate Kawai as salesmen. They were given a mission to degrade morale among workers and incite conflict with their employer. For these purposes, they, for example, initiated a labor union for salesmen and distributed flyers with negative information on the company. Kawai came to recognize Nippon Gakki's conspiracy after some of the union members became suspicious about these men's intentions. Kawai eventually dropped a lawsuit against Nippon Gakki, so this incident did not turn into a criminal case, and the details of Terentyev's secret activities remained uninvestigated ("Bareta sangyō supai" 1961; "Sangyō supai no keiji sekinin" 1964).

This incident, however, drew attention to a number of similar cases, which might earlier have been dismissed simply as heated competition in the corporate world, as one discrete subcategory of crimes that required proactive legal treatment. In 1964, for instance, Terentyev involved himself in another incident in which he and his agency stole confidential information from Dai-Nippon Printing and sold it to its rival company Toppan Printing while at the same time trying to sell it back to Dai-Nippon Printing. Seven people, including Terentyev, were arrested on such charges as theft and the obstruction of business, and all were found guilty the following year ("Sangyō supai no keiji sekinin" 1964; "Terenchefu ni sannen" 1965). Accordingly, in the early 1960s, publications on industrial spies—weekly and monthly journals and monographs—proliferated, reporting major and minor spying incidents, revealing spies' strategies and tools, and providing legal advice for the protection of corporate information.

My aim here is not to fathom the exact extent to which industrial spies threatened Japanese companies. I am more interested in the rise of the discourse of industrial spies as an object of great fear. Numerous publications invoked the fear of these new postwar figures, resorting to sensational titles, subtitles, headlines, and expressions, such as "conspiracy" (*bōryaku*), "secret maneuver" (*an'yaku*), "trap" (*wana*), and "war" (*sensō*; Kimura 1963; Nakae 1963). They implied that anyone, even the most industrious worker at a company, could turn into a spy and that any company could be the target of espionage activities in contemporary Japan, which, under the terms of article 8 of the Articles of Agreement of the International Monetary Fund, was proceeding with the further liberalization of international trade, inspiring more and more intense feuds among companies—not only within Japan but also in the international arena. It was around this time that Kajiyama Toshiyuki's first spy novel, *Black Test Car*, became a bestseller of the year (1962), selling 200,000 copies, and Daiei released its film adaptation. Kajiyama quickly earned the reputation of an authority on industrial spies and actively shared his expertise backed by thorough fieldwork. According to him, companies' intelligence activities were in reality much more dumbfounding, and *Black Test Car* in fact could be read as a work of reportage (Kajiyama 1963c). By strategically and effectively blurring the line between fiction and reality, Kajiyama participated in the construction of a discourse of the vulnerable Japanese corporate world targeted and manipulated by industrial spies.

Reviewing these numerous spy-related publications, we realize that the fear of spies inspired not necessarily animosity and contempt but fascination and enjoyment. These publications constantly mentioned industrial spies' extraordinary experiences unconstrained by national borders and trivial everyday concerns. It was common for them to indicate or imply the prominent presence of intelligence organizations and agents overseas—in the United States and Hong Kong, for example—and their advancement to Japan, the growth of an international market for confidential corporate information, and the large-scale money transactions that were occurring there. One journal article even stated that industrial spying offered a perfect amusement for white-collar workers who were performing "boring jobs" ("taikutsu na shigoto") while "sensing their boss's gaze on their backs" ("senaka ni uwayaku no me o kanjinagara"; "Sangyō supai to himitsu hogohō" 1964).

Furuya Tatsuo's 1963 monograph entitled *Hong Kong Group* (*Honkon gurūpu*) is one excellent example in this regard. As the title suggests, Furuya warns readers about spies from Hong Kong and maintains that they have hubs in Kobe and Yokohama—the two largest port cities in Japan with a number of foreign, including Chinese, residents (the cultural meanings of these port cities will be examined in chapter 4)—and that they take every opportunity to steal information and technology from major Japanese corporations. By identifying them as "present-day ninja" ("gendai no ninja") and by sharing with readers their artful techniques, such as wiretapping, secret photographing and taping, wearing disguises, and fabricating documents, as well as the elaborate devices crafted for these purposes, Furuya underscores the thrilling, mysterious, and glamorous nature of spies' activities.

What interests me most about this book is that the author implies that he himself is a spy. He maintains that during the war, he was director of the Japanese Imperial Navy's intelligence agency located in Shanghai, namely Nanjō Agency, and that he now works for a secret organization that aims to collect information on espionage, security, contraband traffic, and so on. While insisting that his mission is to help Japanese companies defend themselves from encroachment by foreign spies, he does not reveal his exact identity or occupation and seeks to adopt the mysterious aura of the spy himself, thereby making the boundaries between intelligence and counterintelligence vague and almost meaningless. On the back cover of the book, we see a photo of Furuya standing on an urban street on a rainy day, looking into the distance, dressed in a double-breasted suit and wearing a hat, which had already long ceased to be a must-have item for a regular businessman in Japan. Part of the caption on the back cover reads:

> The pioneer of espionage in Japan. As far as appearances go, he does not look like an intelligence agent at all. He is just a grey-haired, slender, middle-aged man. But the way he speaks in his deep voice while watching every corner is accompanied by an unusual mood.
> ... Now, taking advantaging of his wartime experience, he supervises a public intelligence organization. There is much speculation about this organization—gathering security-related information, cracking down on drugs and smuggling, etc.—but the truth is unknown. (Furuya 1963)

When this secretive dandy with an obscure career talks about his connection with a number of intelligence agents, referring repeatedly to such exotic locales as Hong Kong, Shanghai, Macao, Kobe, and Yokohama; his memories of maneuvers in China during World War II; and espionage on a global scale, we have to wonder whether he is sincerely advocating a Japan free from spies. On the contrary, it appears to be the case that he is luring readers into a world of espionage rife with excitement and unpredictability and seeking to fashion a sense of admiration and awe toward spies' and, of course, his own undercover business.

Katayanagi and his lover Reiko in *Black Weapon* are idealized and hyperbolized embodiments of industrial spying born out of this context. Their stylish, urban appearance and lifestyle, therefore, should not be reduced to questions of taste and luxury but need to be interpreted as cultural codes that indicate their intertextual relations with other industrial spies represented by the media. These codes insinuate their extensive transnational network; the freedom and mobility with which to travel throughout Japan, Asia, and beyond; their daily interactions with foreigners and people in high positions; and the cultural refinement necessitated and nurtured by all these.

The significance of these cultural codes for the contemporary Japanese audience was much greater than we can imagine today because few citizens had opportunities for international travel back then. Even after Japan regained independence and sovereignty in 1952, the government had strictly limited the issuing of passports to those going overseas for business, academic, and other officially approved purposes due to the fear of foreign-currency outflow. International travel had been reopened only in April 1964, just two months before the release of *Black Weapon*. In a country where regular citizens could not yet easily cross national borders, spies allowed those young Japanese born in the postwar era to imagine the various foreign countries to which they had never been but might travel someday while reminding more senior Japanese, raised in the prewar era, of the cities that they had visited or in which they had lived when they were able to travel freely within the empire. The transnational and transcultural mobility that spies were thought to enjoy was antithetical to the discipline and rules of highly bureaucratized and stratified industrial society and therefore captivating. Reading stories and watching films about spies who cleverly used connections and resources across the country and beyond, challenged the corporate elite, revealed their greed and secrets, and undermined the seemingly unalterable social hierarchy in industrial society from without were safe and exhilarating forms of entertainment.

Osaka as a Modern Industrial City

Just as place has mattered to the appreciation of *Susaki Paradise* and *Blue-Sky Girl*, so does it to the appreciation of *Black Weapon*. The film is set in the city of Osaka and its northern suburb Senri New Town. The meanings of the places in *Susaki Paradise* and *Blue-Sky Girl*—Susaki-Bentenchō and Akihabara in the former and Izu and Aoyama in the latter—were built upon meanings and images already circulating in late-1950s Japan (e.g., Akihabara as a newly emerging "electric" town and Izu as a well-known resort town for wealthy Tokyo urbanites). On the other hand, *Black Weapon*, although set in Osaka, seeks to keep the audience from applying its widely shared knowledge of the city to the appreciation of the film, asking them to focus instead on its anonymous nature as a modern, hyperindustrialized city.

Osaka possesses a rich history of commercial prosperity and vigorous popular culture dating to the era of Toyotomi Hideyoshi in the sixteenth century. As such, it has inspired many filmmakers' imaginations. When we observe Osaka-set films made in the 1950s and 1960s, one general trend catches our attention. That is, they often view Osaka nostalgically as a reservoir of the values and sensitivities that many Japanese urbanites had shared but were quickly losing with the acceleration of high-speed economic growth. Especially in comparison to Tokyo, this second-largest metropolis generated the perception that it had not succumbed entirely to the anonymity inherent to industrialization and urbanization and had managed to preserve more organic ways of living backed by its long history.[9] For example, *My Town* (*Waga machi*, 1956), adapted from Oda Sakunosuke's novel of the same title and directed by Kawashima Yūzō, showed the warmhearted and unreserved but sometimes crude interactions among residents in a working-class neighborhood of old tenement houses in central Osaka. *Bonchi* (1960; the title refers to the young son and heir to a merchant family in Osaka) and *Matriarchal Family* (*Nyokei kazoku*, 1963), both adapted from the novels of Osaka-born author Yamasaki Toyoko and directed by Ichikawa Kon and Misumi Kenji, respectively, took up as a main theme the intense familial ties and conflicts within merchant families in the prestigious Semba district. *Ōshō* (1962; the title refers to one of the *shōgi* pieces, the loss of which decides the match), based on a play written by Hōjō Hideji and directed by Itō Daisuke, portrayed the life of legendary *shōgi* player

Sakata Sankichi from Tennōji, who was passionate about his loves but lacked the industriousness and financial artfulness indispensable to everyday working life.[10]

Compared to these Osaka-set films, *Black Weapon* is quite an anomaly because it is completely indifferent to participating in the reinforcement of the cultural images of the Osaka constructed by local authors and the national media. *Black Weapon* does not address any themes, like those mentioned above, that highlight the historical and cultural particularities of the city or its rivalry with Tokyo. The characters in this film, including Katayanagi and Reiko, do not employ, build upon, or recall any character types strongly perceived as representative of Osaka (or the Kansai region more broadly), such as the independent-minded, frugal merchant played by Nakamura Ganjirō in Kawashima Yūzō's *The Shop Curtain* (*Noren*, 1958); the irresponsible son from a wealthy family, or *bon-bon*, played by Morishige Hisaya in Toyoda Shirō's *Hooray for Marriage, or Sweet Beans for Two* (*Meoto zenzai*, 1955); or the chatty and candid middle-aged woman with an overwhelming personality, played by Naniwa Chieko in Toyoda's *A Cat, a Man, and Two Women* (*Neko to Shōzō to futari no onna*, 1956) (Cronin 2017).

Even more noticeable is that none of the main characters in *Black Weapon* speaks the Osaka dialect, which is probably the most essential marker of Osaka's distinctiveness and which non-Kansai-native actors in Osaka-set films usually try to mimic—with varying success. They do not use any accent, intonation, vocabulary, syntax, tone of voice, speech pattern, or conversation style specific to Osaka. All the conversations take place in the so-called standard language, or *hyōjungo*, a variation of Japanese that the Meiji government artificially created as part of the centralization project for the newly born nation-state, based on the language spoken by the educated class in Tokyo's "high city." In fact, the audience cannot be sure that the film is set in Osaka until about seven minutes in, when Katayanagi brings up the name of the city as the place to go home to during his driving date with Reiko. The only two characters who speak the Osaka dialect are the owner of the bar where Katayanagi and Reiko meet for the first time and the young cleaning woman working in Reiko's apartment building, both of whom make only brief appearances and play minimal roles.

It would be short-sighted, however, to conclude that the actors and actresses were simply too lazy to learn the Osaka dialect. Tamiya

Jirō was born in Osaka and raised in Kyoto, so he was a native speaker of the Osaka (or broader Kansai) dialect. Indeed, he demonstrated his fluent and natural Osaka dialect in several Daiei films, such as *Matriarchal Family* and *Women's Medal* (*Onna no kunshō*, 1961). Both films featured other well-known Kansai-native actors, including Kyō Machiko, Nakamura Ganjirō, Naniwa Chieko, and Nakamura Tamao; and those who were not native speakers of the dialect, such as Wakao Ayako and Kanō Junko, all mastered it to an acceptable level. The refusal to use the Osaka dialect in *Black Weapon*, therefore, seems like a conscious decision of those involved in the making of this film as part of the effort to present it not as a film *on* Osaka—a film about tradition, community, customs, or "human sentiment" (what is referred to as *ninjō*) specific to the city—but a film simply *set in* Osaka.

It is interesting to note the location sites for this film. The film carefully avoids showing any metonymic sites that regular moviegoers would have associated with the city, such as the Shinsaibashi shopping street, with its high-end retailers; the historic neighborhood around Hōzenji Temple (Hōzenji Yokochō); the Tsūtenkaku tower and Jan-Jan Yokochō street in Shin-Sekai, filled with down-to-earth bars; Osaka Castle; Shitennōji Temple; Sumiyoshi Grand Shrine; and so on. The flashy neon signs over Dōtonbori River do appear with superimposed images of Katayanagi as he wanders the city after losing his job at Dai-Nihon, but only briefly. Instead of these uniquely Osakan places, to which the national and local media has given specific meanings in relation to their histories (whether premodern or modern), we see a factory, office buildings, offices, busy streets and intersections, and freeways. In *Black Weapon*, Osaka signifies neither excess nor lack. It appears as an anonymous, unmarked modern industrial city where people work for survival and where corporate rivalry prevails. The film uses Osaka as one example of modern industrial cities in advanced capitalism—akin to Tokyo, Nagoya, Chicago, Los Angeles, or London—in order to illuminate their shared experiences characterized by an obsession with money and permanent growth, a strict class structure, competitive markets, disposable workers, and the atomization of individuals.

In this sense, the use of Osaka in *Black Weapon* resembles that in Mizoguchi Kenji's *Osaka Elegy* (*Naniwa erejī*, 1936), though all the actors and actresses speak a quite heavy Osaka dialect in the earlier film. Made at a time when the Japanese economy was overcoming the large-scale recession of the early 1930s through the colonization of Manchuria, *Osaka Elegy* represented this massively industrialized metropolis as a space where class- and gender-related tensions manifested under the interlocked system of capitalism and patriarchy. The experience of the protagonist Ayako, played by Yamada Isuzu, was by no means unique to Osaka but epitomized the experiences of many urban, working-class women, who had to work to survive but also had to face all kinds of gender-based discrimination and harassment at work and home.

The Placelessness of Senri New Town

The anonymity of the modern industrial city is reinforced by the landscape of one location that appears repeatedly in the film: suburban Senri New Town, developed by the Osaka prefectural government, 7.5 miles north of Osaka Station. Kuronuma (Kaneko Nobuo), the Taiyō executive against whom our protagonist seeks to retaliate, lives with his family in a large house there. Katayanagi drives through this town in his Benz, plotting against Taiyō and collecting information useful to his mission. When the film was released in 1964, Senri New Town was truly a brand-new town: construction had started just a few years earlier. While suburban development in the Osaka-Kobe region had already advanced in the interwar period, as we see in the Hanshin-kan (the region "between Osaka and Kobe"), pursued by the private commuter-train companies Hankyū and Hanshin (Hara 1998), Senri New Town was Japan's first large-scale suburban development carried out by the public sector. The acceleration of migration to Osaka from rural Japan in the 1950s, the exacerbating problem of overpopulation, the shortage and poor quality of housing in the city, and sharply rising rent and real estate prices all spurred the prefectural government to take measures to alleviate these social problems. The prefectural government looked to Senri Hills—a large, gently hilly area stretching between the cities of Suita and Toyonaka. While the southern tip of this area had been developed in the 1920s as an exclusive neighborhood modeled after Letchworth Garden City in England, the rest remained undeveloped, except for a few agrarian communities. Based on careful urban planning in collaboration with researchers, academic associations, and private offices, the prefectural government envisioned the creation of an enormous manufactured community of approximately 4.5 square miles in this area easily accessible from downtown. Senri New Town celebrated its inauguration in November 1962, right after the first group of residents, chosen by lottery from many applicants, moved into Satakedai—the southernmost neighborhood in the new town (see map 3.1 and figure 3.3).[11]

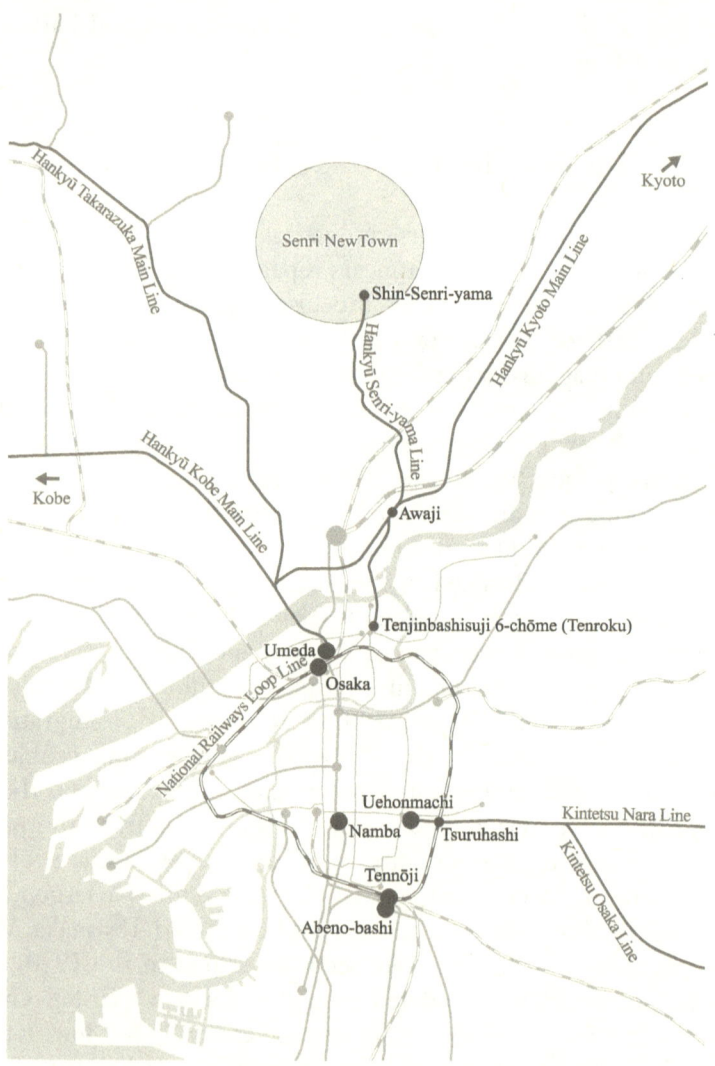

Map 3.1. City of Osaka and Senri New Town (circa 1964).

Figure 3.3. *Black Weapon* (1964). Location shooting was conducted in Senri New Town. Here, we can see condominiums built by the prefectural government in the neighborhood of Takanodai.

Location shooting for *Black Weapon* was conducted mainly around Satakedai and Takanodai, both close to Shin-Senri-yama ("New Mount Senri") Station on Hankyū's Senri-yama line, which had opened in 1963.[12] Senri New Town today has expanded far north of this station and is a well-established, mature community with not only residential but commercial and business functions, directly connected by both the Hankyū and Kita-Osaka Kyūkō lines to Osaka's central areas, including Umeda, Yodoyabashi, Shinsaibashi, Namba, Tennōji, Tenroku, and Kitahama. As of 1964, however, Shin-Senri-yama Station was the northernmost station in the community, and the rest was still far from completion. Development would later be hastened by the selection of Senri as the venue for the 1970 Osaka Expo.[13] What we see in the film is Senri New Town in its very early history—wide roads and freeways with little traffic, unpaved streets, countless brand-new condominium buildings almost indistinguishable from one another, houses with wide yards allocated in a planned manner, hills with immature trees, and unobstructed views of the sky.

Those of us who live in contemporary industrialized and postindustrial countries in the twenty-first century take completely for granted this type of artificial suburban landscape. In Japan's case, following Senri New Town, both the public sector (e.g., the Public Housing Corporation and prefectural and municipal governments) and the private sector (e.g., train and real estate companies) built a number of large-scale suburban communities throughout the high-speed growth era and beyond, including Tama in western Tokyo, Senboku in southern Osaka, Suma and Seishin in northwestern Kobe, and Tsukuba in Ibaraki. There is no shortage of their representation in the national and local media. Many (including myself) grew up in such a town or have at least visited one of them. But this was not the case in the early 1960s. The artificial and exceptionally well-organized landscape of Senri New Town (which few contemporary viewers could likely identify) must have surprised and impressed the audience, since their images of the city were constructed mainly from central neighborhoods in major metropolises, whether Osaka, Tokyo, Kobe, Yokohama, or Nagoya, where narrow shopping streets developed in a disorderly way (or organically, depending on one's perspective), right beside or above train or subway stations, crammed with small retailers, restaurants, and bars with flashy and almost vulgar signs. The urban space around Akihabara Station, discussed in chapter 1, was a perfect example of the representation of such a central neighborhood in Tokyo.

When we compare the landscape of Senri New Town to that of such urban centers as Akihabara, we recognize that the former, as the product of a meticulously calculated and newly launched project, is void of historically accumulated meanings and memories. Or, we can also argue that it possesses the feature of what Edward Relph (1976) has called "placelessness"—the absence of any distinctiveness engendered and solidified by the immediate experiences of those who live and work in that place and care for it. This placelessness is characterized by an astonishing resemblance in the appearance and atmosphere of such places across the country and even the world. Relph sees placelessness as a crucial feature of the urban landscape of modern societies, where the construction and maintenance of places tend to be dictated by political and economic forces that do not necessarily have direct ties with those places but take profitability and functionality as the most important goals (e.g., big-capital corporations). Among the various landscapes that Relph points out as concrete manifestations of placelessness, particularly relevant for our discussion here is "subtopia," as it refers exactly to the numerous large-scale suburban communities that developed quickly in the post–World War II world (105–9; and it is not a coincidence that the Canada-based geographer established this concept in the 1970s after experiencing firsthand the massive urbanization and suburbanization of the previous few decades in North America).

If we consider Senri New Town as a place associated with a sense of placelessness, we understand why the makers of *Black Weapon* chose it as a main location for corporate battles and intelligence activities. It symbolizes Osaka as an unmarked modern industrial city. Its tidy, sanitized, well-organized, and futuristic landscape hardly exhibits any specific locality, hardly encourages the audience to mobilize their memories or intertextual knowledge of the city. This landscape seems interchangeable with many other suburban developments within and beyond contemporary Japan. As such, it conspicuously attests to the standardizing and homogenizing effect of industrial society, which is enabled by the systems of mass production and mass consumption and prioritizes efficiency and productivity. When we watch our protagonist drive through this landscape in his Benz, we almost forget he is in Osaka and focus instead on the global nature of espionage, that is, espionage as a phenomenon ubiquitous throughout industrialized countries as it is embedded in the system that fuels an unquenchable desire for permanent economic growth and requires ceaseless competition over limited resources and markets.

Uehonmachi Station: The Return of History

This is not to say, however, that the film is dominated entirely by "placelessness." There is one more place in Osaka that makes an extensive and memorable appearance, namely Kintetsu Railway's Uehonmachi Station, located in central Osaka (see map 3.1). After helping Katayanagi secure the confidential information about Taiyō's refrigerator, Reiko becomes disillusioned by the corporate world's greed and decides to retire as an industrial spy and return to her hometown of Ise (Mie Prefecture), departing from this station. Appearing at the very end of the film and represented as a place with distinctive and irreplaceable local histories and memories, Uehonmachi Station abruptly subverts the images of Osaka that the film has so far consolidated as an anonymous industrial city.

Kintetsu Railway is the largest private train company in Japan in terms of the length of rail (more than three hundred miles). The company is headquartered in Tennōji, Osaka, and its train network extends into the Kansai and Chubu regions, connecting Osaka to Kyoto, Nara, Mie, and Nagoya. It is now one of the five major private lines in the Osaka metropolitan area (the other four are Hankyū, Hanshin, Keihan, and Nankai). It is used as a commuter train in the major cities, but also its long-distance express trains carry urban passengers from these cities to tourist sites in Yoshino, Asuka, Ise, Shima, and so on. As of 1964, Uehonmachi was one of Kintetswu's two terminals in Osaka (the other was Abenobashi in the south), and it was linked to such destinations as Nara and Ise-Nakagawa through its Osaka and Nara lines. When the film was released, there was also a city-run trolley station right by the Kintetsu Station, from which one could transfer to multiple lines leading to the other major stations in the city. Serving as a center of public transportation in the city, the neighborhood around Uehonmachi Station back then enjoyed lively traffic throughout the day and enormous commercial prosperity.[14]

Uehonmachi Station is located at the heart of the area called Uemachi Daichi, or "uptown plateau," located in the eastern part of the city, stretching about six miles, from Osaka Castle in the north to Sumiyoshi Shrine in the south. After defeating the Toyotomi clan at the Siege of Osaka in 1614 and 1615, the Tokugawa government organized residential districts for warriors and merchants just south of the castle and nine temple towns further south on this plateau (because of this, to this day Osaka Prefecture enjoys by far the highest concentration of temples by area).[15] In sum, Uehonmachi in the 1960s was a place that evoked a long history and provided what Dolores Hayden, in her exploration of the landscape of Los Angeles, calls "an overload of possible meanings" like "a weave where one strand ties in another" (1997, 18). In this sense, Uehonmachi stood in stark contrast to Senri New Town.

In the film, we first see the inside of the station, on the ground floor. Reiko comes up to this floor via a stairway, probably from the basement of the Kintetsu Department Store attached to Uehonmachi Station. Then, Katayanagi, who has just arrived at the station looking for her, finds her around the ticket office. Behind the ticket office, we see the ticket gate and, beyond that, the bay platforms. Reiko explains to Katayanagi that she wants to be alone and start her life over in her hometown (see figure 3.4). She also confesses that she is scared of the cruelty that Katayanagi demonstrated when he staged the fake

Figure 3.4. *Black Weapon* (1964). Reiko plans to board the train at Uehonmachi Station to go back to her hometown in Ise.

kidnapping of the son of the Taiyō executive, implying that she can no longer think about a future with him. While this conversation takes place, the camera does not focus exclusively on the lovers but moves around the inside and outside of the station, crammed with men and women, old and young. Focus shifts slowly from one person or group to another, including students gathering at the kiosk, passengers boarding a train, leaving a train, and passing through the ticket gate, people using the station as a meeting place, a mother carrying a baby, and a girl playing with a doll. Some are walking, some are running, and some are just standing. Many of them do not seem to be extras hired for the film but regular, local urbanites who happened to be there at the time of the location shooting. Their movements are far from uniform. They are a disorganized and spontaneous crowd.

Moreover, all over the station's interior, we see advertisements for businesses and cultural institutions in Osaka (for example, a local doctor's office), some run by Kintetsu (for instance, Kintetsu Real Estate), and some located along the Kintetsu line (the Yamato Museum in Nara and Daidō Steel in Nagoya). The unprompted presence of the large crowd, backgrounded by numerous advertisements with their concrete information about local sites, provides a striking degree of historical and geo-cultural specificity to this place and to the people there. Together, it all dramatically and abruptly alters the atmosphere of *Black Weapon*. A film that has so far underscored the uniformity and monotony of the modern industrial city now looks like a documentary film illuminating the actuality and heterogeneity of the people who have incidentally crossed one another's paths on their ways to work, school, shopping, movie theaters, restaurants, bars, temples, shrines, home, and so on. Here, Uehonmachi Station is represented as a unique place that cannot be mistaken as or replaced by any other place.

Reiko's departure from Uehonmachi Station needs to be understood within this context. The film has so far established industrial spies as cosmopolitan urbanites, detached from local contexts, and therefore when we first hear her speak about her return to her hometown, or *inaka*, which in Japanese refers not only to one's hometown but also to the countryside in general as a concept antonymous to the city, we have some difficulty reconciling this woman's urbanity and her *inaka* origin. They seem incompatible, especially because her hometown Ise is not just any *inaka* but home to the Ise Grand Shrine, with more than a thousand years of history. Then, we recognize one simple fact: this spy has her own personal history, just as those individuals visiting or passing through Uehonmachi terminal have their own histories. She does not detail her past at all, but that is not important. What demands our attention is that her movement from Uehonmachi to Ise by Kintetsu prompts us to imagine the specific historical network of the exchange of people, goods, and money that the city of Osaka has built since the premodern era and the millions of people like her, whether workers, students, travelers, drifters, or runaways, who have moved to, visited, lived in, and left Osaka for innumerable reasons. Now, Osaka is no longer an unmarked industrial city dominated by "placelessness" but a city with an idiosyncratic history; it is an economic center of the nation-state, a hub of transportation, a destination for migration, and a place where people like Reiko seek to build a life and achieve success.

The film's emphasis on the uniqueness and irreplaceability of Uehonmachi Station culminates in the final shots that follow. Aware that it is impossible to change Reiko's mind, Katayanagi bids her farewell and leaves the station without seeing her off. Now, we finally see the station building from outside (see figure 3.5). Osakans used to call this gorgeous six-story building (with one additional floor in the basement and two in the penthouse) by the nickname "Daiki." It was built in 1926 by the Osaka Electric Railroad Company (Osaka Denki Kidō), the predecessor of Kintetsu, and "Daiki" was the abbreviation of this company's name. Mikasaya Department Store occupied the basement

Figure 3.5. Black Weapon (1964). The exterior of the Daiki building at Uehonmachi Station appears at the very end of the film.

and the first three floors, fulfilling (and creating) busy middle-class suburban commuters' everyday needs, but withdrew in 1935 as Daiki chose to launch its own department store. The combination of terminal station and department store is one leading model for urban/suburban development in modern Japan, and Daiki, together with other railway companies in Osaka such as Hankyū, was one of the pioneers of this model at the national level. The building miraculously survived the US bombings during the Pacific War while many other parts of the city were reduced to ashes. It soon revived as Kintetsu Department Store, and by 1960 it had grown into a major destination in the city, with the average number of customers per day exceeding twenty thousand (Kinki Nihon Tetsudō Kabushiki-gaisha 1960, 257). As of 1964, the building was still under full use and serving as a powerful metonymic site that recalled to many Osakans the modern historical evolution of the city and their personal memories of it (see figure 3.6).

The choice of the Daiki building at Uehonmachi Station, with its diverse historical meanings, as the site of these final shots is suggestive. The film seems to demonstrate yearning for an "authentic place" (Relph 1976), a place not yet defaced or absorbed by the standardizing and homogenizing forces of industrial society, and the Daiki building is used as an indication of this yearning. Of course, the question remains whether there is such a thing as an authentic place in an urban center such as Uehonmachi, which is undoubtedly

Figure 3.6. The Daiki building. This building appeared in a picture postcard as a site representative of urban Osaka.

a product of the advanced technologies of industrial capitalism, and, even if there is, whether it makes sense to view the Daiki building as such a place. But I am not trying to verify the authenticity of this place nor confirm that this question is relevant for the appreciation of this final sequence. Instead, I want to emphasize that industrial society's mass production system, which sees humans mainly as an abstract collective of worker-consumers and turns them into calculable data, tends to lead people to search for a space—whether physical or metaphorical—where they can feel that organic human relations based on immediate and spontaneous interactions are preserved, valued, and fostered and that they are exercising control over their own experiences without being mediated by larger anonymous entities. In this final sequence, it appears that *Black Weapon* has identified the possibility of such a space in Uehonmachi in central Osaka and employs its saturated history and heterogeneous memories as a way of communicating the anxiety of the seemingly unrelenting standardizing and homogenizing forces of industrial society. Although Katayanagi cannot stay in this place, determined as he is to return to the competitive corporate world, these images of Uehonmachi Station and the Daiki building provide respite at the very end of this otherwise extremely somber spy film.

4

Yokohama Romance

The Cold War, Revolution, and Asian Solidarity in Ezaki Mio's *A Warm Misty Night* (1967)

Far beyond the ocean
Great dark waves rise
I always view the ocean here
I dream on this beach
Bad dreams, about the war in that country
People and children cry
I wonder where happiness is

>—"Far beyond the Sky" ("Tōi sora no kanata ni"),
>sung by Itsutsu no Akai Fūsen (1969)

My friend, in the darkness before dawn
My friend, burn the fire of fight
The dawn is close, the dawn is close
My friend, beyond this darkness
My friend, tomorrow is brilliant

>—"My Friend" ("Tomo yo"), sung by
>Okabayashi Nobuyasu (1968)

❦

Japan's high-speed economic growth continued throughout the 1960s. Prime Minister Ikeda Hayato's "income doubling plan," which he introduced in the aftermath of the 1960 Anpo protest to alleviate the ideological and political divisions within Japanese society, successfully doubled both the nation's GNP and per-capita income and did so even faster than the expected ten years. The LDP government also enhanced social security through the introduction of universal health care and national pension systems, thereby consolidating the foundations of the welfare state. Ikeda and his LDP quite successfully mitigated the intense conflict between capital and labor that existed in the 1950s by transforming the working masses into beneficiaries of the postwar economic system. The next prime minister, Satō Eisaku, also from the LDP, would manage to form three cabinets in a row, remaining in power for almost eight years, from 1964 to 1972—the second-longest tenure in the history of modern Japan (by consecutive days in office), after Abe Shinzō's three cabinets between 2012 and 2020. This was possible precisely because of the economic (and to some degree political) stability whose seeds had been planted by his predecessor.

On the other hand, in the second half of the 1960s, it became increasingly evident that the Japanese economy heavily relied on American imperial projects in Asia for continued growth. As the United States deepened its involvement in the Vietnam War through the bombing of the communist north, Japanese companies massively benefited from war-related procurements of the US forces, gaining opportunities for further investment and technological innovation. While the peace and antiwar movement that attracted hundreds of thousands of participants throughout Japan in this period could not end the war or alter the fundamental political structure dominated by the pro-American LDP, it called public attention to Japanese complicity in and acquiescence to America's aggression in Asia as well as Japan's subordinate and colonial status within the Cold War geopolitical system. By the late 1960s, it had become extremely difficult to sustain the innocent narrative that postwar Japan with its new constitution had revived itself as a pacifist state committed to international cooperation, redirecting its people's energy toward economic reconstruction and growth.

In this chapter, I discuss a Nikkatsu film made amid the Vietnam War and examine the tension that Japanese society experienced between desire for economic profit through alliance with the United States and solidarity with Asia through critique of the war. The film is *A Warm Misty Night* (*Yogiri yo kon'ya mo arigatō*), directed by Ezaki Mio and released in 1967.[1] This film features Ishihara Yūjirō, without doubt one of the best-loved and most charismatic male stars in the history of Japanese cinema. The film is an adaptation of the 1942 American film *Casablanca*—which was released in Japan in 1946 and enjoyed enormous popularity, just as it did in the United States and many other countries. As in *Casablanca*, a triangular relation among one woman and two men (or, to put it another way, a homosocial relation between two men who love the same woman) constitutes a crucial foundation for the plot in *A Warm Misty Night*. But the site of this triangular relation has been shifted from the northern African city ruled by the pro-Nazi Vichy regime during World War II to 1960s Yokohama during the Vietnam War. Yūjirō, as the counterpart to Rick, the role in *Casablanca* played by Humphrey Bogart, plays the owner of a successful nightclub at Yokohama Harbor who wavers between love for his former fiancée and ideological sympathy for her current husband, a man from an unidentified Southeast Asian country.

While we readily recognize the anti-Nazi political message in *Casablanca* (i.e., the unsympathetic representations of the Nazis and the heroic representations of the Resistance), it is not so easy to identify the same degree of political implications in *A Warm Misty Night*, for it does not directly reference politics in contemporary Japan and Asia. However, intertextual knowledge of *Casablanca*, particularly concerning Rick's tacit support for the Resistance and friendship with his former lover's husband mediated by a shared ideology, encourages us to read *A Warm Misty Night* as more political than it first appears, and the method of historicization certainly helps us conduct this reading. In this chapter I aim to discern the meanings of the key elements that constitute the film—including the setting (Yokohama Harbor), the occupation of the protagonist played by Yūjirō (nightclub owner and provider of support for illegal overseas migrants), and, of course, the triangular relationship into which he is drawn—within the geopolitical and economic context of Japan in the late 1960s, especially as it involves the Cold War and the Vietnam War. My aim is to read this romance film as a manifestation of the tension between desire for the economic perks of the American military presence and solidarity with the struggle against American imperialism in Asia.

I start with a discussion of Nikkatsu's "mood action" (*mūdo akushon*) films, the genre to which *A Warm Misty Night* belongs. I explain the implications of the term *mood* in popular culture in postwar Japan and how the film was intended to create a soothing and romantic mood for a mature audience by relying on the exotic image of the port city Yokohama. Then, resorting to the notion of "contact zone" propounded by Mary Louise Pratt, I articulate the absent presence of the US forces in the film's seemingly apolitical "moody" representations of Yokohama and how the protagonist appears as a prosperous business owner who economically benefits from American GIs and officers—that is, an accomplice to American imperialism in Asia. This is followed by a discussion of the process by which this male protagonist is gradually persuaded by his former fiancée to support the revolution in which her Southeast Asian husband is involved. The final section addresses the question of his former fiancée's infertility and demonstrates how the film, while showing sympathy for the revolution through the trafficking of this Japanese woman between the Japanese protagonist and the Southeast Asian revolutionary, at the same time seeks to defend her purity by foreclosing the possibility of the couple producing multiethnic children.

Nikkatsu "Mood Action" Films

Ishihara Yūjirō's career as an actor started with the 1956 Nikkatsu film *Season of the Sun* (*Taiyō no kisetsu*), in which he played only a minor role. This was a film adaptation of the Akutagawa Prize–winning novel written by his older brother Ishihara Shintarō ([1955] 2011). The crude representations of reckless and selfish young people from urban middle-class families and the explicit treatment of such topics as sex and pregnancy scandalized Japanese society. Both the novel and the film were perceived as symptoms of the advent of a new postwar generation whose young people enjoyed abundant time for personal pleasure and prioritized their emotional impulses and material desires over duty to family and community. The media soon dubbed this new generation the *taiyōzoku*, or "sun tribe," and Yūjirō, together with his brother Shintarō, became one of those celebrities seen as its representatives. As discussed in chapter 1, as of 1956 (the same year as the release of *Susaki Paradise Red Light* and the publication of the famous economic white paper), the majority of working people had yet to feel the perks of the economic growth that was just launching, and therefore the number of people who could indulge themselves in the kind of lifestyle depicted in *Season of the Sun* was extremely limited both socioeconomically and geographically. The film, however, alerted the general audience across the country to the rapid change happening in a small segment of urban Japan and presented one concrete, tangible manifestation of economic growth.

Yūjirō quickly gained national stardom in the second half of the 1950s. The films that featured him as protagonist, such as *Crazed Fruit* (*Kurutta kajitsu*, 1956), adapted again from Ishihara Shintarō's ([1956] 1980) eponymous novella; *I Am Waiting* (*Ore wa matteru ze*, 1957); and *Man Who Causes a Storm* (*Arashi o yobu otoko*, 1957) brought box-office success to Nikkatsu, which had just resumed film production a few years earlier after dissolving its wartime merger with Daiei. As Michael Raine (2001) points out, Yūjirō and Nikkatsu intentionally and successfully replaced his earlier image of a rebellious, delinquent young man with that of a rough but kind older brother, thereby expanding his fan base to those who had been appalled by the *taiyōzoku*'s antisocial and aggressive representations. The commercial success of Yūjirō prompted Nikkatsu to discover "second Yūjirōs," namely Kobayashi Akira, Akagi Keiichirō, and Wada Kōji. Together with Yūjirō, these stars, promoted as the "Diamond Line" (*daiyamondo rain*), would sustain the golden age of Japanese cinema in the 1950s and contribute to consolidating the popular association of Nikkatsu with dramas and action films targeting teen and young-adult audiences (Nikkatsu Kabushiki-gaisha 2014, 78–83).

Even with Yūjirō's charismatic popularity, however, Nikkatsu could not cope effectively with the problem that all the film production companies faced in the 1960s, that is, the sharp decline in the number of moviegoers. The growing diversification of entertainment during the high-speed growth era broadly and the rapid dissemination of televisions in particular, starting in the late 1950s, drew many viewers away from movie theaters. While the total movie box office exceeded 1.1 billion in 1958, it dropped below 700 million in 1962, and this phenomenon would steadily continue throughout this decade (Matsumoto 2012, 50–55). All film production companies tried to overcome this problem through drastic rationalization, which naturally fueled conflict between management and workers. As for Nikkatsu, in 1962, the year the company celebrated its fiftieth anniversary, its contract workers, frustrated at poor work conditions, formed a labor union and deepened their confrontational attitude toward management, demanding better compensation and criticizing CEO Hori Kyūsaku's autocratic business style. In the same year, worsening performance forced the company to stop paying dividends to stockholders. In 1964, although its film production branch was still profitable, the company sold its exclusive theater in Marunouchi in central Tokyo to Mitsubishi Estate to pay off the debt accumulated in its real estate branch, which was followed by the disposal of other exclusive theaters in Ryōgoku and Kanda (Nikkatsu Kabushiki-gaisha 2014, 120; Matsumoto 2012, 70–80).[2]

It was around this time that Yūjirō's "mood action" films—action films combined with melodramatic elements related to adult relationships—emerged as a strategy to revive Nikkatsu and reach out to a new pool of more mature moviegoers. According to film critic Watanabe Takenobu (1982a, 23), Nikkatsu began the production of melodramatic action films featuring Yūjirō in 1963, and they can be identified as "mood action" films retroactively. But it was in an advertisement for *Sunset Hill* (*Yūhi no oka*) in 1964 that the company first used this expression. This was a new subgenre that Nikkatsu distinguished within its action-film genre—the genre that this film production company had strongly pushed since the late 1950s with the four stars in the "Diamond Line" and such actresses as Kitahara Mie, Ashikawa Izumi, and Asaoka Ruriko.

The term *mood*, or *mūdo* in Japanese, requires a bit of explanation. Here, I want to point out the two related but different meanings that gained cultural currency in 1950s and 1960s Japan. On the one hand, in 1950s Japan, "mood music" mainly from the United States was gaining popular recognition as a new genre of music. This easy-listening, soothing orchestra music, led by, for instance, Percy Faith, David Rose, Victor Young, Andre Kostelanetz, and the Anglo-Italian Mantovani, was welcomed in Japan, just as in the United States and elsewhere, because it incorporated elements of jazz and classical music but arranged them in a manner much more accessible to mainstream audiences, thereby serving as perfect background music for uncomplicated relaxation and comfort.[3] It also stimulated regular Japanese people's imagination of, and longing for, middle-class American life, about which they had come to learn during the occupation era and in which, they believed, citizens fully enjoyed their leisure time after work, backed by material wealth. A 1956 article on mood music published in *Swing Journal*, a well-known monthly journal specializing in jazz, viewed Japanese consumers' interest in "mood" and the American lifestyle positively, associating it with Japanese society's desire for "improvement" (*kōjō*), by which the article no doubt meant improvement in quality of life ("Saikin no ryūkō mūdo myūjikku" 1956).

On the other hand, "mood" also went through heavy localization within postwar Japan's specific cultural and social context and thereby acquired new meanings. Inspired by jazz, Latin, Hawaiian, and other foreign music genres, Japanese songwriters wrote songs for Japanese singers with mellow melodies in slow and medium tempo, and these were called "mood popular songs," or *mūdo kayōkyoku*. For example, Frank Nagai was singing American jazz songs under contract to the occupation forces when he began his career as a singer in the late 1940s, but he switched to Japanese original songs in the 1950s after being discovered by Japanese composer Yoshida Tadashi, who would create a number of memorable popular songs in the next several decades. The ballads he sang in his soothing, deep voice were described as possessing "mood" ("Frank Nagai no miryoku" 1958). In the 1960s, Nagai, together with other singers like Matsuo Kazuko and groups like Wada Hiroshi and Mahina Stars, helped to establish the genre of mood popular songs.

Japanese songwriters and singers used this new genre as a medium to express affects deriving from romantic relations set in various places within Japan, particularly urban downtown neighborhoods. There are abundant examples, such as Frank Nagai's 1957 massive hit "Let's Meet in Yūrakuchō" ("Yūrakuchō de aimashō"—Yūrakuchō is a neighborhood in central Tokyo, right next to Tokyo Station); "Tokyo Nightclub" ("Tōkyō naitokurabu," 1959), a duet by Nagai and Matsuo Kazuko; Mikawa Ken'ichi's "Yanagase Blues" ("Yanagase burūsu," 1966—Yanagase is an entertainment district in Gifu) and "Niigata Blues" ("Niigata burūsu," 1967); "Otaru no hito yo" ("A woman from Otaru," 1967) by Tsuruoka Masayoshi and Tokyo Romantica; and "In

Nagasaki It Rained Again Today" ("Nagasaki wa kyō mo ame datta," 1969) by Uchiyamada Hiroshi and Cool Five.

Because these songs were set in specific, familiar, and quotidian places within Japan, their lyrics tended to address the crude, realistic affects that unavoidably accompanied relationships, such as sorrow, worry, and loneliness, rather than joy, pleasure, and hope. Reflecting this, the melodies tended to be in minor chords, melancholic and pensive. Listeners could project their own experiences or read multiple possibilities into these songs—an extramarital relationship, a breakup due to class difference, socioeconomic insecurity for those working in the bar and nightclub industry, and so on. At the same time, mood popular songs' exotic tunes helped to neutralize the crudity and reality of the affects portrayed in the lyrics and made it possible to represent them as romanticized urban fictions. In this sense, mood served as a tool of what Paul Roquet has called "somatic self-discipline" (2016, 9–14) since it allowed the moderate glorification of everyday lives in modern industrial society rife with unbearable difficulties and frustrations (or memories thereof), bathing them in mellow, sweet comfort as if they were bearable or even desirable.

The "mood" in Yūjirō's new genre films was aligned with this second sense of the term. Compared to his earlier action films, these films were less busy and violent and focused more on the subtle, complex, and sometimes dark affects of adult men and women who had gone through physical, psychological, and socioeconomic hardships and their struggles to come to terms with their own pasts. By incorporating mood into action, Nikkatsu sought to appeal to both those looking for mainstream action films with familiar conventions, such as Yūjirō's showy fights with his enemies, and a more mature audience interested in his melodramatic romance with the heroine, usually played by Asaoka Ruriko. Furthermore, Yūjirō was already in his thirties in the mid-1960s, and his physique was quickly changing. Nikkatsu could no longer sell him simply as the young, slim, and handsome star that he had been. "Mood action" was also suitable as a response to his maturing appearance.

Many of Yūjirō's mood action films were set in port cities throughout Japan. They sought to create mood through extensive location shootings and elaborate sets that aimed to convey the atmosphere of these port cities. For example, *Red Handkerchief* (*Akai hankachi*, 1964), which Watanabe Takenobu regards as the masterpiece of mood action films (1982a, 33), is set in Yokohama (see figure 4.1). Yūjirō plays an ex-cop who mistakenly shoots and kills a suspected drug trafficker and ends up working construction in Hokkaido but returns to Yokohama three years later to investigate the plot behind the shooting incident, set by his former colleague. In *Sunset Hill* (1964), a young yakuza in Tokyo, played by Yūjirō, falls in love with the lover of his "big brother," kills a man who threatens to reveal their affair, and runs away to Hakodate, a port city on the southern tip of Hokkaido. In *Black Strait* (*Kuroi kaikyō*, 1964), Yūjirō is a Yokohama yakuza loyal to his boss who travels to Kobe on his orders to search for a man who ran away after embezzling money. In Kobe, Yūjirō learns from this man that his boss simply wanted to manipulate his loyalty and even pressured his father to commit suicide several years earlier. Furious at his boss's betrayal, Yūjirō returns to Yokohama, determined to exact revenge. In *A World for Two* (*Futari no sekai*, 1966), he plays a suspect in a murder case. After spending fifteen years in the Philippines as a fugitive, he goes back to Nagasaki to find the true murderer before the statute of limitation expires.

Yūjirō travels around these cities and visits their ports, train stations, and downtown streets while engaging in romance with the heroines (all played by Asaoka Ruriko except in *Black Strait*, which stars Toake Yukiyo) and confronts evil and merciless enemies. Viewers

Figure 4.1. *Red Handkerchief* (1964). The film was shot in Yokohama. "Mood action" films starring Yūjirō, including this one, sought to create mood through visual images of port cities throughout Japan.

are given various opportunities to observe and scrutinize the urban landscapes offered by these cities. Here, we have to remind ourselves of one important commonality among the cities Yūjirō travels through in these mood action films—Hakodate, Yokohama, Kobe, and Nagasaki: their ports were all among those that the Tokugawa government opened for trade with Western countries in the 1850s. The 1854 Convention of Kanagawa first opened Hakodate and Shimoda (in present-day Shizuoka Prefecture), then the 1858 Harris Treaty opened Yokohama, Hyōgo (that is, Kobe), Nagasaki, and Niigata. Although these were bilateral treaties with the United States, the Tokugawa government signed similar treaties with other Western countries (Britain, France, Russia, and the Netherlands) as well, thereby agreeing to trade with them through these ports. Upon the opening of these ports, the Tokugawa government established "foreign settlements" for businesspeople, merchants, diplomats, and clergy from these countries where they enjoyed extraterritorial privileges and developed autonomous administrative and economic spaces.[4]

On the one hand, the foreign settlements were a clear symbol of the unequal legal relations between Japan and the Western powers in the nineteenth century, when the latter were becoming increasingly aware of Asia's vast potential as a market. The political scientist Turan Kayaoğlu (2010) has called this form of domination based on the imposition of unequal treaties "legal imperialism." The Meiji government endeavored to revise the treaties and demanded the return of these areas to Japanese sovereignty, a goal that would not be realized till 1899. On the other hand, it is also the case that these port cities, because of the visible presence of foreigners—not only Westerners but also Chinese and Indians—since the nineteenth century, developed transcultural urban spaces distinctive from many other cities in modern Japan, characterized by foreign ships, Western-style houses (Yamate in Yokohama and Kitano in Kobe), Chinatowns (in Yokohama, Kobe, and Nagasaki), and various religious buildings such as Christian churches, Guan Yu shrines (*Kanteibyō*, in Yokohama and Kobe), and a mosque (in Kobe).[5] The exoticism of these port cities and their nonconformity to mainstream bourgeois society, particularly Yokohama and Kobe due to their size, have been vigorously addressed in cinematic and literary representations since the interwar years. Mitsuyo Wada-Marciano (2008), who has analyzed films set in Yokohama in the 1920s and 1930s such as Shimizu Hiroshi's *Japanese Girls at the*

Harbor (*Minato no Nihon-musume*, 1933), demonstrates how this port city was imagined as a liminal space that represented the foreign—"a transient, heterogeneous population of outlaw space" (35).

As I mentioned in the previous chapter, after defeat in the war and the collapse of the empire, international travel remained restricted until 1964. This meant that one could no longer travel through those Japanese port cities to other ports of Asia—such as Pusan, Dalian, and Shanghai—and beyond, which were far more exotic and liminal than, say, Kobe and Yokohama for Japanese travelers. Therefore, in postwar Japan, as people lost the mobility they had enjoyed in the era of empire, the exoticism and liminality of these Japanese port cities, or *minatomachi*, became even more precious and seductive. These were among the few places left within Japan that allowed people to have the tangible experience of things foreign and to immerse themselves in the atmosphere of cultural hybridity safely and easily (note that Yokohama and Kobe are about thirty minutes by train from Tokyo and Osaka, respectively). Yūjirō's mood action films took full advantage of these images of exoticism and liminality and used them to consolidate a glamorous and mysterious mood around the struggles of his romantic relationships and professional duties. Below, I discuss in detail *A Warm Misty Night*, which Watanabe has deemed the zenith of mood action films (1982a, 73). I examine more closely the mood that surrounds this film, unpacking the political and socioeconomic conditions beneath that mood and what narratives can be extracted about postwar Yokohama and Japan.

Cosmopolitan Yokohama

The film starts in Kobe—another exotic and liminal port city in the Japanese imagination. Sagara, played by Yūjirō, works for American President Lines, a large, American-owned passenger and freight shipping company. The ship on which he served as the captain has just returned from a long voyage. He calls his fiancée, Akiko (Asaoka Ruriko), from the ship to propose to her, suggesting that they get married immediately. Akiko is a dancer and receives this call at her dance studio. Excited about Sagara's proposal, she rushes to the church that he has specified (which is supposed to be in Kobe, but for the location shooting, Yamate Catholic Church in Yokohama was used).

While in a taxi heading toward the church, she finds a flower vendor on the street. She asks the driver to stop so she can buy flowers for the wedding. As she crosses the street toward the vendor, however, she is hit by a car. Then, the opening credits start. They are accompanied by the mellow-tuned, eponymous theme song, sung by Yūjirō in his tender and soothing baritone voice—a song now considered a standard of mood popular songs. While the opening credits are showing, we see Sagara in his uniform wandering the town, desperately searching for Akiko, who never showed up to the church.

After the opening credits, the setting shifts to Yokohama Harbor four years later. Sagara owns a nightclub named Scarlet, located at the harbor. The audience understands that he ended up not marrying Akiko and started a new business in another port city. Throughout the film, this nightclub appears again and again, serving as the main venue for Yūjirō's interactions with Akiko and the other main characters. It therefore constitutes a crucial part of the total visual image that the film creates of this port city. It is spacious, separated into a bar and a dance floor with a fair number of tables and chairs. One wall of the dance floor is decorated with a large bas-relief world map showing the Pacific Ocean at the center, which is illuminated by dim, fuchsia-tinted lighting. By this wall stands a grand piano, unused. Three white men are clustered by the piano, playing music with a light bossa nova beat: one on guitar, one on flute, and the third on what looks like a bongo. None appears to be a professional musician (the man playing guitar is wearing a sailor uniform). They look more like customers who have ended up jamming as the evening went on. A few people are dancing to the music joyfully. The customers are a mix of races and ethnicities. The camera moves from one table to another showing these customers. At one, two Asian men, one white man, and one white woman play cards accompanied by cocktails, beer, and brandy (judging by the shapes of their glasses; see figure 4.2). At another table, one Black man reads a paperback by Alfred Hitchcock with a glass of brandy to one side and several other English-language paperbacks to the other. At a third table, a Japanese man and woman, seemingly lovers, whisper together while holding hands.

Right after this sequence, three yakuza men in black suits come to the bar and accuse Sagara of hiding the man they are looking for (note that the outlaw and clandestine nature of yakuza is closely associated with port cities). Sagara does not know the man in question

Figure 4.2. *A Warm Misty Night* (1967). Scarlet attracts customers of various racial and ethnic backgrounds.

and easily beats up the thugs. He apologizes to the customers in both Japanese and English for the trouble: "osawagese shite mōshiwake arimasen" and "ladies and gentlemen, so sorry, this trouble." The relaxing atmosphere prevails once again. Sagara moves to the dance floor and starts playing the piano while singing "Fallen Flower" ("Kobore-bana"), another soothing mood popular song, with that gorgeous bas-relief behind him. A white man wearing what seems to be a merchant marine uniform and an Asian man wearing a fez, both of whom seem to be not only customers but also good friends of Sagara's, join him, playing the guitar and bongo, respectively (see figure 4.3). While Sagara plays and sings, an Asian woman in a black

Figure 4.3. *A Warm Misty Night* (1967). Yūjirō's character (*center*) fraternizes with friends at the cosmopolitan Scarlet.

dress, who speaks Japanese with a slight accent, approaches him and says how she enjoyed her encounter with him the other day and that she is free tonight.

Thus, from the very beginning, *A Warm Misty Night* appropriates the historically amassed image of Yokohama and foregrounds its transcultural mingling. In fact, Nikkatsu had repeatedly used the liminal image of nightclubs, bars, and restaurants in this port city in many of their action films prior to *A Warm Misty Night*. In *The Call of the Foghorn* (*Muteki ga ore o yonde iru*, 1960), Akagi Keiichirō, playing a sailor who has just come home to Japan, has drinks with Ashikawa Izumi at the nightclub Casablanca, talking about the mysterious death of the man who was his best friend and her boyfriend. In *Black Scar* (*Kuroi kizuato no burūsu*, 1961), Kobayashi Akira, playing a yakuza who has just been released from prison, dances with a young Yoshinaga Sayuri to mellow jazz at a nightclub called Blue Sky. In *The Wharf of No Return* (*Kaerazaru hatoba*, 1966), which Ezaki Mio directed just seven months before *A Warm Misty Night*, Yūjirō's character, a pianist trapped by a drug-smuggling organization, has a date with Asaoka Ruriko in a lively, racially mixed diner and a romantic restaurant owned by an Italian man, who seems to be a good friend of the pianist (see figure 4.4). Moviegoers fond of Yūjirō and Nikkatsu action films, therefore, had already been quite familiarized with the kind of liminality represented by Scarlet in *A Warm Misty Night*.

Figure 4.4. *The Wharf of No Return* (1967). The Italian restaurant in this film, too, is represented as a space of transcultural mingling in Yokohama.

At Scarlet, just as at those liminal spaces in previous Nikkatsu films, national, ethnic, and racial boundaries do not seem to be crucial factors that dictate the terms of fraternization among the owner, workers, and customers. Japanese and foreign patrons, whether Asian, white, or Black, communicate in English and Japanese and experience transient but friendly and intimate, sometimes sexual, encounters. The details that garnish the mise-en-scène in this sequence—the bongo, brandy (or cognac), Hitchcock, the fez, bossa nova, and so on—are detached from their national, ethnic, or religious origins and contexts and randomly mixed, and this randomness seems more intentional than accidental. The mixture does not permit these details to serve as markers of particular cultural heritages. They are treated as equivalent in their value, in that their primary function is to enhance the cosmopolitanism of Scarlet and, by extension, Yokohama Harbor.

But whether this kind of cosmopolitanism truly existed in 1960s Yokohama is another question. It is a little hard to imagine that a place like this—where visitors from a wide variety of backgrounds fraternize without prejudice or conflict, as global citizens who transcend national, ethnic, and racial boundaries—could exist anywhere in the world. Scarlet should be seen more as a utopian and hyperbolized version of Yokohama as an exotic port city. It is probably safe to argue that popular fascination about things foreign led to the idealization of what contemporary Japanese society expectantly perceived as transcultural fraternization in such an exotic place as Yokohama. At the same time, however, we should also recognize that the exhibition of those cultural items mentioned above in the mise-en-scène of the film attests to the fact that global capitalism in the postwar era had already introduced these items into the Japanese market, or at least disseminated the knowledge of them in society, while cementing the cultural basis on which the audience could appreciate their significance as symbols of Yokohama's cosmopolitanism.

Yokohama as a Contact Zone

While this Yokohama cosmopolitanism filled with "mood" seems to underline equality and harmony, reading it within the historical context specific to 1960s Yokohama (or postwar Japan more broadly) reveals the relations of domination and subordination embedded within. Critical to such a reading is the acknowledgment of the heavy presence of the US forces. Yokohama was the first city in mainland Japan that MacArthur and his forces occupied after their arrival at Atsugi Airbase on August 30, 1945. MacArthur stayed in the city with his General Headquarters of the United States Army Forces, Pacific (USAFPAC) until September 17, when the headquarters was moved to Hibiya, Tokyo. However, the Eighth Army, headquartered in the Customs building in the center of the city, remained in Yokohama and from there administered first the eastern part of Japan and then the entire country. During the occupation, almost all parts of the port and many facilities in the central part of the city that had not been destroyed by the US bombings were condemned (Kurita 2011; Yokohamashi Sōmukyoku Shishi Henshūshitu 2000, chap. 1). The number of condemned facilities totaled 177. These were converted into barracks, apartments, arsenals, post exchanges, storage sites, officers' clubs, schools, cafeterias, theaters, hotels, hospitals, and so on. Many of these facilities were returned to the original owners after Japan regained independence and sovereignty in 1952. As of the time of the release of *A Warm Misty Night* in March 1967, however, twenty-five facilities in the city remained occupied by the US forces under the terms of the Security Treaty. These facilities included North Dock (60.3 hectares), part of the port of Yokohama located at Mizuho Pier, which had become home to the 836th Transportation Battalion, and a large housing complex in Negishi (47.4 hectares), not far from central Yokohama (Yokohamashi Furusato Rekishi Zaidan 2014, 90–95; Yokohamashi Sōmukyoku Shōgaibu 1973, 15, 22–23). Kanagawa Prefecture, in which Yokohama is located, also hosted (and still hosts) US military facilities in Atsugi, Yokosuka, and Sagamihara. It was (and, again, still is) one of the prefectures with the largest concentrations of American bases in Japan.[6]

During the Vietnam War, Yokohama gained further importance as a center of logistic support for the US forces fighting in Vietnam, as the US Navy's Military Sea Transportation Service (MSTS) in Yokohama shipped fuel, equipment, supplies, and troops to Vietnam and other parts of Asia. One controversy this created in Japanese society was that the crews of their tank-landing ships, so-called LSTs, included not only Americans but also Japanese. Starting early in 1965, as the US bombing of North Vietnam intensified, the MSTS's recruitment of Japanese crews began to receive media attention. In April 1965, The *Asahi* newspaper reported that there were seventeen LSTs with Japanese crew members and that about 820 Japanese crew members were already working under contract to the US Navy, transporting military supplies to Vietnam, South Korea, and Okinawa. The article further noted that the MSTS was planning to recruit 380 more Japanese crew members and asked the Yokohama branch of the All-Japan Seamen's Union for support, though the union declined this request out of concern for the safety of workers ("Nihonjin sen'in zokuzoku ōbo" 1965).

This issue was brought up repeatedly in the Diet. Socialists Matsumoto Shichirō and Hanyū Sanshichi criticized the LDP government's condoning of the recruitment of Japanese workers for US military labor as clear evidence of Japan's complicity in actions beyond the framework of the Security Treaty.[7] In today's Japan, the presence of these Japanese workers recruited in Yokohama has faded from popular memory of the Vietnam War, but in the mid-1960s, Yokohama, together with other port cities with a heavy presence of US forces, such as neighboring Yokosuka and Sasebo in Nagasaki, served as a constant reminder to Japanese citizens of their country's complicity in the Vietnam War and the crude reality that postwar Japan's peace and economic prosperity were in fact enabled and protected by its ally's military aggression in Asia.[8]

Therefore, an analysis of the representation of Yokohama in *A Warm Misty Night* entails our recognition of the US forces' absent presence. While US bases and soldiers appear nowhere in the film, and the characters make no direct references to them, we must not overlook this as an absolute absence but consider how the US forces mediated those representations. The recognition of this absent presence leads us to understand Yokohama in the film not simply as a space of cosmopolitanism but as a "contact zone," which Mary Louise Pratt defines as "the space of colonial encounters, the space in which peoples geographically and historically separated come into contact with each other and establish ongoing relations, usually involving conditions of coercion, radical inequality, and intractable conflict" (1992, 6). Whereas the seeming cosmopolitanism of the port in the film foregrounds peaceful and friendly mingling among people of various national and racial backgrounds, the notion of the contact zone directs our attention to unequal power relations between the

American forces and the Japanese in Yokohama. But the film does not show these relations explicitly, so we must identify the tacit references that imply them and discern their meanings with the notion of the contact zone in mind.

One such reference is the nightclub Scarlet as the setting for the film. In Japan during the Vietnam War era, setting a film in a nightclub (or a bar) in Yokohama was in itself a political statement that immediately conjured up the US forces, since base towns like Yokohama back then were filled with American soldiers stationed in Japan and those in uniform returning from the battlefield in Vietnam in fleet ships and entering such ports as Yokosuka and Sasebo, as well as those having a short vacation on so-called R&R (rest and recuperation) leave. Camp Zama, northwest of Yokohama, hosted a center for soldiers on R&R; there, they received money sufficient for a five-night, six-day stay and traveled to such destinations as Tokyo, Yokohama, and Atami (a hot spring resort in Shizuoka Prefecture). Twenty hotels in Tokyo and ten hotels in Yokohama had special contracts with the US forces to accommodate military personnel entering Japan, whose total number, according to several sources, had grown to approximately fifty thousand by 1967 (Havens 1987, 101–2; Shiomi et al. 1969, 290–93; Andō 1967, 7–19). Bars and nightclubs targeting American soldiers in these cities thrived. Dobuita Street in Yokosuka represented probably the best-known concentration of such nightlife, but in Yokohama, too, such bars as StarDust and POLESTAR at North Dock and Golden Cup in Honmoku, a neighborhood close to the Negishi Housing Complex for American military personnel, were frequented by American soldiers looking for fleeting pleasure and consolation.[9] In 1960s Japan, the link between the US forces and the bar and nightclub industry in base towns was so evident that it seems natural to view Scarlet in *A Warm Misty Night*, precisely because of its location right by the harbor, as hinting at the absent presence of US forces.

Confirmation of this point permits us to identify another reference to the US forces: a young bartender working at Scarlet. He is presented as a person of mixed Asian and Black heritage. While working at Scarlet at night, he devotes his days to training, dreaming of success as a professional boxer. Throughout the film, he remains a loyal ally of Sagara. This bartender, called Bill by people at the nightclub, is played by Japanese actor Gō Eiji in blackface. In the

American context, blackface is seen as a derogatory and dehumanizing form of representation rooted in the centuries-long history of racism against African Americans. Blackface is not unheard of in the Japanese context. Japanese people have long been socialized to representations of African Americans and Africans as well as white Americans' blackface performances in American media. Comedians and musicians in Japan occasionally perform in blackface in the national media, sometimes prompting protest (and sometimes prompting no protest at all). The cultural anthropologist John G. Russell (2015) points out that while many cases of blackface in Japan may not derive from a long history of racial animosity, as they do in the United States, they are definitely based on various stereotypes about Black people widely circulating in Japan and beyond. Also, as Russell indicates elsewhere, regardless of the intentions and purposes behind a blackface performance, the very act of painting a face dark to perform the role of a Black person is an expression of the desire to "demarcate the boundaries" of the "alterity" of Black people, to mark them as a racialized group of people essentially different from the Japanese, and, as such, it is a form of racism (2011, 139).[10] In the case of *A Warm Misty Night*, we can add that the fact that a fairly famous Japanese actor was chosen for this role suggests the filmmakers' dilemma over the hope to visually accentuate the alterity of the mixed-race bartender/boxer and the simultaneous need to represent this alterity within the familiarized territory of "mood action" films in order to appeal to a mainstream audience, who were expecting Nikkatsu's well-known stars and the genre's usual conventions.

While recognizing all these issues related to blackface, I also argue that the performance of blackface in *A Warm Misty Night* differs from other common cases in the Japanese media. It is not played for caricature or ridicule. Gō Eiji's performance does not make himself or Black people look comical, foolish, inferior, superior, or extraordinary. None of the characters in the film makes a big deal of his skin color, either. The main significance of this mixed-race bartender/boxer is that he serves as a key figure who connects the film to the politics and history of postwar Japan, especially that of Yokohama as a neocolonial port city controlled by the US forces. Since the early postwar years, the city and Kanagawa Prefecture have dealt with issues associated with children born to American fathers and Japanese mothers, particularly occupation forces personnel and women in the sex industry, or *pan-pan*, as they were derogatorily called. Because this prefecture hosted the headquarters of the Eighth Army and other US bases, the number of mixed-race children was much higher than in other prefectures. The presence of mixed-race children became a topic of public discussion in the early 1950s when those born at the beginning of the occupation era were reaching school age. According to a survey conducted by the Kanagawa branch of the Social Welfare Council in 1952, there were 553 mixed-race children in households in the prefecture, 366 of whom resided in Yokohama. On the other hand, the number of mixed-race children raised in child welfare facilities in the prefecture amounted to 267, and this was more than half of all mixed-race children in such facilities nationwide (Yokohamashi Sōmukyoku Shishi Henshūshitu 2000, 642–45).[11] These children endured severe discrimination and economic hardship as many grew up without fathers and their socially isolated mothers could not rely on support from their families or communities.[12]

Moreover, we need to attend to the working-class nature of boxing as a profession. Because it required few financial resources compared to other sports, boxing attracted young men from economically disadvantaged families and provided them with an opportunity for upward social mobility while its extremely rough and brutal nature placed them at risk of serious injuries, permanent brain damage, and sometimes death (Sugden 1996). Postwar Japan was not exceptional in this regard. There are many stories, factual and fictional, of men mired in poverty winning fame as successful boxers, from Harada Masahiko (under the ring name Fighting Harada) and Saitō Seisaku (who became the comedian Tako Hachirō), both of whom excited boxing fans in the early 1960s (Harada 2018; Sasakura 1999), to Jō Yabuki in Chiba Tetsuya's popular manga, *Tomorro's Jō* (*Ashita no Jō*). Among these men was Yamanaka Akira, born in 1946 to a Japanese mother and an African American soldier in Yokohama. He had six siblings but was the only mixed-race child and grew up without knowing his father. His mother died when he was in his second grade while he was at a sanatorium for tuberculosis. He spent his childhood at several orphanages because his Japanese stepfather could no longer support him financially. While living in a welfare facility and working in a factory after graduating from middle school, he was scouted by the famous Kyōei Gym, run by Kanehira Masaki, and decided to pursue a career as a boxer, attracted by the "hope to explore life" on his own ("jinsei o kirihiraite ikeru to iu kibō"; Yamanaka 2001, 56). He made his debut in 1962 with the ring name Jō Akira. Although his career as a professional boxer was brief, his experience certainly confirms the meaning that boxing had for men from his social class and seems to have served as a model for Bill in *A Warm Misty Night*.[13]

Cognizance of the nightclub and the mixed-race bartender/boxer as references to the absent presence of the US forces in 1960s Yokohama naturally forces us to mobilize greater sensitivities to the issues of race and class in our examination of the representations of Scarlet, to look beyond its seemingly peaceful and egalitarian cosmopolitanism, and to imagine the complex and multitiered relations of power operating inside that nightclub. We need to direct our attention to the problem of inequality embedded in interactions and negotiations between the people of various social backgrounds who gather and work at Scarlet. For example, we can think about the people like Bill who face discrimination due to their racial origins, are excluded from mainstream society, and have come to Scarlet looking for employment; the American soldiers and officers who relish their free time in Yokohama while enjoying social and economic privileges backed by America's military power and the strong dollar; the people who build romantic relations with those men; those who sell their sexual services to them pressed by economic need; and the men in that clandestine world who manipulate and exploit these people. These were among the people commonly present in base towns since the occupation era, and to examine Scarlet as a "contact zone" with the US military is to recognize this nightclub as a representative urban space that implies the complex social mingling of these people.

Furthermore, this type of politically oriented reading of Scarlet within the Cold War context allows us to highlight this film's intertextual relations with other films made around the same time that represented the US military presence in communities with bases in a far more explicit manner and to corroborate that this was indeed an issue about which Japanese society cared deeply. Such films include Imamura's famous *Pigs and Battleships* (1961); the same director's *History of Postwar Japan as Told by a Bar Hostess* (*Nippon sengoshi: Madamu onboro no seikatsu*, 1970), in which Akaza Etsuko, owner of a bar named Onboro (or "Rickety") in Yokosuka, shares stories of survival and encounters with American soldiers; and Takechi Tetsuji's *Black Snow* (*Kuroi yuki*, 1965), a dark, hopeless film about rape, murder, and corruption involving prostitutes, pimps, and American soldiers around Yokota base in Tokyo.[14]

The Dream of Revolution

If we accept Scarlet as a contact zone within which unequal power relations prevail, what role does Sagara—the nightclub's owner, played by Yūjirō—play in this urban space, and what relations does he build with the people there, particularly US military personnel? For this, it is useful to pay attention to the economic boom that the Vietnam War brought to Japanese society. Although the Japanese government did not like to publicize the fact that the Vietnam War opened up lucrative markets in Asia and the Pacific for the Japanese economy, this was common knowledge in contemporary Japan. In the second half of the 1960s, America's heavy involvement in the former French colony solidified a system under which Japan took responsibility as an important supplier for various demands created by the American war effort—similar to what had happened during the Korean War back in the early 1950s. Japan's direct procurement of goods (e.g., sandbags, shoes, cement, cameras, petroleum, and food) and services (e.g., repair of airplanes and ships) for the US forces rose dramatically in this period. At the same time, so-called "indirect procurement" also expanded as Japan actively increased sales of semiprocessed materials and capital goods to American allies in Asia, including South Korea, Taiwan, the Philippines, and Thailand, all of which also received a large number of procurement orders from the US forces.[15] This direct and indirect procurement bolstered Japanese corporations' further capital investment and technological innovation, allowing the nation to demonstrate its outstanding production capacity. It is not a mere coincidence that Japan's GNP became the second largest in the world in 1968.

The bar and nightclub industry in base towns was one of those industries that benefited from the Vietnam War. This is proven by so-called "yen sales," which referred to cashing checks issued by the US forces in Japanese yen. The yen thus cashed was used by American military personnel stationed in or visiting Japan. Yen sales rose sharply in the late 1960s with the increase in American soldiers on R&R. An *Asahi* article in July 1967 reports that, in the first six months of that year alone, yen sales amounted to $179,822,000, a 26 percent increase over the previous year ("Tanomi no tsuna wa 'kikyūhei'" 1967). Of course, consumption by American military personnel included not only eating and drinking but also lodging, shopping, and many other activities, and it is hard to identify exact breakdowns. But it is reasonable to assume that young soldiers, coming from Vietnam and hoping to enjoy temporary relaxation and consolation in peaceful and prosperous Japan, spent a fair amount of money on drinks, dance, and encounters at bars and nightclubs.

Within this economic context, it is almost impossible to view Sagara as an innocent nightclub manager who simply offers a cosmopolitan and peaceful space for customers of diverse backgrounds to gather. He is a business owner who ingeniously draws on the growing presence of American military personnel in Yokohama and their desire for drink and pleasure during the Vietnam War. Here, his former status as an employee of American President Lines hints at the connections that he might have with Americans, and we suspect that these connections are helping him secure customers for Scarlet. He parasitically benefits from the base-related service economy, and therefore he is complicit in the reproduction of America's neocolonial domination of Yokohama. In this sense, this clever and successful businessman is mirroring the postwar Japanese state itself, which has never missed an opportunity to insist on its contribution to peace in Asia and the world while at the same time taking full advantage of the economic booms triggered by America's wars in Korea and Vietnam.

If nightclub owner is Sagara's public face, he has another face unknown to most people at Scarlet. He runs an underground business as a *nigashiya*, which literally means a "shop that helps [someone] run away." He assists those who need to leave Japan urgently but cannot do so through legal means by getting them fake passports and visas and finding clandestine but safe means of travel. Desperate individuals, such as a yakuza man embroiled in a gangland war and a business owner who embezzled his own clientele's money, come to Sagara seeking help. His former fiancée, Akiko, who disappeared in Kobe four years ago, is one such individual. One night, she shows up at Scarlet without knowing that it is run by Sagara. She is now married to a man named Nguyen (Nitani Hideaki). He needs to return immediately to his home country in Southeast Asia with Akiko to help the revolution that has just started there but cannot use the official air routes from Tokyo and Osaka because of interference by his country's government agencies. Rumors that the owner of Scarlet runs a *nigashiya* have drawn the couple to Yokohama, in hopes he can help them return to Nguyen's country by a sea route through Singapore. When they enter the nightclub, Akiko realizes that its owner is the man she hoped to marry back in Kobe. Sagara initially rejects their request. He cannot forgive her betrayal.

The film is never clear about which Southeast Asian country Nguyen is from. Indeed, it gives us confusing clues. On the one hand, his name, Nguyen (阮), is one of the most common Vietnamese surnames. Also, his revolutionary friend, who tries to help Nguyen return to their home country but gets killed during their fight with yakuza hired by their government, is called Tran (陳), which is another common Vietnamese surname (in Japanese, it is pronounced "Chan"). Also, there is a brief scene in which the two converse in French when they reunite in Yokohama, again suggesting their origin in this former French colony in Indochina (though it is hard to hear exactly what the two are saying, the screenplay clearly indicates that their conversation is supposed to take place in French; Ezaki et al. 1967). On the other hand, Nguyen has a large Filipino flag hanging on the wall right above his desk in the room where he and Akiko are staying in Yokohama, suggesting this is the homeland to which Nguyen is trying so desperately to return (see figure 4.5).

Figure 4.5. *A Warm Misty Night* (1967). The film gives confusing clues regarding which Southeast Asian country the revolutionary Nguyen is trying to return to.

It is unclear whether this is a conscious decision made by the filmmakers or a mistake deriving from a lack of simple research on the countries of Southeast Asia. In either case, the mix-up of the two Southeast Asian countries in this manner is puzzling because, despite their commonality as former Western colonies, their positions within the Cold War geopolitical order, their bilateral relations with the United States, and the images that people in Japan had of these countries were completely opposite in the mid-1960s. Vietnam was the victim of American military aggression and imperial ambition. America's war there prompted, in Japan as in many other parts of the world, various forms of peace and antiwar movements, represented by the Citizens' League for Peace in Vietnam, or Beheiren—a nationwide, nonpartisan civic organization that managed to enlist massive popular support in the second half of the 1960s (Avenell 2010; Sasaki-Uemura 2001). Contrastingly, the Philippines was one of the United States' most loyal Cold War allies in Asia and the Pacific. Through the 1947 Military Bases Agreement and the 1951 Mutual Defense Treaty, the United States had integrated its former colony into its capitalist block designed to contain revolutionary waves—reminiscent of Japanese integration into the same bloc through the 1951 Security Treaty. During the Vietnam War, President Marcos, in support of America's effort to contain communism, dispatched the Philippine Civic Action Group, a combat engineer battalion, thereby securing military and economic aid from the United States (Celoza 1997, 99–106).

How, then, can we make sense of the mix-up of these two countries? In what way does this mix-up relate to contemporary Cold War geopolitics? It appears that by giving two of the most common surnames used in a country where a revolution is in progress (Vietnam) to men who are supposed to be from a country known as a loyal Cold War ally to the United States (the Philippines), the film, whether intentionally or not, transplants revolutionary identity into the latter country and fosters an imagined Third World and Asian solidarity between the two. It creates the perception that the revolution that started in the former French colony is now spreading to one of the most loyal US allies in Asia and that the pro-American government there is under attack. Of course, this is quite contrary to what was happening in reality, as President Marcos of the Philippines managed to secure his political, economic, and military ties with the United States through the Vietnam War, solidified his anticommunist attitude, and guaranteed the longevity of his authoritarian regime, which lasted until 1986. But within the historical context of 1960s Asia, in which the United States was making strenuous efforts to prevent and discredit revolutions through military intervention, economic assistance, intelligence services, puppet governments, academic discourse, and cultural representations, the film's narrative of an alternate history of revolution—as something imminent and pressing, something that has grown to attract concerned and passionate patriots like Nguyen and Tran—can be seen as an attempt to bring discord to the widely circulated narrative of the US military in Asia as the defender of the free world, which had been endorsed by the United States and its allies, including the Japanese government.

Stirring Asian Solidarity

As mentioned, Sagara initially refuses to offer any help to Nguyen and Akiko. But Akiko later visits Scarlet once again, without Nguyen this time, and tries again to persuade him. The strategy that she takes is to appeal to his conscience and his consciousness of the economic quandary of the world's disadvantaged, which she observed when he was still working for American President Lines. She says, "I knew you in the past. Whenever you came home from a voyage, you told me about poor countries [*mazushii kuni*] in Southeast Asia, the Middle East, and Africa. You always said things couldn't go on like that and you would have to do something. When you left on a voyage, you took toys from Japan with you and gave them to children over there."

In this statement, we can observe two different but related sensibilities newly arising in Japan in the 1960s. The first is a sensibility about the so-called Third World. By this time, the dream of decolonization in the early post–World War II era had been quickly replaced by the reality of the neocolonial forms of domination deeply embedded in the global economy controlled by the former colonial powers. While modernization theory from the United States understood poverty and the political instability that often accompanied it as discrete problems intrinsic to each national community, objections from the Third World intensified, calling for the treatment of these problems as legacies of centuries-long colonial exploitation. It was in 1965 that Kwame Nkrumah, then the president of Ghana, published his *Neo-colonialism: The Last Stage of Imperialism*, accusing the West of a new type of colonialism that no longer showed interest in direct territorial acquisition but aimed to preserve hegemony through economic and financial means. In Japan in 1967, the same year as the release of *A Warm Misty Night*, the renowned political scientist Okakura Koshirō, also an active member of the Japan AALA (Asia, Africa, and Latin America) Solidarity Committee, published the second edition of his *Introduction to the Issues of Asia and Africa* (*Ajia Afurika mondai nyūmon*) with Iwanami Press, in which he enlightened the Japanese reader about the notion of neocolonialism while referring to Nkrumah and other political leaders and theorists from the regions. Akiko, speaking about "poor countries in Southeast Asia, the Middle East, and Africa," has internalized this new way of recognizing the struggles of the former colonies and is convinced that the revolution that is waiting for her husband's return is part of these struggles necessary for disentangling existing neocolonial relations.

Furthermore, when Akiko admires Sagara's concern for children in the "poor countries," she is perceiving Japan, which is geographically part of Asia, not as belonging to the Third World but as a developed country, just like the United States and Western European nations, capable of providing economic assistance to the Third World. In her understanding, Japan is clearly separated from the rest of Asia by the extent of its economic development and political stability, and this is the other sensibility that I want to point out. This sensibility must be understood in relation to the post–World War II "discovery" of persistent mass poverty in the Third World as a problem that required intervention and developmental policy by advanced nations in North America and Europe (Escobar 2011). In Japan ten years earlier, at the early stage of high-speed growth, when most people were still striving to reconstruct their lives in the aftermath of the war, there would have been no room for this kind of sensibility to spread (for example, could we imagine anyone in *Susaki Paradise* or *Blue-Sky Girl* talking about Japan's responsibility for helping "poor countries" in Asia?). It is undoubtedly a product of the confidence and material affluence brought by the acceleration of high-speed growth in the 1960s. Backed by these two sensibilities, Akiko urges her former fiancé to support the revolution, presenting it as a moral responsibility that a Japanese person with a lucrative business, disposable money, and broad connections should fulfill.

However, Akiko's strategy to underscore the link between the revolution and the neocolonial condition of the Third World does not work on Sagara. He tries to quiet her. But she continues: "I know more about what you used to do in Japan. You invited the mixed-race [*konketsu*] children who ran away from orphanages to your ship, found foster parents using your own money. . . . You always said you wouldn't want to make our children feel miserable and that was why you worked hard." Akiko now seeks to redirect Sagara's attention to the legacies of the US occupation of Japan, for which she believes he will demonstrate more personal concern (since he works with one of those mixed-race people at his own nightclub). In so doing, she connects this domestic issue to the neocolonialism that her husband is tackling in the unnamed Southeast Asian country, alluding to the US forces' accountability for both problems. This is also her tacit critique of Sagara, whose prosperous business at Yokohama Harbor is inconceivable without the presence of the US forces. By pointing out the contradiction between his invocation of (or at least sympathy for) a just society at the ideological level and his economic reliance on the US forces at the practical level, Akiko tries to appeal to his sense of guilt and conscience. Despite Akiko's effort, Sagara still refuses to have a conversation with her. He even denounces Akiko's eloquence, which she seems to have acquired in the past four years as a revolutionary's wife.

Later in the film, however, he opens up to her and decides to help her and her husband leave Japan by finding a ship heading toward Singapore. The decisive moment comes when she least expects it. Sagara is alone at the empty Scarlet after business hours, playing the piano with the large bas-relief of the world map at his back. Akiko comes in. She has just found in his office the wedding ring that he bought for her four years ago. This recalls her love for him and undermines her dedication to her husband and commitment to the revolution in Southeast Asia. Now, as she faces him alone at Scarlet, she cannot help expressing her long-repressed emotions. In order to make up for the loss of the past four years and to resuscitate their shared memory, she starts listing the things that he liked when they were together in Kobe: "Sidewalks after rain, children's toys, a lonely gorilla, bright summer sea, a negro boxer, thick-soled shoes, disentanglement puzzles impossible to disentangle, jockeys at a local horse track, a party where no one is left . . ."[16] Then, she moves on to the things she liked: "And then, my favorite things. The tiny brooch you gave me, the dunes in Tottori I visited with you, the 50-yen curry rice I ate with you, the gloves you forgot to take with you . . ." While making this statement, she stands up and begins walking toward him. The camera shows both Akiko and Sagara alternately in close-ups. Akiko is relaxed and smiling, looking determined to embrace her love for Sagara once again after the four-year break, whereas Sagara maintains a stern facial expression, indicating his hesitation to forgive and accept her back. Akiko gently touches the piano that he is playing. Then, she stands behind him and caresses his shoulder a little reluctantly. Sagara stands up, holds her tightly, and kisses her passionately.

While this sequence might make us believe that they are now happily reunited (at least Akiko feels that way), this is not the case. Right after this reunion, Sagara begins looking in earnest for a ship willing to take Akiko and Nguyen to Singapore. He soon finds a ship bound there that has made an unscheduled stop at Yokohama due to the medical emergency of a crew member. Using his old connections as an employer at American President Lines, he manages to convince the captain to take them to Singapore. The yakuza men, however, quickly learn of this plan and try to prevent Nguyen and Akiko from leaving Yokohama. Sagara, in collaboration with Nguyen and Bill, fights back against them and takes the couple to a small boat ready to carry them to the ship offshore. Sagara helps not only Nguyen but also Akiko get on the boat, which greatly perplexes Akiko since she has already made her decision to stay with him in Yokohama. Ignoring her confusion, Sagara wishes Nguyen good luck and says farewell to both. Akiko has no power to alter the fate assigned to her by Sagara. Although aware that Akiko wants to stay with Sagara, Nguyen gratefully accepts Sagara's offering of Akiko. The boat leaves. As his character walks away from the harbor, Yūjirō's theme song begins to play. When their boat vanishes from view, Sagara throws the ring into the water, and here ends the film.

The question remains: Why did Akiko's enumeration of their favorite things, which she believed would serve to awaken their mutual love again, actually lead Sagara to give up on her permanently and to support Nguyen's revolution? What Akiko identifies are things over which one cannot claim ownership (e.g., "sidewalks after rain" and "bright summer sea"), things that had already perished and existed only in their memories (e.g., "the 50-yen curry rice"), and things that were trivial and inexpensive (e.g., "the tiny brooch" he gave her). She carefully and consciously avoided mentioning anything expensive and lasting. The values of the things that she mentioned cannot be objectively measured. They cannot be exchanged for other things of equivalent value in the market. Their value can be appreciated only between them in the realm of personal affection. These things, therefore, mark a contrast with the things that Sagara had come to prioritize in the past four years—the luxurious, profitable nightclub, which has enormous exchange value in the market, as well as his clandestine business of *nigashiya*, which yields a substantial supplementary income. While Akiko lists their favorite things as a demonstration of her unchanged love for Sagara, for him this ironically serves as a critical indicator of his money-obsessed, materialistic way of life in the base town. Although Akiko previously tried in vain to remind him of the contradiction between his care for the disadvantaged and his economic connection to (or parasitic reliance on) the US forces, this time she unintentionally achieves this goal and thereby manages to arouse his latent political consciousness by implying that there are valuable things that are unmeasurable in the market but may provide him with a sense of fulfillment.

Homosociality and the Infertile Body

The triangular relation in *A Warm Misty Night* is almost parallel to that in *Casablanca*. In both films, the emotionally broken, financially comfortable, and politically aware but inactive male protagonist (Rick/Sagara) cannot forget about his old lover (Ilsa/Akiko) and the city where they were happy (Paris/Kobe). He unexpectedly meets her in another city affected by war and a military presence (Casablanca/Yokohama), confirms that they still love each other, but eventually cedes the woman to his male rival (Victor/Nguyen), who loves her as much as he does. The protagonist and his rival share a political ideology (anti-Nazism / Asian solidarity), but the rival is more active, courageous, and ambitious than the protagonist. By transferring ownership of the woman he loves most to his rival, the protagonist seeks to realize vicariously the political goal that he cannot realize on his own. Moreover, in both films, the protagonist and his rival each appear as a figure who represents his own national community. Using his former lover as the intermediary, the protagonist demonstrates moral support and solidarity from his own country (the United States / Japan) for his rival's country (Czechoslovakia / unnamed Southeast Asian country) against the common enemy (German Nazism / American imperialism). This is a typical homosocial relation in that the trafficking of a woman serves to enhance the ideological, political, and emotional bond between two men.[17] In this final section, I further elaborate the meanings of the triangular relation and the "traffic in women" in *A Warm Misty Night*.

In modern Japan, traffic in women was employed in several critical historical moments as a strategy to complement the masculine project of creating (or imposing) friendship between Japan and other parts of Asia. In 1920, ten years after the annexation of Korea and just after the March First Movement for Korean independence, the Japanese government married Masako of the Nashimoto family, a branch of the imperial family, off to Yi Un, the last crown prince of the Korean Empire, for the "unification of Japan and Korea," or *naisen ittai*.[18] In 1937, the Kwantung Army arranged a marriage between Hiro of the Saga family, a branch of the long-established aristocratic Fujiwara clan, and Pujie, the younger brother of Puyi, the last emperor of the Qing dynasty and the emperor of Manchukuo, to demonstrate cooperation between the Japanese empire and the Manchu state that had been established by the Japanese. If we shift our attention to postwar Japan, there is the case of Nemoto Naoko. When she was working at a high-end nightclub in Tokyo, her beauty was discovered by Kubo Masao, the CEO of a trading company, Tōnichi Bōeki, who was looking for business opportunities in Indonesia as the governments in Tokyo and Jakarta were negotiating over wartime reparations. Kubo introduced Nemoto to President Sukarno, and in 1962 this nineteen-year-old woman left Japan for Indonesia to marry the president, who was then fifty-seven years old and already had two wives, and was given a new Indonesian name, Ratna Sari Dewi Sukarno (Sukarno 2010). The movement of Akiko from Japan to Southeast Asia in *A Warm Misty Night* inevitably reminds us of these Japanese women treated as gifts from Japan to other parts of Asia for the purpose of alleviating political tensions, making alliances, and/or reinforcing an imagined pan-Asian harmony.

Unlike Nashimoto Masako, Saga Hiro, and Nemoto Naoko, however, Akiko has one distinct reproductive challenge: infertility. This provides important context for her sudden disappearance four years earlier and the trafficking of her between Sagara and Nguyen. As mentioned earlier, she was hit by a car on the day she was supposed to marry Sagara in Kobe. It was Nguyen's car, but he could not take her to a hospital because he did not want his enemies to identify his whereabouts. He treated her using his own connections, but this car accident left her infertile. This tormented her because she could no longer have children with Sagara. In deep despair, she decided never to see him again and married the very man who ruined her health and future. But we see none of this in the film. We learn of these details behind the car accident only through Nguyen's narrative.

The film represents the heroine with this reproductive condition as an incomplete person who requires compassion and even forgiveness. This is clear when we observe how her infertility is revealed to Sagara. This occurs halfway through the film, right after he, Akiko, and Nguyen escape an attack from the yakuza hired by the Southeast Asian country's government. The three are hiding in an empty church (although this is supposed to be in Yokohama, the location shooting was conducted at Reinanzaka Church in Minato Ward in Tokyo). The walls are covered from top to bottom with gaudy paintings of Jesus, the saints, and angels, including one mural of the Annunciation. Standing against the mural on the right side facing the altar, Nguyen begins to narrate what happened to her in the past four years. Akiko's infertility occupies the center of his narrative. Akiko tries to stop him. But he insists that she is "obliged" ("gimu ga aru") to let Sagara know the truth and continues as she dissolves into tears (see figure 4.6). The decorative setting inside the church, which seems like an outcome of the filmmakers' conscious effort to foreground the religious and spiritual nature of this space, makes Nguyen's narrative sounds like

Figure 4.6. *A Warm Misty Night* (1967). Nguyen (*right*) "confesses" Akiko's infertility to Sagara (*left*), while Akiko (*center*) collapses into tears.

a well-staged confession. This confession presents not only Nguyen's act of injuring Akiko but also her infertility as that which needs to be absolved by Sagara.

Sagara, however, cannot easily accept Akiko's unproductive body. Since the very beginning of the film, the audience has been made aware of Sagara's obsession with reproductive prosperity. It has long been his dream to build a family with three boys and two girls, and Nguyen also knows of this dream. The film stresses his emotional ambivalence and conflict with alternating close-up shots of Sagara and a statue of Mary holding the baby Jesus. Nguyen impatiently urges Sagara to forgive her, but Sagara postpones a decision by using as an excuse their hazardous situation. He says, "This is a battlefield. Rather than love and forgiveness, survival is more important" ("Koko wa senjō da. Ai dano yurusu dano, sonna koto yori ikiru koto no hō ga saki da").

Sagara does later decide to give up Akiko, as discussed in the previous section. When Sagara held and kissed her at Scarlet after being reminded by Akiko of the things that they had liked (that is, when Akiko thought they were finally reunited), he had already heard Nguyen's confession. If we interpret Sagara's decision in light of the knowledge of Akiko's unproductive body, we can argue that Sagara has ceded her to Nguyen not only because he wanted to show his support for the revolution in Southeast Asia but also because he found little value in the infertile woman who could not give him children. When he said "three boys and two girls" four years ago, he may have been expressing his innocent wish for a large, bustling household. But now that he has transformed himself into a successful businessman with large assets, progeny have become not only desirable but also necessary for the preservation of the economic capital that he has accumulated. Akiko's unproductive body has made it easier for him to offer her to the Southeast Asian revolutionary as a proof of their friendship.

We also need to consider the meaning that Akiko's infertility bears for the sexual union between her and Nguyen. Most importantly, the prospect of reproduction is foreclosed for this married couple. This is to say that mixed-race children will never be born between this Japanese woman and the Southeast Asian revolutionary. In modern Japan, just as in many other modern states, nationalist discourse since the nineteenth century has often imagined female bodies as a source of national strength, drawing direct correlation between biological reproduction and the social reproduction of economic and military power. We can observe this conflation most conspicuously in the state campaign during the Asia-Pacific War to boost the birthrate and population (Frühstück 2003; Takaoka 2011). But female bodies, because they exist in the material world as part of the lived experiences of those who own them, have also been feared as susceptible to penetration by unwanted, alien blood. Through the reading of Johann Fichte and Étienne Balibar, Ann Laura Stoler has pointed out that *métissage*, or crossbreeding, serves as a marker of the existence of an "interior frontier" within the nation-state or empire, where the purity of the community reveals its imagined foundation and is constantly proven unstable and volatile (2002, 80). *A Warm Misty Night* appears to seek to contain the rise of an interior frontier and to protect the purity of the beautiful heroine and her homeland of Japan by rendering her infertile and keeping her from bearing a mixed-race child like Bill the bartender.

The question of nationality in relation to mixed-race children also seems relevant here. First, Japan's Nationality Law, established in 1950, refused (and still refuses) to recognize dual nationality. It is likely that Akiko, married to a foreign revolutionary who might take up an important position in his home country's government if the revolution succeeds, has already surrendered or will be asked to surrender her Japanese nationality (note that Nemoto Naoko surrendered her Japanese nationality when she married President Sukarno). Second, until its 1984 revision, the same law remained patrilineal and gender discriminatory, denying those born between Japanese mothers and foreign fathers Japanese nationality. These two legal points imply that even if, by any chance, Akiko overcomes her reproductive challenge and manages to have a child with Nguyen, this child would never be granted Japanese nationality. Thus, the film carefully precludes the possibility of "contamination" by alien blood in two steps—by depriving the heroine of her reproductive ability and by alluding to the legal system that would keep any child of this couple from claiming Japanese nationality and the various rights that accompany it.

In this way, *A Warm Misty Night* demonstrates two different attitudes toward Ngyuen's homeland in Southeast Asia—pan-Asian solidarity between Sagara and Nguyen through the mediation of Akiko and obsession with the defense of the purity of the Japanese nation through her infertility. These seem inconsistent and even contradictory, but it is not difficult to make sense of them if we take into account the two different perceptions of Asia that much of postwar Japanese society shared. As we have seen in the previous section, pan-Asian solidarity was a response to the growing aggression committed by the US forces in Vietnam and the Japanese government's complicit relations with the United States. It is also true that postwar Japan, through defeat in the war, the collapse of empire, and the subsequent US occupation, detached itself from Asia, sealed over its past as a multiethnic empire, and established a self-recognition as an ethnically homogeneous state. The residents from former colonies—Korea and Taiwan—were deprived of their Japanese nationality by the 1951 San Francisco Peace Treaty and marginalized as aliens as though they had been allowed to stay in Japan by the benevolence of the Japanese state. As high-speed economic growth gained momentum in the 1960s, Japanese society developed an increasingly instrumental view of Asia, perceiving it predominantly as a market for Japanese products, a supplier of raw material, and a recipient of Japan's developmental aid.[19] Meanwhile, the entry of people from Asia to Japan, whether as workers, immigrants, or refugees, was strictly controlled, which reinforced the myth that the Japanese were living in a socially harmonious and culturally insulated community essentially different from the rest of Asia (Oguma 1995). It was only in the 1980s that Japanese society, spurred by a growing labor shortage, began seriously discussing the possibility of accepting foreign workers—whether Asians or Japanese descendants from South America—and coexisting with them. The two issues surrounding Akiko—her trafficking for pan-Asian solidarity and her infertility for the purity of the Japanese nation—were a reflection of the uneasy, complex relationship that postwar Japan had with Asia in the 1960s: sympathy for Asia at the emotional and ideological level amid the Vietnam War (that is, desire for a regional identity beyond the nation-state) and fear of ethnic and cultural hybridity at the practical level (that is, belief in the ethnically and culturally homogeneous nation-state as a natural and organic unit).

While *A Warm Misty Night* points to this dual attitude toward Asia in a quite elusive manner, Ōshima Nagisa's *Sing a Song of Sex* (*Nihon shunkakō*, 1967), released just a few weeks earlier than *A Warm Misty Night*, addresses it far more explicitly and violently. In this film, Kaneda Sachiko (Yoshida Hideko), a Korean Japanese high school student from Gunma who has come to Tokyo for a college entrance examination, appears as a person who challenges postwar Japan's belief in ethnic and cultural homogeneity. Slipping into a party organized by middle-class Japanese students where they are singing American protest songs, such as "We Shall Overcome" and "This Land Is Your Land," Kaneda, out of the blue, begins singing an old song about the plight of Korean "comfort women" in Manchuria, namely "Mantetsu kouta." The Japanese students praise this song but are completely ignorant of its historical context (i.e., Japan's colonial past and the presence of Korean Japanese in postwar Japan). They ask who wrote that song, wondering whether it is an African or Japanese folk song. Meanwhile, a few male students carry her away, and when she comes back a few minutes later, she is wearing not her school uniform but a gaudy, sleeveless dress, and tears are dropping from her eyes, both of which imply that she has been raped by those Japanese students. This rape clearly alludes to the fact that mainstream middle-class Japanese society, while critical of America's aggression in Asia and Japan's complicity in it, was simultaneously insensible to the identities of other Asian people living within Japan. Immersed in postwar Japan's conviction in ethnic and cultural homogeneity, these male students are not capable of imagining that Kaneda might not be Japanese but of another ethnicity. For them, she is simply a woman, devoid of a social and historical background, who can be used to satisfy their sexual desire and to enhance their homosocial bonding. At the end of the film, however, another character, Taniyama Takako (Koyama Akiko), shouts repeatedly that "Japanese people's homeland is Korea" ("Nihonjin no furusato wa Chōsen desu"), an alternative historical view to the one that insists on Japan's ethnic and cultural homogeneity and thereby seeks to relativize Japanese fetishism for purity and harmony.[20]

Looking at the dual attitude toward Asia in *A Warm Misty Night* through *Sing a Song of Sex* in this way, we realize that it actually contains a serious contradiction that could result in extreme brutality. Thus, this Yokohama-set "mood action" romance film references the conflicting and entangled desires that Japanese society experienced during high-speed growth: to enjoy economic prosperity under American military tutelage, to demonstrate solidarity for people in Asia, and to defend the purity of the national community. The image of high-speed growth that this film presents, therefore, is by no means optimistic or bright but communicates the layers of the problems that postwar Japan had to tackle regarding its position within Cold War Asia.

5

Waiting for Spring in Shiretoko

A Postscript to High-Speed Growth in Kumashiro Tatsumi's *The Light of Africa* (1975)

There were too many sad things
I wanted to travel somewhere far away
I put all my memories in my pocket
And took a train alone

—"I Am Wind" ("Watashi wa kaze"), 1975,
sung by Carmen Maki & OZ

Beneath the shadow of the wings flows the savannah
In a rising cloud of dust pass by many dramas
I go searching to the Africa of my dreams
I want to encounter the wilderness people have forgotten

—"I Want to Go to Africa" ("Afurika e ikitai"),
1975, sung by Arai Yumi

THE EARLY 1970S WAS A time of economic turmoil for Japan. In August 1971, President Nixon announced the termination of the US dollar's convertibility to gold, thereby ending the Bretton Woods system, which had contributed to stabilizing the war-torn economies of Western Europe and Japan. The subsequent introduction of a floating exchange rate brought panic and pessimism to the business world in Japan as it could no longer rely on the beneficial fixed rate of 360 yen to the dollar for export. At home, Prime Minister Tanaka Kakuei's 1972 plan for "Remodeling the Japanese Archipelago," aimed at rural reinvigoration, invited fierce land speculation by corporations, punishing consumers with high inflation. Then came the 1973 oil crisis. Sharp increases in the price of crude oil further destabilized Japan's economy, which, like that of many other industrialized countries at that time, had come to rely heavily on imported oil from the Middle East to maintain massive production throughout the postwar years. This further exacerbated inflation and led to a decline in industrial production and business investment. In 1974, Japan's GDP shrank for the first time in postwar history, marking the end of almost two decades of high-speed growth.[1]

In mainstream narratives of economic history, the 1973 oil crisis and the second oil crisis of 1979 often signify both a crisis and an opportunity. These narratives stress the concerted efforts made by the government, bureaucrats, corporations, and workers to adjust swiftly and flexibly to the rapidly changing global economic environment. For instance, in its description of Japanese responses to the two oil crises, the Economic and Social Research Institute, a think tank administered by the Cabinet Office, emphasizes how the Japanese economy, prompted by these crises, successfully transformed into a major producer of high-technology and high-added-value manufactured goods such as automobiles and semiconductors, thereby steadily increasing its trade surplus, especially with the United States. This narrative also maintains that the harmonious and cooperative relationship between management and workers was a key factor in the Japanese economy's performance by pointing out the flexibility demonstrated by unique "Japanese-style management," or *Nihonteki keiei*, which refers to such features as lifetime employment, seniority, and company unions (Kojima 2011, 27–30). In this narrative, the two oil crises are presented as a difficult but necessary and somewhat welcome trial that the Japanese economy had to overcome to move on to the next developmental stage, namely the stable growth of the 1980s.

In order to examine the relation between this economic condition and its manifestations in the cultural realm, the final chapter of this book analyzes *The Light of Africa* (*Afurika no hikari*), a film directed by Kumashiro Tatsumi and released by Tōhō in 1975. My purpose is not to reiterate the triumphant narrative of this historical event. While I agree that the oil crisis did mark a critical turning point for the Japanese economy in the long run, I also find it important to appreciate properly how those who lived through this event experienced the large-scale recession that it brought. During this period, companies enforced rationalization, bankruptcies increased, job vacancies dropped, and unemployment soared. Yet prices skyrocketed, leading to severe stagflation—inflation coupled with a recession. In January 1974, facing an increase in wholesale prices of almost 30 percent over the previous year, Fukuda Takeo, the minister of finance, called this phenomenon a "frenzy," or *kyōran* ("Bōtō wa kyōran jōtai" 1974). Furthermore, in the early 1970s, Japanese society had already been dealing with various consequences of intense capitalist development, such as industrial pollution and overcrowded cities (and dissolving rural communities as the other side of uneven development). Throughout the postwar years, the LDP government, the business community, and workers had aspired to an affluent society realized and sustained by permanent growth, but this vision of society was quickly losing grounds for justification. Instead, a sense of malaise dominated as the nation became increasingly aware of the ephemeral nature of growth and the high price they had to pay for the economic success of the past several decades.

The Light of Africa helps us delve into this sense of malaise at the end of the high-speed growth era. The film depicts the process by which two men who come to a small fishing town in Hokkaido to find work and save money for a trip to Africa are gradually defeated by the hard work conditions, the cold and snowy weather, and cruel treatment from local fishermen and give up their dream. The plot of the film is hopeless, its tone depressing. The visual images, captured by location shooting in Rausu in the Shiretoko region of eastern Hokkaido, give us an awfully cold and miserable impression. Through an examination of the representations of these two men, the competing images of Rausu in the media, the meanings of Africa as a fantasy, and the implications of male-male intimacy, this chapter details how the film translates a social atmosphere specific to the time, characterized by economic uncertainty, skepticism of Japan's present state, and anxiety for its future.

I begin with an examination of the film's main actor, Hagiwara Ken'ichi, a quintessential cultural icon who inspired many young people's fascination in the 1970s and makes *The Light of Africa* unmistakably a product of post-oil-crisis Japan. I then move to a discussion of the film and demonstrate how, through the representation of the two drifters, it highlights the issues of precarity in capitalist society, which resurfaced in Japan in the aftermath of two decades of high-speed growth. I then contrast the meanings ascribed to the two places in the film, Rausu and Africa: the former is represented as an economically depressed rural community, a consequence of the state's economic policy aimed at urban development, while the latter is fantasized about by the two men as a land of happiness and opportunity. Last, I address the question of intimacy between the two men. I argue that the film relativizes the heterosexual, middle-class nuclear family that functioned as a basic social and economic unit sanctioned by the state during high-speed growth and thereby implicitly declares the end of this national event.

Shōken Meets Kumashiro Tatsumi

Many call Hagiwara Ken'ichi endearingly by his nickname Shōken, which literally means "Little Ken." According to Hagiwara's autobiography, his friends started calling him by this nickname when he was still commuting to middle school in Tokyo from his home in Saitama Prefecture. A delinquent student more interested in fashion, parties, and going out with girls than study, Hagiwara became acquainted with students at a Korean high school near his middle school. A graduate from this middle school, whose Japanese name was Ken, was called Dai-Ken, or "Big Ken," because he was an excellent fighter and remained influential at school even after graduating. Hagiwara got along with Dai-Ken, frequented bars and clubs with him, and often took responsibility for calming down his short-tempered friend whenever he got into a fight. Because of his close relation to Dai-Ken,

Hagiwara earned the nickname Shō-Ken although his real name was not Ken'ichi but Keizō. This short, memorable, and catchy nickname circulated among his fans once he began his career in the world of entertainment (Hagiwara 2008, 41–45).

Shōken first gained national fame as the lead vocalist of the Tempters, a rock band categorized within the genre of "Group Sounds"—a Japanese interpretation of a wide variety of American and British rock music styles, influenced by Elvis Presley, the Ventures, the Beatles, the Rolling Stones, and so on. Shōken was only sixteen years old when the Tempters released their first single record, "Unforgettable You" ("Wasure-enu kimi"), in October 1967. Japan at that time was engulfed by a massive Group Sounds boom, which had been accelerated by the Beatles' visit to Tokyo in June 1966. Shōken's impish appearance and sweet and slightly husky voice allowed the Tempters to grow quickly into one of the most popular Group Sounds bands at that time. In 1968, at the height of their popularity, the Tempters produced a series of hits, including "Please, God!" ("Kami-sama onegai!"), "Emerald Legend" ("Emerarudo no densetsu"), and "Mother" ("Okāsan"). Among the numerous Group Sounds bands that emerged and disappeared in the late 1960s, the Tempters, together with the Spiders and the Tigers (with charismatic vocalist Sawada Kenji), is now considered most representative of that genre.[2]

After his band broke up in 1970, Shōken formed a new rock band named PYG with Ōguchi Hiroshi from the Tempters, Sawada Kenji and Kishibe Osami (now Kishibe Ittoku) from the Tigers, Ōno Katsuo and Inoue Takayuki (who would later be in charge of music for *The Light of Africa*) from the Spiders, and Harada Yūjin from Mickey Curtis & the Samurai—aiming for more authentic and less commercially oriented rock music. Meanwhile, Shōken began pursuing a career as an actor. *A Promise* (*Yakusoku*, 1972) is one of the first films in which he secured critical acclaim. The film was directed by Saitō Kōichi, who, although not prolific, would later create such impressive films as *Weight of the Journey* (*Tabi no omosa*, 1972) and *Tsugaru Jongara-bushi* (1973, the title refers to the Tsugaru region's folk songs to *shamisen* accompaniment), portraying the beautiful landscape of rural Japan, not unmediated by the capitalist economy at the end of high-speed growth, without sentimentalizing it. In *A Promise*, Shōken played a lonely man named Akira who falls in love with a woman on a train while traveling along the snowy Japan Sea. The film depicts their brief affair over a few days until this woman, who turns out to be a convict out on parole to visit her mother's grave, returns to prison. Although they promise to meet again once she is released in two years, this promise is never fulfilled because right after the woman goes back to the prison, Akira is arrested for an armed robbery. His performance as the passionate but antisocial protagonist opposite the well-established star Kishi Keiko earned him recognition as a serious actor with great potential. *Kinema junpō* selected *A Promise* as the fifth-best film of the year. After this, Shōken would go on to work with many other directors, including not only Kumashiro Tatsumi but Ichikawa Kon, Shinoda Masahiro, and Kurosawa Akira (Hagiwara and Suga 2010).

The early to mid-1970s, when Shōken was gaining critical acclaim and massive popularity, saw the possibilities for organized political resistance and social change diminish. Labor unions had determined to cooperate with capital to better benefit from the country's growing economy during the high-speed growth era and therefore could not effectively counter the efforts at rationalization and restructuring employers pursued during the oil-crisis recession. The new left, which had appealed in the previous decade to a wide range of supporters concerned about such issues as regimented higher education, the corporatization of society, the Vietnam War, the Anpo system, and military bases, became increasingly sectionalized and violent (as demonstrated, for instance, in the United Red Army's Asama-Sansō incident in 1972), thereby alienating ordinary citizens. Because many citizens desired stability within the ever-expanding industrial society, the LDP coalition with big capital successfully reinforced their rule throughout the 1970s, presenting corporate-managed life as the most effective way of achieving success and curtailing visions of an alternative society.[3]

For many people who spent their adolescence in the 1970s, Shōken embodied a shared frustration with the banality of society and with the political conservatism it fostered. He presented himself as unamused, cynical, short-tempered, and somewhat irritated. He disliked, or pretended to dislike, fawning over his fans, flattering directors and producers, and pleasing interviewers with expected responses. He did not hesitate to express his personal opinions about other actors, directors, and the world of show business in general, using candid, often inflammatory language. Observing this, a writer for a weekly journal said that people discovered in his rudeness "humanity" (*ningensei*) "not yet contaminated, not yet fully controlled" ("mada osen sarete inai, mada kanri sarekitte inai"; Nishiyama Tadashi 1974). Another writer, after an interview with Shōken in which he said he had no "purpose of life" (*ikigai*) in a cold tone, concluded that it was that kind of "jaded appearance" (*sameta fūbō*) that appealed to filmmakers (Kamura 1974; see figure 5.1).

On screen, Shōken was not at all interested in maintaining his earlier image as a young Group Sounds pop idol but chose to play characters with complex, eccentric personalities: the aforementioned lonely traveler Akira in Saitō's *A Promise*; Mokutarō in Ichikawa Kon's

Figure 5.1. Hagiwara Ken'ichi. Shōken was enthusiastically supported by young people in the 1970s (Kamura 1974, 185). Courtesy of the publisher.

The Wanderers (*Matatabi*, 1973), one of three men who, pressed by poverty and uprooted from their hometowns, live a drifting life in Tokugawa Japan; Haruo in Shinoda Masahiro's *The Petrified Forest* (*Kaseki no mori*, 1973), a medical intern who feels suffocated by the authoritarian world of medicine and seeks a sense of achievement by plotting a murder in collaboration with his girlfriend; and, of course, Jun in *The Light of Africa*, who dreams of going to Africa to begin life anew. These characters are all discontent with their own social environments, strive to improve them—often in an awkward manner—but lack recourse to collective action beyond their private sphere, and consequently encounter an insurmountable reality.

An article by the journalist Ikeda Shin'ichi (1975) gives us insight into Shōken's popularity in relation to the social atmosphere of the time. In his provocative article, Ikeda maintained that since defeat of the 1960 Anpo protest, what he called "democratic feudalism" ("minshuteki hōkensei") had been solidified. While a democratic political system was maintained, family origin, family assets, and social status, over which individuals had no control, reemerged as crucial factors for determining one's success in society (by which he implicitly refers to rule by the LDP and elite bureaucrats), just as in prewar Japan. Leftist resistance was no exception to this trend. Ikeda was quite cynical about Minobe Ryōkichi, elected in 1967 as the governor of Tokyo, backed by the Socialists and Communists. Although Minobe's victory exhilarated leftist and progressive citizens and contributed to building a network of so-called "progressive communities" (*kakushin jichitai*) in urban Japan in the 1970s, including Kyoto Prefecture, Osaka Prefecture, and the city of Yokohama, Ikeda pointed out that Minobe was a "son of good family" ("ryōke no o-botchan"): his father was Minobe Tatsukichi, a renowned legal scholar from Tokyo University who had established the famous "emperor organ" theory in prewar Japan.

According to Ikeda, Shōken was creating so much excitement precisely because he was the antithesis to post-1960 Japan's democratic feudalism. He was from Yono in Saitama Prefecture (now part of the city of Saitama), a modest suburban town north of Tokyo; grew up without a father; was a delinquent student; and dropped out of high school. He won success in the entertainment industry despite a lack of connections and money. Contrasting him to another actor, Ishizaka Kōji, who grew up in Denen Chōfu, a wealthy neighborhood in Ōta

Ward in Tokyo, and graduated from the prestigious Keiō High School and Keiō University, Ikeda explained that the masses were tired of the predictability of nepotistic and conformist elite culture and found in Shōken something essentially new and resistant. If Ishihara Yūjirō in his early career in the late 1950s symbolized the urban middle-class youth culture enabled by the reconstruction of the national economy, and if Tamiya Jirō in his spy films in the 1960s embodied the anxiety of mushrooming industrial society at the height of high-speed growth, then Hagiwara Ken'ichi in the 1970s spoke for a society that had become disenchanted with the promises of high-speed growth in the earlier decade, such as the ever-growing economy, equal opportunity, and upward social mobility.

Shōken worked with director Kumashiro Tatsumi for the first time on *The Failure of Youth* (*Seishun no satetsu*, 1974), a year before *The Light of Africa*. Kumashiro had been already recognized as a talented filmmaker in the genre of "roman porno" (*roman poruno*), which Nikkatsu launched in 1971 to reinvigorate its financially declining business through the mass production of low-budget soft-core films.[4] Although Kumashiro's first film, *Front-Row Life* (*Kaburitsuki jinsei*, 1968), which dealt with love and tension between a middle-aged exotic dancer and her daughter, failed commercially, his 1972 *Sayuri Ichijō: Following Desire* (*Ichijō Sayuri: Nureta yokujō*) was critically acclaimed, ranked eighth on *Kinema junpō*'s annual list of best films, and enabled him to consolidate his fame as a young, talented "roman porno" director. Set in Osaka (more precisely, in Noda Hanshin, a working-class commercial district in the northwestern part of the city), this film depicts the rivalry between the exotic dancer Ichijō Sayuri, playing herself, and a younger, ambitious dancer named Harumi (Isayama Hiroko) and their resistance to police harassment.[5] Shortly after its release, the film critic Satō Tadao (1972, 31) commended it as a powerful realist film rooted in the lives of "regular people," or *shomin*, similar to Imamura's *The Insect Woman* (1963). *Twisted Path of Love* (*Koibito-tachi wa nureta*, 1973), another well-known *roman poruno* film by Kumashiro, details the sexual encounters of a young man who returns to his rural hometown with no particular purpose in life. It features Nakagawa Rie, who, by appearing in many such films, supported Nikkatsu's temporary resurgence in the 1970s.

These characters—Ichijō and Harumi in *Following Desire* and the young man and his friends in *Twisted Path of Love*—as well as many other characters in Kumashiro's films are misfits in mainstream society (meaning that they do not belong to or are excluded from the industrious corporate world), frustrated by the present, and jaded and cynical about the future. In this sense, it is not surprising that Kumashiro and Shōken found each other and made their first film, *The Failure of Youth*, since both had been speaking for discontented youth as director and actor respectively. In an interview conducted in 1975, Shōken mentioned that he had been "blown away" (*futtonjatta*) by *Sayuri Ichijō: Following Desire* and that there had been no other film as "lively" (*ikiiki to shita*). After persistent attempts, he continued, he successfully convinced Tōhō, which had proposed to make a film with him, to hire Kumashiro, who was then a Nikkatsu employee, as the director. *The Failure of Youth* was thus made, and Shōken, in that interview, expressed his strong sense of fulfillment that they had made it "painstakingly, scene by scene" ("ichi bamen ichi bamen kurō shite"; Fukuoka 1975, 114–15).

The Failure of Youth is adapted from Ishikawa Tatsuzō's (1968) novel of the same title, which was first serialized in the *Mainichi* newspaper in 1968. Shōken plays an ambitious and intelligent but financially struggling law student named Etō Ken'ichirō. Aspiring to economic success and entrée into upper-class society, Ken'ichirō studies hard to pass the bar exam. Meanwhile, in order to make a living, he works as a private tutor for a young woman from a modest family (Momoi Kaori) and begins a sexual relationship with her. She claims that she is pregnant by him and demands that he takes responsibility for her and the baby that will be born soon. But he has a fiancée from a bourgeois family, whose father is financially supporting him, and he ends up killing his pregnant girlfriend. At the end of the film, the police discover his crime, and his dream of upward social mobility crumbles. By representing this unfulfilled and irritated male protagonist as a former student activist who became disappointed in politics after the failure of the 1970 Anpo protest, the film effectively appealed to urban youth immersed in a strong sense of defeat.

The issues dealt with in *The Failure of Youth*, such as disillusionment with the rigid social order, struggle against economic plight, and thwarted dreams and ambitions, would be explored more intensely in the second film on which Shōken and Kumashiro collaborated the following year: *The Light of Africa*, adapted from the novel of the same title written by Maruyama Kenji (1974), a recipient of the prestigious Akutagawa Prize. The film is about two men who wish to go to Africa—Jun (Shōken) and Katsuhiro (Tanaka Kunie)—for reasons they never articulate. To get there, they first travel to a small fishing community in Hokkaido and take jobs to save money while waiting for an opportunity to catch a tuna-fishing ship heading to the continent in the spring. Maruyama's original novel describes the two men's financial struggle and emotional frustration in an elegant, unsentimental, and detached style, but Kumashiro's film completely alters that tone. It underscores the weakness and odiousness of the humans who are placed in conditions of material deprivation, showing in an unpretentious manner their quotidian activities, such as desperately looking for jobs, drinking cheaply at bars, fighting with local men, being beaten up by them, freezing in an apartment with no heat, having sex, masturbating, and so on. As film critic Saitō Masaharu has said, this is a film about *dame otoko-tachi*, or "good-for-nothing men" (1975, 37), a theme that Kumashiro had repeatedly addressed since beginning his career as a director. By the time the film was made, the effects of the economic recession caused by the 1973 oil crisis had been strongly felt in every corner of Japanese society, and, as the rest of this chapter shows, the two "good-for-nothing men" in *The Light of Africa* fully exhibit the anxiety that plagued people in Japan at that time.

Jobless Men in Hokkaido

The Light of Africa starts with a brief title sequence. Jun and Katsuhiro are crossing a long concrete bridge on a dark, foggy, gusty winter day. At the foot of the bridge are patches of snow. After this bridge scene, we find them walking in deserted open land. Once the film title appears, the land is covered by snow and ice. They are listening to Russian broadcasting on a portable radio, which informs us that they are somewhere in Hokkaido, the northernmost island of the archipelago. Each of them is wearing an unfashionable thick winter jacket and knit hat and carrying a duffle bag. Despite the terribly depressing weather, they appear cheerful. They are laughing and roughhousing, playfully hitting each other with their bags and chasing each other. The audience assumes they have come to Hokkaido with a high degree of hope and optimism.

The rest of the film, however, is dedicated to showing the two men's irredeemable failures, one after another, and how these gradually defeat their initial optimism, leading them to the realization that their dream of going to Africa is too bold and unviable. Upon arriving at the fishing town in Hokkaido, they find out that residents there—fishermen, cops, and gamblers—are rough, cold, and hostile to strangers and have no intention of welcoming them into their community. In order to fund a trip to Africa, they start working for a squid-fishing boat with local men, but work on the cold Sea of Okhotsk turns out to be excruciating for part-time fishermen like them. Jun quickly gives up, connects with a man named Anabuki (Fuji Tatsuya) who runs a gambling house, and becomes a guard there for easy money. Meanwhile, Katsuhiro, who continues to work on the fishing boat, becomes seriously ill due to the hard labor and harsh weather. The doctor suggests that he go on a retreat to a warm place. Initially reluctant, he soon recognizes the limits of his health and decides to go home (we do not know where but assume that it is someplace warmer). Jun stays, but the police crack down on the gambling house, and he loses his job. The men who lost money at the gambling house now direct their anger at Jun, who no longer enjoys Anabuki's protection, and try to lynch him on a boat. Spring is around the corner, but he flees the town without realizing his dream of going to Africa (at the end of the film, however, a superimposed caption informs us that Jun finally managed to embark on a ship heading to Africa three hundred days after his escape from the town).

The Light of Africa is dominated by a dark, dismal, and depressing atmosphere. This can be attributed to the fact that the film deals directly with the precariousness immanent to work in a capitalist society. Although Jun and Katsuhiro, both of whom seem unemployed, come to Hokkaido to earn money for their trip to Africa, they have no concrete job prospects. They first have to go to the fishermen's union and ask around about vacancies. Even after securing jobs, they do not know exactly how long those jobs will last, how much they can save in a week or a month, or whether they can save enough before the spring comes. In fact, neither of their jobs—squid fishing and gambling-house security—is secure or stable, and they sell their labor power on completely unpredictable terms. Both men lose their jobs for unexpected reasons—the deterioration of Katsuhiro's health and the crackdown on Jun's gambling house—and have to give up their dream. While it may seem that the precariousness that they face has to do with these men's personal traits of recklessness, dissoluteness, and irresponsibility, this is actually the fundamental nature of employment in capitalism, which workers have had to cope with since industrial capitalism became the dominant organizing principle of society. This type of floating population is entailed by capital for its expansion as an essential part of the reserve army of workers, who can be absorbed into the active laboring population during an economic boom (like high-speed growth) and can be disposed of during a recession (like the oil crisis), allowing employers to keep workers' wages relatively low.[6]

The Keynesian social and economic policies that advanced capitalist states adopted for reconstruction and growth in the post–World War II era were attempts to minimize precariousness and to bring greater security and predictability to workers' lives. These included full employment, enhanced welfare provisions, and, in the case of large Japanese firms, lifetime employment and promotion based on seniority. The large-scale recession in the early 1970s, however, revealed the vulnerability of the system created through these policies and the brutal nature of the capitalist economy. As both individual consumption and industrial demand dropped amid steep inflation, cash-strapped companies pursued various forms of rationalization, including furloughs, hiring freezes, the firing of part-time and temporary workers, the solicitation of voluntary retirement, and the reinforcement of subcontracting (Ōhara Shakai Mondai Kenkyūjo 1976, 101–11). The number of unemployed reached one million in 1975 (an increase of 260,000 over the previous year), and the unemployment rate hit 1.9 percent. The next year, these figures would rise to 1.07 million and 2 percent, respectively (see table 5.1). While the unemployment rate of 1.9 or 2 percent does not seem especially high, the "unemployed" in governmental statistics in Japan includes only those fifteen years of age and older who (1) are not employed, (2) can start working immediately if a job becomes available, and (3) are actively seeking a job (such as going to an employment security office). Anyone not actively looking for a job due to illness, injury, childrearing, caregiving, or another reason is not considered unemployed. This means that the actual number of those who want or need to work for survival but lack jobs is much higher than official statistics show.

Table 5.1. Number of Unemployed and Unemployment Rate in Japan

Year	Number of Unemployed Individuals	Unemployment Rate (%)
1971	640,000	1.2
1972	730,000	1.4
1973	670,000	1.3
1974	740,000	1.3
1975	1,000,000	1.9
1976	1,070,000	2.0

Based on data provided by the Statistics Bureau of Japan (https://www.stat.go.jp/data/roudou/longtime/03roudou.html).

While Tanaka Kakuei's cabinet and his LDP, backed by economic growth and pressured by the leftist opposition, had promised to further enhance social security by identifying 1973 as "the inaugural year of welfare," or *fukushi gannen*, and did manage to implement several important policies such as fully subsidizing medical care for people seventy years of age and older, the recession that started later the same year hindered this project.[7] Now that more than forty years have passed since that recession, we can confirm that it was the beginning of the process by which the Fordist compromise between capital and labor would gradually collapse over the next several decades and be replaced by a neoliberal regime characterized by flexible accumulation (Harvey 1990, 141–72). Indeed, during this recession, the strong feeling was ubiquitous in Japanese society that some fundamental change was occurring in the postwar economic structure that the state and corporations had striven to build since the 1950s. The media, citing economists and other pundits, described this with such sensational expressions as "fearful negative growth" ("kyōfu no mainasu seichō"), "[greatest] national hardship since the Mongol invasions [of the thirteenth century]" ("Mōko shūrai irai no kokunan"; "Kinkyū daitokushū" 1974), and "the worst economic catastrophe of the postwar" ("sengo saiaku no keizai hakyoku"; Shimizu Ikkō 1974), and thereby encouraged the masses to come up with effective strategies for self-defense without relying much on the government or employers.

To us, looking at this event many decades after, these fear-mongering expressions may seem a little exaggerated, since it is indeed the case that the LDP government did not undertake full privatization until the 1980s. As Richard Reitan (2012) has shown, however, the uncertain economic circumstances of the mid-1970s undoubtedly prepared the ground for the dissemination of neoliberal economic thought. It was around this time that the economist Nishiyama Chiaki, who had earned his degree at the University of Chicago and would later introduce works by Friedrich Hayek and Milton Friedman to Japanese readers, published his *Liberal Economy* (*Jiyū keizai*). In this book, he called for a "free society" ("jiyū shakai") in which individuals could maximize their potential without restrictions from above while assailing the welfare state as based on "bureaucratism by the elite" ("erīto ni yoru kanryō-shugi") and society as a mere "fiction" ("kyokō"; Nishiyama Chiaki 1974, 102–4).

As I pointed out at the beginning of this chapter, it is true that the 1973 oil crisis, at the macro level, provided Japanese corporations with an opportunity for continued growth and innovation with limited resources, and this would later be exalted as "Japanese-style management" in and outside Japan (Vogel 1979). But when they were enforcing "rationalization" and "streamlining," there had to be people who were forced to become parts of the reserve army of labor constituted by the unemployed and marginally employed, and Jun and Katsuhiro in *The Light of Africa* are among these people. Their living and working conditions indicate the end of the era of growth, in which Japanese society tried to convince itself that the "growing pie" was smoothly and effectively reducing contingencies of work (or in which the dominant discourse of growth and prosperity managed to keep the precarious nature of capitalism from surfacing). These two men draw our attention to the (re)emergence of flexible and mobile labor with no guarantee of security, which was becoming a reality for many workers at that time and would dominate Japan's labor market in several decades.

Here, it is interesting to compare the precariousness observed in *The Light of Africa* to that in *Susaki Paradise Red Light*, examined in chapter 1. In the earlier film, by Kawashima Yūzō, we see jobless and penniless young people drifting from place to place for daily survival, which is quite similar to *The Light of Africa*. In fact, both films begin with scenes in which the protagonists are crossing a bridge, indicating the liminality of their social status and the uprooted nature of their lives. But there is a major difference between these two in the movement and mobility of the protagonists. In *Susaki Paradise*, made in the mid-1950s, when reconstruction from the war was still underway, the young couple of Yoshiji and Tsutae drift around only a small part of Tokyo, while in *The Light of Africa*, made about twenty years later amid the oil-crisis recession, Jun and Katsuhiro's movements have taken them as far as Hokkaido. We do not know exactly where in Japan they are from, but given that Hokkaido seems like a completely unknown place to them we can speculate that they have come from outside this island prefecture, crossing the Tsugaru Strait. Furthermore, Hokkaido is simply a stopover place for their final destination, Africa. Implied in their long-distance movement (and their desire for it) are the dramatic developments in the means of transportation during the high-speed growth era—the high-speed train, airplanes—and the consequent affordability of domestic and international travel. Now, even unemployed men like Jun and Katsuhiro can travel quite lightly to Hokkaido, an island prefecture remote from the major metropolitan areas, and believe in the dream of "going to Africa," which would have been almost inconceivable for most Japanese twenty years earlier.[8] At the same time, their strong commitment to escaping Japan and sailing to Africa testifies to the extent of the severe recession that Japan was undergoing at that time and their deep disillusion about their opportunities and future in Japan.

Rausu: Rural Japan Unromanticized

Although *The Light of Africa* does not make it explicit which town in Hokkaido Jun and Katsuhiro settled in, it is a common knowledge that the location shooting was conducted in Rausu, a small port town on the east side of the Shiretoko Peninsula with a population of about 8,200 in 1975. The monthly journal *Scenario* (*Shinario*) published a series of articles on this film to mark its release in June 1975, and a few mention the location. One article, written by the producer Okada Yutaka, explains how the crew, in search of snow and drift ice, started the location shooting at Rausu port in March (Okada 1975). Another article consists of an informal discussion of the film among Shōken, Kumashiro, assistant director Hasegawa Kazuhiko, and cameraman Himeda Shinsaku, which took place in April in Rausu in the middle of the location shooting ("Zadankai: *Afurika no hikari*" 1975). The film's opening credits also acknowledge support from the town and its tourist association.

Shiretoko Peninsula, on which Rausu is located, had already been nationally recognized for specific cultural meanings by the mid-1970s. Both Rausu and Shari (on the other side of the peninsula) attracted tourism as affluent middle-class travelers became fascinated with discovering "unexplored spots," or *hikyō*, outside the hyperindustrialized and overpopulated metropolitan areas. The recognition of the peninsula was made definite by a massive hit song, "Sentiment of Travel in Shiretoko" ("Shiretoko ryojō"), released in 1970 by Katō Tokiko, who was then in her twenties and already a renowned singer-songwriter. The song was written in 1960 by Morishige Hisaya, the multitalented actor, singer, and comedian, when he stayed in Rausu for the shooting of *Creatures That Live at the End of the World* (*Chi no hate ni ikiru mono*, 1960), a film about an old man who stays alone with cats in a small cottage by the Sea of Okhotsk all winter to protect the fishing nets from being gnawed by mice. The song was a thank-you gift from Morishige to the residents of the community, who gave the crew various support during the long shooting. It gradually gained fame as a mellow, nostalgic tune that celebrated the beautiful landscape of the peninsula. Deeply moved when she heard it in a bar in 1970, Katō recorded her own version and released it as a single, which had great commercial success, selling more than a million copies ("Morishige Hisaya, Katō Tokiko no 3-jikan" 1971).[9]

Katō's unpretentious, calm, and soothing voice perfectly suited the song's nostalgic and sentimental lyrics and melody. While there is no doubt that this is one reason her rendition enjoyed so much popularity, it is also true that the timing of the release of the song worked in its favor. Earlier the same year, the debt-burdened Japanese National Railways, or Kokutetsu, had launched a nationwide campaign that encouraged tourism throughout Japan, named "Discover Japan." Prior to this campaign, Kokutetsu had boosted its transportation capacity for the 1970 Osaka Expo by increasing the number of cars on the Shinkansen's Hikari Express from twelve to sixteen. In October 1970, it completed the electrification of the main line between Kita-Kyushu and Kagoshima, meaning that all the main lines from Tokyo to Kagoshima, through Nagoya, Osaka, Hiroshima, and Hakata, amounting to 910 miles, were now electrified. It was planning to extend the Shinkansen, whose service was still limited to the leg between Tokyo and Shin-Osaka, further west to Okayama and then to Hakata within a few years (and it was indeed extended to Okayama in 1972 and to Hakata in 1975). Kokutetsu started the "Discover Japan" campaign as a way of continuing to create demand as it actively invested in its nationwide network (Nihon Kokuyū Tetsudō 1974, 148–50).

In this campaign, Kokutetsu encouraged tourism by promoting "Japan's rich nature, beautiful history and tradition, and scrupulous kindness" ("Nihon no yutaka na shizen, utsukushii rekishi ya dentō, komayaka na ninjō"; Nihon Kokuyū Tetsudō 1974, 148). Instead of conducting a nationwide campaign, it targeted young unmarried women in the major metropolitan areas of Tokyo, Nagoya, and Osaka, who were most likely to have disposable money and time for leisure, and stimulated their curiosity in rural Japan (as well as "old cities" like Kyoto, Nara, and Kanazawa) by effectively using innovative advertisements designed by the powerful public relations company Dentsū (Sasaki Shun'ichi 1972, 5–7). By this time, the large-scale and long-term migration of young workers to cities had aggravated the economic and cultural gap between the city and the countryside to an irremediable degree and threatened rural communities' sustainability. Kokutetsu's "Discover Japan" campaign was an attempt by state bureaucrats, the corporate world, and the mass media to capitalize on this unevenness (instead of remedying it) and to commodify the images of the rural Japan while naturalizing such unevenness as something to relish and to take pride in.[10]

The image of Shiretoko nature invoked by Katō Tokiko's "Sentiment of Travel" fit comfortably within the rural Japan that Kokutetsu was selling to urban consumers through the "Discover Japan" campaign. The song is written from the points of view of an urban male traveler visiting Shiretoko with his friends (first and second verses) and a woman living there (third verse). The song tells of a romantic encounter between the two. "When the rugosa rose blooms on the cape of Shiretoko" ("Shiretoko no misaki ni hamanasu no saku koro"), the song begins, "please think of us" ("omoidashite okure oretachi no koto o"). After the first verse references Kunashiri Island (one of the islands that had been occupied by the Soviets since the end of the Asia-Pacific War), seen from the hill that the traveler climbs, the second verse goes like this:

Isn't this the sentiment of travel? The more I drink, the more I feel like drifting
When I go to the beach, the moon shines above the waves
Hoping to hug you tonight for sure
I walk toward the shade of the rock, and then, smiles a *pirka* [pretty girl] (Katō [1971] 1994)[11]

In the final verse, on the day of the traveler's departure, the local woman asks him not to forget her, calling him a "whimsical crow" ("kimagure karasu-san") and referring to herself (and probably Shiretoko as the feminized land) as a "white seagull" ("shiroi kamome"). Just as the "Discover Japan" campaign did, this song depended on a clear binary between the urban visitor as the subject who consumes the nature and culture of rural Japan and the local resident as part of the object of the desire for this consumption.

Shiretoko in *The Light of Africa* differs strikingly from the Shiretoko sung of in "Sentiment of Travel" and the rural Japan that the "Discover Japan" campaign touted. Shiretoko, or the town of Rausu more precisely, in *The Light of Africa* is a place of labor, livelihood, and survival, just like any other place in a modern society. Jun and Katsuhiro are not financially comfortable tourists looking for extraordinary and memorable experiences. They have to work and save to go to Africa. They do not have time or money with which to indulge themselves in this town's natural beauty or to learn about its cultural heritage. There is no exotic, beautiful woman eager to show them around the beach, the port, or the mountain. The woman they meet and have sexual encounters with at the beginning of the film is a jaded, vulgar, money-loving bar waitress (Momoi Kaori), far from the *pirka* in "Sentiment of Travel." When Jun and Katsuhiro meet this woman—named Fujiko—at a gloomy local bar for the first time, she is flirting passionately with another male customer. Fujiko tells these two unfamiliar men, who are watching them enviously, to bring money if they wanted to do the same. Furious at her rudeness, Katsuhiro replies that they do not want to sleep with such a "sow" ("mesu buta").

While they are having this conversation, a song called "Virgin Blues" ("Bājin burūsu") is playing in the bar, sung by Nosaka Akiyuki, who is probably best known outside Japan as the author of *Grave of the Fireflies* (*Hotaru no haka*; Nosaka [1968] 1972) but was also a singer, politician, and TV celebrity. The song begins,

> Throb, throb, throb, throb, her blood throbs
> Plum and cherry both open up
> Throb, throb, throb, throb, her blood throbs
> The sheltered girl can't sleep (Nosaka [1999] 2011)[12]

Although it is not very explicit, the song appears to be commenting on the sex industry and the frenzy and cunning that it incites, with such expressions in the rest of the lyrics as "yokubari babā" (a greedy old lady), which surely indicates a brothel manager, "osake o nondara zeni kanjō" (settling a bill when finished drinking), and "otoko to onna no damashiai" (a man and a woman cheating each other). If "Sentiment of Travel" projects onto Shiretoko the image of a pure, uncontaminated land on the periphery of the nation-state, using the metaphor of a "pirka" as an innocent virgin, *The Light of Africa*'s use of "Virgin Blues" for the scene with the explicitly sexual conversation between the men and the bar waitress seems like a critical response to "Sentiment of Travel." "Virgin Blues" rejects such romanticism and reminds us of the pervasiveness of the sex industry throughout Japan and the apparent fact that sexual service is exchanged for money as a commodity no matter where one lives, whether in the city or country. This effectively makes us recognize Shiretoko not as a utopian land outside the temporality of modernity or a fancy vacation destination divorced from everyday life but as an integral part of the economic system of contemporary Japan.

This recognition prompts us to delve further into the gloomy representations of the town and its residents in the rest of the film within the material context of the national economy. Here, I want to emphasize that when urban Japan was fascinated with the nature and culture of rural Japan, the latter was becoming increasingly concerned about the problem of "depopulation" as an undesirable consequence of high-speed growth. The national census conducted in 1965 had revealed that while the population was steadily growing at the national level, more than half of the forty-six prefectures (Okinawa was still under US administration back then) and more than three-quarters of the 3,376 local communities had faced a population decline over the previous five years (Jichi Daijin Kanbō Kikakushitsu 1972, 12). The growth of the country's population, which would last until 2010, was enabled mainly by the (over)growth of the major metropolitan regions along the Pacific and the Inland Sea. In the second half of the 1960s, the LDP government, bureaucrats, lawmakers, and local governments perceived this as a social problem that entailed urgent public intervention, circulating the term *kaso*, or "depopulation," to raise national awareness and to highlight the shared nature of the wide-ranging population-related problems that many rural communities were coping with throughout Japan. In 1970, the Diet passed the Emergency Measure for Dealing with Depopulated Areas Law (Kaso chiiki taisaku kinkyū sochihō). The law authorized financial assistance from the central and prefectural governments for those communities designated as "depopulated areas," the definition of which was based on each local government's financial health and the speed at which its population was declining (Jichi Daijin Kanbō Kikakushitsu 1972, 11–67).

In 1972, Tanaka Kakuei ran for LDP president with his ambitious plan for "remodeling the Japanese archipelago," *Nihon rettō kaizō*. Coming from a rural village in snowy Niigata Prefecture, Tanaka, unlike many elite LDP politicians, did not possess a celebrated family lineage, an illustrious academic history, or strong connections with the political world in Tokyo. He was alarmed by agrarian and fishing communities left behind by high-speed growth as well as the plight of young people who, just like himself, were forced by poverty to leave their hometowns for jobs in cities. For him, these were not just social but personal problems. In his "remodeling" plans, Tanaka promoted the industrialization of rural Japan (that is, more equal distribution of capital throughout the nation-state) and the improvement of the traffic network throughout the archipelago (Tanaka 1972). Once he had formed a cabinet as the sixty-fourth prime minister in July 1972, Tanaka established an advisory council to put the remodeling plans into practice. These plans, however, incited a speculative fever, the result of which was the deepening of the subordination of rural Japan to urban money. This speculative fever and the oil crisis, which occurred right after, fomented high inflation. With Tanaka's resignation the following year, the remodeling plans dissipated without achieving their promised goals.

What *The Light of Africa* is communicating to the viewer is the distress of rural Japan at the time when the dream of rural revitalization was quickly being replaced by the reality of inexorable uneven development. The men in town, most of whom are fishers, do not seem to have permanent, stable jobs. During the day, they wander through town without much to occupy them. At night, they go out to local bars for drinks and to the gambling house where Jun works. Like Jun and Katsuhiro, they are always cranky, which can be read as an indication of their frustration when enduring various work-related contingencies. They are mean to Jun and Katsuhiro and constantly pick fights with them, seeing these outsiders with no money and connections as a perfect outlet for the rage that they cannot express in any other way (see figure 5.2). Yet these men never talk about leaving their hometown for cities in pursuit of greater opportunities since the end of high-speed growth no longer allows them to indulge in straightforward dreams of urban success. In this regard, Sayoko (Takahashi Yōko)—a young granddaughter of the fisherman who owns the squid-fishing boat on which Katsuhiro works—is exceptional. She is bored and hopeless helping her grandfather's modest fishing business. She hopes that Jun will take her away with him, but she leaves the town alone at the very end of the film when she realizes that he has no such intention. Yet she does not seem particularly happy about her endeavor, nor does she seem to have any concrete plans. No one except Jun sees her off at the train station. A few small bags are all she carries. The film by no means suggests a bright future for her, instead implying that she will undergo a precarious, lonely life just as Jun and Katsuhiro do in Rausu.

The landscape of Rausu observed in *The Light of Africa* underscores the resignation shared by these town residents, too. The film

Figure 5.2. *The Light of Africa* (1975). A local man picks a fight with Jun at a pachinko parlor.

carefully refrains from showing any fancy tourist sites; we see only the sites of the everyday lives of regular working people, such as Jun and Katsuhiro's tiny one-room apartment, fishing families' jerry-built residences, bars, restaurants, the harbor with fishing boats, a jail, a pachinko parlor, a family-owned clinic, a public bathhouse, the fishermen's union, and so on. All these places are old, shabby, and dark (see figure 5.3). To be clear, while many Hokkaido communities were already facing the challenge of depopulation in the 1970s, Rausu was not designated as a "depopulated area" until 2010. But the film presents the landscape of Rausu not as unique to this town but as typifying declining provincial communities in 1970s Japan. In fact, there are a fair number of similar cinematic representations from this time. It might remind some people of the landscape of a rural fishing town in Chiba with a sketchy porn movie theater in another of Kumashiro's films, *Twisted Path of Love* (1973), and others of the windy fishing village in Aomori with its worn-down shacks and wretched bar in Saitō Kōichi's *Tsugaru Jongara-bushi* (1973) or the Tohoku community exhausted by the drain of male workers who left for cities on *dekasegi* (temporary migrant labor) in Shindō Kaneto's *My Way* (*Waga michi*, 1974). Together with these landscapes, Rausu in *The Light of Africa* indicates not the vibrancy and fulfillment of its residents' lives (as the "Discover Japan" campaign would have done) but the tedium and enervation of their routines. When repeatedly shown this landscape, we cannot help thinking about the enormous

Figure 5.3. *The Light of Africa* (1975). Although shot in Rausu, the film shows only sites of the everyday lives of regular working people.

price that Japanese society had to pay for the industrialization and urbanization of a handful of metropolitan areas while policymakers, bureaucrats, and corporations in cities, especially Tokyo, mobilized populations and resources in rural regions in the name of national growth.

Longing for Africa

Jun and Katsuhiro constantly talk about their plan to go to Africa but never elaborate in concrete terms what meanings Africa bears for them. While the two men genuinely believe that they can start their life anew and enjoy some kind of success and happiness only if they manage to go to Africa, we never learn what about Africa so appeals to them, what they want to do there, how they will make a living, which part of Africa they want to go to, or what they know about it (after all, do they know that Africa is a continent, not a country?). It seems that, to them, Africa is a nebulous dream at most. What, then, should we read into their great longing to go there?

First, Japanese society had been in the midst of an unprecedented boom in "exploration," or *tanken*, since the late 1960s. Academics (especially anthropologists), journalists, amateur explorers, and the like wrote enthusiastically about their experiences exploring the kind of places around the globe to which an ordinary middle-class Japanese person dared not go. Between 1967 and 1968, Sannō Shobō—a well-known press in Tokyo—published the five-volume *Exploration of Hidden Places* (*Hikyō tanken*) series, with travelogues written by various Japanese people about their explorations of seas, mountains, and deserts all over the world (Kazami et al. 1967; Kobayashi Daiji et al. 1967; Ōmori et al. 1967; Aoyagi et al. 1968; Satō et al. 1968). Bungei Shunjū published the eight-volume *Contemporary Adventure* (*Gendai no bōken*) series in 1970 (Umesao 1970; Fukuda 1970; Ishihara 1970; Itokawa 1970; Murayama 1970; Kawakita 1970; Agawa 1970; Izumi 1970), with an ambitious editorial team consisting of well-known intellectuals including Umesao Tadao (anthropologist), Ishihara Shintarō (novelist), Agawa Hiroyuki (novelist), and Itokawa Hideo (rocket scientist). In an article in the *Asahi* newspaper on September 16, 1974, Nitta Jirō, who had written numerous novels about mountain climbing, pointed out the proliferation of exploration-related publications and maintained that the "massification" (*taishūka*) of exploration was ongoing (Nitta 1974).

Second, in these publications, Africa was repeatedly imagined as a "savage" and "uncivilized" place, enticing the reader's curiosity, and as one of the ultimate destinations for the most ambitious adventure. The Sannō Shobō series mentioned above, for example, included Sekine Yoshirō's essay on his cross-continental drive along the equator in Africa and Suzuki Keiko's essay on her climb of Kilimanjaro. In 1972, two graduates and one student from Notre Dame Seishin University—a women's university in Hiroshima—secured funding from the *Sankei* newspaper's "Adventure Plan" competition (Umesao Tadao was one of the judges) and left for Africa. Upon the conclusion of the trip, these amateur explorers published *Record of a Surprising Africa Adventure* (*Afurika bikkuri bōkenki*; Kosaka and Hamaguchi 1974). Around the same time, the young explorer Kamion'yu Takashi died at the age of twenty-two in a desert in Mali without achieving his goal of crossing the Sahara alone on camel. His travelogues, published soon after his death, stimulated young people's fascination with the Sahara (Kamion'yu 1975a, 1975b).

Especially insightful among these publications is the introduction that Umesao Tadao, then a Kyoto University professor and an active explorer himself, wrote for the eight-volume *Exploration and Adventure* (*Tanken to bōken*) series, published by the Asahi newspaper company in 1972. This explains why the idea of exploration had come to capture Japanese minds so strongly in the past decade or so. He first defines his contemporary time (the early 1970s) as "the era of experience" (*taiken no jidai*) and points out that many Japanese have begun visiting every corner of the world, even places considered the "periphery" (*henkyō*). Next, he maintains that while in the past only those activities that aimed for scientific discoveries were viewed as authentic exploration—that is, exploration was monopolized by professional researchers—the liberalization of travel abroad since 1964 has enabled regular citizens with no academic knowledge or training to enter the field of exploration. The Kyoto University professor approves of this trend, finding in it Japanese people's vital energy to discover "evidence" (*akashi*) of their own existence. He states:

> Our present-day world is still uneven [*fukinshitsu*]. The globe has not been covered entirely by an artificial climate dome. By escaping the quotidian idleness of civilized life [*bunmei seikatsu no nichijō-teki an'itsu*], humans can recuperate their humanity in the brutality of nature. Isn't that what exploration is about? (Umesao 1972, 16)

Umesao does not further articulate this point but is undoubtedly speaking about the regimentation of everyday life in advanced capitalist society and how that begets conformism while depriving people of opportunities for thrilling and unforeseen experiences, which he believes are the essence of human life. He establishes a dichotomy of civilization, to which he believes Japan belongs, and savagery, to which he believes Africa belongs, and sees the latter as a remedy for the problems created by the former.

Here, we should remember the industrial spy boom, which occurred in the 1960s, prior to the exploration boom. As we have seen in chapter 3, the industrial spy boom was a manifestation of the anxiety Japanese people were feeling about the complex and enigmatic structure of highly industrialized society as well as the powerlessness and alienation of individuals amplified by that structure. For those who spent extremely disciplined everyday lives dictated by corporate values, industrial spies who plot against gigantic corporations, cunningly beguile greedy executives, and disclose the dark secrets of business operations were like heroes who embodied in an exaggerated and embroidered manner the kind of desire that ordinary workers could never dare to put into practice on their own. The industrial spy boom, therefore, was one way for the masses in a country where economic growth was gaining momentum to come to terms with their ever-expanding industrial society.

On the other hand, the exploration boom occurred in the early 1970s, when high-speed growth was reaching its final phase. By this time, corporate control and the standardization that it fostered had been firmly established and were seen as something inevitably generated by economic growth, something now unavoidable if one were to continue enjoying the perks of that growth. Accordingly, people's attention shifted from the inside to the outside of industrial society, which they wanted to believe was not yet entirely governed by corporate values. The "Discover Japan" campaign, launched in 1970, was an attempt to find (or artificially create) such an outside within the nation-state and thereby contributed to reinforcing the fantasy of the periphery, whereas the exploration boom imagined similar places beyond the boundaries of the nation-state—the African desert, the Himalayas, the Polynesian islands, and the Amazon rainforest, for example. In this sense, the "Discover Japan" campaign and the exploration boom of the 1970s were two cultural phenomena fostered by the same desire that people in an advanced capitalist society shared for "nature" and "wilderness" as opposed to hypermodern "civilization" governed by mass production and consumption.

This is the cultural environment within which Jun and Katsuhiro in the film long for Africa. The two men, who lack stable jobs in the oil-crisis recession and are prevented from entering (or going back to) a secure middle-class life, cannot hang onto their hope for the postwar industrial society. Even if they abided by its rigid laws and endured the dull repetition of corporate life, there would be no guarantee that they could benefit from it. Their longing for Africa is linked to their wish to escape the corporate world in Japan and search for a place of greater freedom. For Jun and Katsuhiro, Africa is not a concrete place constituted by living and working people but an abstract, intangible place that exists in their imagination. Because of this, the political, economic, and social conditions within which Africa found itself in the 1970s—whether the anticolonial and postcolonial struggle in Mozambique and Angola, the racial conflict in South Africa and Rhodesia, or the military dictatorship in Uganda—do not enter their consciousness (and in this sense "Africa" in this film is quite different from the Africa that Akiko talks about in *A Warm Misty Night*). The Africa that they envisage is simply beautiful and comforting, detached from its material context.

Jun and Katsuhiro's longing for Africa is visually represented through three brief shots of the continent's natural landscape with wild animals. These shots, each of which lasts only a few seconds, appear out of the blue, unconnected to the plot. In the first shot, which comes just a few minutes after the title sequence, giraffes run gracefully across the savanna (see figure 5.4). The second and third shots, in the middle of the film, show moving rhinos and buffalos, respectively. Each of the shots of the African landscape is sandwiched by scenes of the two men's miserable lives in Hokkaido. The first appears between a scene in which a skirmish that the two men were

Figure 5.4. *The Light of Africa* (1975). Images of the natural scenery of Africa are contrasted with the harsh reality that Jun and Katsuhiro face in Hokkaido.

dragged into by local fishermen at a bar develops into a physical fight on the street and one in which they are freezing in jail the next morning (see figure 5.5). The second comes between a scene in which Jun takes care of a sick Katsuhiro in their cold apartment and one in which Jun masturbates alone in the apartment. The third comes between a scene in which Jun bathes Katsuhiro in a public bathhouse and one in which the latter receives an injection at a clinic.

Figure 5.5. *The Light of Africa* (1975). Jun and Katsuhiro are detained in jail due to a street fight in which they were involved. This shot comes right after a shot of giraffes in Africa.

Observing these three shots of the African landscape and the scenes that sandwich them, we immediately notice that the two spaces—Africa as a symbol of freedom and Rausu as the suffocating reality—are placed in such a way as to provide a remarkable contrast. The bar, jail, apartment, bathhouse, and clinic are all closed, human-made spaces indispensable to social life and the governing of society. Jun and Katsuhiro's activities there include fighting, detention, care of a sick person, and treatment of a disease, all of which connote constraints, responsibilities, and needs that hamper freedom and mobility. On the other hand, all three shots of Africa show open, wild spaces. We see no humans, only animals, which live according to their instincts. There is no single element in these shots that suggests life struggles. This contrast between these two spaces is further strengthened by their colors and sounds. The scenes of Hokkaido—indoor, in winter, and/or at night—are dominated by dark, heavy colors. They are full of unpleasant sounds produced by the characters' mumbling, yelling, accusing, and scolding, which cannot always be clearly heard but are indistinguishable from raucous noise and therefore quite irritating. The shots of Africa are a pale, yellowish orange, which conjures up images of the gentle light of sunrise or sunset. They are accompanied by complete silence or quiet background music. They provide us with fleeting moments of repose and temporarily take our attention away from the bleak, freezing landscape of the northern island and Jun and Katsuhiro's constant antagonism.

Africa in *The Light of Africa* is similar to the blue sky in *Blue-Sky Girl* (discussed in chapter 2) in that both serve as ideologies that create meanings for one's experience and dictate how one thinks, acts, and interprets experiences. Just as Yūko in *Blue-Sky Girl* was able to interpret her lonely life in Tokyo as a trial necessary for future happiness by fantasizing about the blue sky, so do Jun and Katsuhiro seek to tolerate the destitution and ostracism they face by fantasizing about Africa. However, while Yūko is fully determined to transform her environment through her own effort, aims for upward social mobility within 1950s Japanese society, and achieves this goal through her marriage to the handsome and rich Mr. Hirooka, the two men in *The Light of Africa* are not interested in success in the competitive capitalist world but have bet on a dream that seems far less realistic but far more entertaining and exciting precisely because of its unrealistic nature. This can be explained by the different historical contexts within which Yūko and the two men are placed. While in the late 1950s the government, bureaucrats, business community, and national media were all orchestrating a new era of growth, bolstering the idea that industriousness and incessant effort would enable an affluent society, such enthusiasm for economic growth had already disappeared by the mid-1970s. A multitude of social problems spawned by postwar industrialization and the end of high-speed growth were eroding popular faith in the foundational notions that the modern world had embraced, such as growth, progress, and development. Thus, the gap between Yūko in *Blue-Sky Girl*, who says she can always see the "blue sky" even with her eyes closed, and Jun and Katsuhiro in *The Light of Africa*, who face so much difficulty getting to Africa, indicates not only their relative physical distance from these objects but also the different degree of confidence they demonstrate in the attainability of their dreams.

"Stranger Intimacy" and the End of an Era

Male-male friendship provides an important motif for *The Light of Africa*. Jun and Katsuhiro need each other to make their dream of going to Africa come true since their life in Rausu is rife with uncertainties and disappointments: their financial situation is shaky, many people in town demonstrate explicit antipathy toward them, and they have no clear idea concerning exactly when they can leave the depressing fishing town. They live together in a small one-room apartment, which imposes physical intimacy upon them. Their intense, often physically expressed affective relation catches the audience's attention from the very beginning of the film. They sleep beside each other in that tiny apartment. They walk with their arms around each other's shoulders. They sit huddling together. They fight a lot, which obviously involves constant physical contact. When Katsuhiro gets sick, Jun dedicatedly cares for him. He presses his own face to Katsuhiro's to check his temperature. He tries to apply a rectal thermometer. Jun also carries Katsuhiro to a public bath. When Katsuhiro has incontinence, Jun cleans him up and consoles him with a gentle touch. Thus, intimate exchange at the physical level is a crucial component of the friendship between the two men in *The Light of Africa*.

A Warm Misty Night, discussed in the previous chapter, also addressed the issues of male-male friendship. Unlike that in *The Light of Africa*, the friendship between Sagara and Nguyen in that film, however, manifested indirectly through their support for the revolution in Southeast Asia and had to be mediated by the act of trafficking the woman whom both loved. The only direct physical contact that the two men shared was when they shook hands in the final sequence, right before Nguyen and Akiko's departure from Yokohama Harbor. In *The Light of Africa*, too, traffic in a woman functions to solidify male-male friendship, but in this film, the traffic is executed in a much more direct manner, which involves actual physical communication between the two men. While Katsuhiro makes love to bar waitress Fujiko, Jun waits for his turn right next to Katsuhiro. Katsuhiro's intercourse with Fujiko ends quickly, but Jun is not particularly eager to sleep with her next. He instead directs his attention to Katsuhiro. After Fujiko leaves the room to take a bath, Jun, snickering, asks Katsuhiro how it was. They have this conversation while lying together in bed. It appears as if Jun had already satisfied his sexual desire through Katsuhiro as a proxy. This is undoubtedly the scene in which intimacy between the two men is underlined most intensely (see figure 5.6).

It seems that Shōken deliberately chose to represent male-male intimacy in this exaggerated manner. In an interview published in the September 1973 issue of *Kinema junpō*, answering a question about

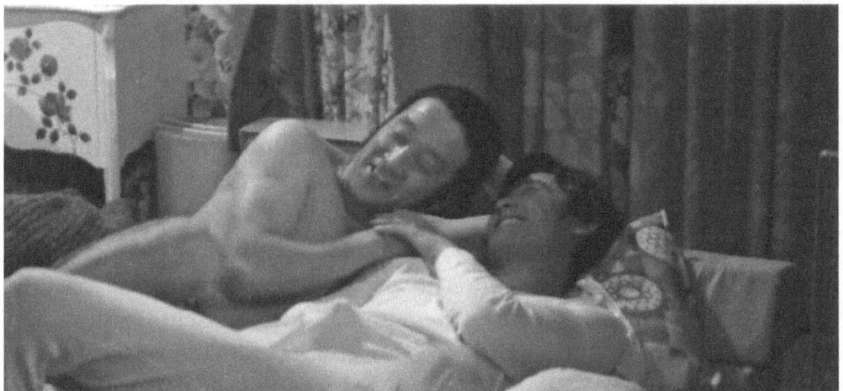

Figure 5.6. *The Light of Africa* (1975). After Katsuhiro makes love to Fujiko, Jun and Katsuhiro enjoy intimate time alone together.

what kind of film he wanted to make next, he made the following statement:

> Then, a *Midnight Cowboy*-like men's love story. Concretely, a story about homosexual people [*homo no hito-tachi*]. Personally, I am not interested, but come to think about it, homosexuals [*homo*] have lots of men's embarrassment, men's odiousness, and men's kindness. I think they embody men's romanticism. They are complete outlaws and are living with a disconsolation that they don't know where to take, and that they can't share with their wives. They are interesting. (Fukuoka 1973, 115–16)

The following year, Shōken worked with Kumashiro Tatsumi for the first time and starred in *The Failure of Youth*. The theme of male-male intimacy, or "homosexuals," can already be observed in this film. The college student that Shōken plays, who at the end kills his girlfriend due to his ambition for economic success, displays deep affection for his best friend (Kawarasaki Kenzō) through physical contact that imitates a rugby practice and therefore does not threaten or challenge their identity as heterosexual men. *The Light of Africa*, released almost twelve months after and looking a bit like what can indeed be called "a *Midnight Cowboy*-like men's love story" (or perhaps a *Scarecrow*-like men's love story), intended to further advance this theme of male-male intimacy.

Despite Shōken's fascination with "homosexuals," however, *The Light of Africa* did not become a film about homosexual men in the strict sense. Both Jun and Katsuhiro sexually objectify women and sleep with women. While *Midnight Cowboy* alludes to the homosexual desire of the Texan cowboy Joe (Jon Voight) by encouraging the viewer to imagine his backstory through flashbacks (Lang 2002, chap. 5), nothing in *The Light of Africa* indicates any backstory related to repressed sexuality, closeted identity, or sexual experience with other men in the past. They both seem like uncomplicated heterosexual men who desire women. But we should be aware that Shōken was using the term *homosexual* not as a concept related to one's sexual orientation, particularly the object of sexual desire, but to refer to an intense and excessive male-male friendship that seemed to deviate from what society considered normal—taking a male friend's temperature rectally, for instance. Of course, within the context of 1970s Japan (and in many parts of the world including the United States back then), this use of *homosexual* was not unusual at all, and my aim here is not to accuse Shōken of a misuse of the term. But this demonstrates not only the limits of the understanding of human sexuality in Japan at the time but also the paucity of appropriate and precise language with which to describe various forms of intimacy.

Another good example of this can be found in the critic Ono Kōsei's evaluation of the film. In an article published in *Kinema junpō*, he stated that all Jun and Katsuhiro did in the film was to "act like big babies, wanting to go to Africa" ("Afurika ni ikitai nā to dada o konete iru") and expressed his discomfort with an "impotent men's paradise, in which they flirt with each other tenderly" ("yasashiku ichatsukiau otokotachi no inpotentsu tengoku"; Saitō Masaharu and Ono 1975, 143). Ono reacted to the issue of "homosexuals" in a manner quite different from Shōken, but we should note that Ono's reaction, too, derived from the fact that there was no proper language available for the description of male-male intimacy. This led him to disinterest and rejection, rather than fascination, and to the belief that the film was not worth serious consideration.

How, then, should we—those of us who are trying to appreciate this film more than forty-five years after its release—understand the intimacy between Jun and Katsuhiro, whom Shōken believed were "homosexuals" and whom Ono called "impotents"? It requires a language that permits us to capture its complexity and historical relevance. The historian Nayan Shah's discussion is helpful here. In *Stranger Intimacy*, Shah examines various forms of intimacy nurtured among the people who migrated from Asia and Mexico to the North American West in the first several decades of the twentieth century. According to him, the analysis of their movements and interactions entails critical awareness of the three "conceptual stabilizations" that researchers privilege, whether consciously or not, when documenting historical events: "permanence over transience," "the nuclear family household," and "polarized sexuality" (Shah 2011, 6–9). "Permanence over transience" refers to the presumption that immigrants' ultimate goals are to settle and start life anew in their destination. This presumption makes us believe that movement to that destination is just a temporary phase for their ultimate goal and therefore overlook the relations, interactions, and solidarities that take place during this phase, which often are transient and unstable, as unworthy of serious examination.

The privileging of settlement is linked to the second conceptual stabilization. Many of us living in modern society share the idea that the nuclear family is the basic unit of social life and the site where intimacy is nurtured, and this idea obscures the affective and physical ties and various forms of household structures that existed among immigrants, which commonly exceeded the boundaries of nuclear families. Finally, by "polarized sexuality" Shah means the simple understanding that human sexual desire and activities can be (or should be) clearly divided into either heterosexuality or homosexuality. He is critical of the use of sexuality as a normative category and argues that human sexualities in reality are contradictory and incoherent and therefore can never be neatly explained within the hetero-homosexual dichotomy. By pointing out these three conceptual stabilizations, Shah calls attention to the complex realities of sexual practices, friendships, companionships, and domestic lives in migrant communities while admonishing us against the prejudices that prompt us to categorize certain relations as aberration and therefore unimportant.

These three conceptual stabilizations offer insight into the question of intimacy in Japan during high-speed growth, since many Japanese people at that time understood intimacy in close association with the image of the middle-class nuclear family, taking for granted the idea that it should be nurtured between a heterosexual man and woman who were united (or were to be united) through the institution of marriage. This understanding did not emerge naturally but was shaped and reinforced by a variety of public and private forces governing society, especially the state and corporations. As we have seen in chapter 2, large corporations in Japan during high-speed growth promoted a strict gender division of labor within the family, thereby enlisting male breadwinners' total devotion to corporate life, which necessarily entailed physical and emotional maintenance offered by caring, full-time housewives. State organizations endorsed this corporate practice by privileging the nuclear family constituted by a husband with full-time work, a homemaker wife, and their unmarried children, regarded as the "standard family," or *hyōjun kazoku*, for purposes of taxation, social security, and public services.[13]

We should learn from Shah's study to recognize properly as intimacy a variety of affective and physical ties that existed (or might have existed) outside the "standard family"—a category manufactured for particular political and economic purposes. This means that we need to resist the impulse to define the cohabitation of Jun and Katsuhiro in *The Light of Africa* with superficial, reductive, and somewhat disdainful language such as "homosexuals" (not in its original meaning but in the way Shōken used it in his interview) and "impotent men," as this would shut down the possibilities of further analysis. Instead, we should note that it is the prescriptive notion of the "standard family" that helped to solidify this perception and accept their cohabitation as one genuine form of intimacy. What they are doing is to eat and sleep in the same room, worry about their household budget, fight over mundane issues, and nurse and be nursed by each other. These affective and reproductive activities in their private sphere do not qualitatively differ from what a heterosexual couple and their children do for one another in "standard families." The main difference is that the intimacy Jun and Katsuhiro practice has no legal, administrative, or social recognition.

It is suggestive that *The Light of Africa* represents a form of intimacy placed outside the realm of the "standard family" within the context of a small fishing-port town in Hokkaido in the mid-1970s. By drawing our attention to the intimacy that develops between two working-class drifters in a provincial fishing community far from the nation-state's major metropolitan areas, the film subverts and decenters the institution of the standard family—that is, the urban and suburban middle-class nuclear family on a corporate salary—as well as the ideologies that have endorsed it, such as proper and respectable gender and parental roles within family and society as well as individual devotion and sacrifice to these collectives. The observation of the intimacy between the two men, who care for each other just like family members living in the same household, inescapably demonstrates that the middle-class nuclear family is by no means the only form of intimacy and that its dissemination is intricately linked to the social arrangements that facilitate it. When reminding ourselves of the interdependent relation between postwar Japan's corporate society and the middle-class nuclear family during high-speed growth, we can argue that by relativizing this form of intimacy, *The Light of Africa* tacitly pronounces the end of this historical event and encourages us to expand our imagination to the microhistories—not just different intimacies but different experiences broadly—that might have been obscured in the shadow of the grand narrative of postwar prosperity.

Coda

IN THESE FIVE CHAPTERS, I have examined five films made during the era of high-speed growth and its aftermath: *Susaki Paradise Red Light* (1956), *Blue-Sky Girl* (1957), *Black Weapon* (1964), *A Warm Misty Night* (1967), and *The Light of Africa* (1975). The main goal of this examination has been to construct narratives of high-speed growth using these films as historical sources. At the broader theoretical level, I wanted to explore the historicity—that is, the historically conditioned nature—of cultural artifacts. While it is still quite common to treat culture—including film, literature, and music—as expressing a discrete set of essential values and ideas, often national, ahistorical, and detached from the realm of politics and the economy, I have been more interested in how culture is generated within a specific material context and how it in turn relates to and shapes that context. Instead of viewing culture as a system of reference that dictates and prescribes one's thinking and behavior in a society, I have dealt with it as a way for people living at a specific moment of history to make sense of the transformations they are experiencing in that society and to communicate their observations of these transformations.

At the more practical level, through the examination of these films, I have shown the possibility of alternatives to narratives widely accepted in Japan today that tend to represent postwar history as a story of great achievement, focusing on the prosperity and peace enabled by high-speed growth. For this purpose, I have adopted the methodology of historicization, placing the significance of these films within their specific political, economic, and social contexts and considering their intertextual relationships with other contemporary cultural and intellectual texts. The five films dealt with in this book were all meant for the entertainment of mainstream audiences and did not express explicit political agendas or messages, but careful historicization has allowed us to make meanings out of seemingly apolitical plots, subjects, settings, visual images, and locations and to see how they reference events, relations, and ideas in contemporary Japanese society.

Using this method, I have read these five films as cultural texts that exhibited anxiety and tension related to the intense and massive capitalist development that occurred from the 1950s to the 1970s. Made only eleven years after Japanese defeat in the war, *Susaki Paradise* addressed the issues of the tardiness of reconstruction from wartime damage and uneven development within the city of Tokyo through the representations of Susaki and Akihabara. Meanwhile, *Blue-Sky Girl*, made around the same time as *Susaki Paradise*, drew our attention to uneven development between the city and countryside within the nation-state and the plight of the working-class girls and boys who had to leave their rural hometowns to find work in Tokyo. By the time *Black Weapon* was made in 1964, high-speed growth had gained momentum, and this film depicted the growing powerlessness of workers vis-à-vis corporations and voiced their frustration with regimented industrial society through the figure of the loner industrial spy who challenges corporate executives. *A Warm Misty Night* was made at the time of the American bombing of North Vietnam. This film highlighted the tension experienced by a nightclub owner in Yokohama between a desire to benefit economically from the presence of American bases and a sense of pan-Asian solidarity with victims of the American war in Vietnam. Finally, *The Light of Africa*, a product of the oil-crisis recession in the mid-1970s, portrayed the precarious nature of work in capitalist society and the economic predicament of rural Japan, imagining Africa as a land free from the needs and constraints of everyday life. Although the topics vary, I hope these chapters have helped the reader view the history of high-speed growth with more complexity and nuance. High-speed growth was by no means a linear progression toward greater happiness and material wealth; rather, it was a confusing, disquieting, and inconsistent process, which demonstrated various contradictions intrinsic to the capitalist economy.

Since the bursting of the "bubble economy" in the early 1990s, Japanese society has endured a prolonged period of economic stagnation—what some call the "lost three decades," which might well become the "lost four decades." With the gradual disappearance of security in the workplace and the rapid spread of a neoliberal discourse of self-responsibility and self-help in the past few decades, such issues as unemployment, marginal employment, poverty, gender-based discrimination, exploitative employers, inhumane work conditions, and uneven development within the nation-state have received great social attention. But it would be wrong to suppose that these arose suddenly and began threatening people's lives and livelihoods only in the aftermath of the bubble economy. These are fundamental problems with an economic system driven by permanent desire for capital accumulation, and, as such, they have existed throughout the history of modern Japan, thereby forming a salient undercurrent of historical experiences (though the scale and the concrete manifestations may have differed depending on the period). As this book has shown, the high-speed growth era was not exceptional. There is a tendency to overlook or underestimate the persistence of these problems when we look at high-speed growth primarily as a national event, emphasizing, for instance, growth, development, modernization, and industrial society as key concepts around which to give meaning to experiences, articulate their links, and create narratives. In this book, I have insisted on the importance of resisting the impulse to accept uncritically the grand narrative dictated by these concepts and highlighted the heterogeneity of the experiences of high-speed growth.

To be clear, my study is by no means the first to undertake this kind of project. On the contrary, my argument in this book undeniably has built upon studies produced by scholars and writers over many decades. Among them, I especially want to acknowledge two as having motivated me to look at the history of high-speed growth with skepticism: the economist Kumazawa Makoto (1981, 1986, 1996) and the journalist Kamata Satoshi ([1973] 1983), both of whom witnessed firsthand the immense social change that occurred in Japan during high-speed growth. The former has dedicated himself to recording in numerous works the workplace culture in postwar Japan that enabled high-speed growth but also came to control every corner of regular workers' lives through the normalization of corporate values, whereas the latter, in his famous reportage based on his experience as a seasonal worker at Toyota, has poignantly critiqued the system of mass production that mobilized workers to full exhaustion for greater productivity. Their work taught me sensitivity to the details, whether of individual experiences or local manifestations, that a grand narrative of history might overlook or fail to grasp while providing me with models of how to communicate these details with both imagination and solid evidence. What I have wanted to do in this book is to validate that the concerns these people and other researchers and writers shared about postwar Japanese society and its economic growth were in fact well documented in cinematic texts, too, and thereby to contribute as a cultural historian to enriching the scholarship that they have built.

I am not insisting, however, that the narratives I have presented in *Cinema of Discontent* are the only correct ones or that they should replace other narratives. When constructing counternarratives of postwar history, I have sought to establish their accuracy and validity through careful historicization, close reading, and intertextualization of the cinematic and other cultural texts, but my own imagination and insights have also played a significant role in the construction of these narratives (just as in the case of Maruyama Masao's practice of *shisōshi*, or the "history of ideas"). Some might call these prejudices and biases. I am aware that the narratives presented in this book are just a few among many existing and potential narratives concerning postwar history. Other cultural historians or film studies scholars analyzing the same films, or other films produced during the same period, might produce narratives entirely different from mine. I am pointing out this self-evident fact, with which few researchers and readers will disagree, because accepting the multiple possibilities of historical narratives based on diverse interpretations is one of the most basic assumptions that should be shared for the analysis of not only cultural texts like film and literature but all kinds of historical texts. In postwar Japan, just as in other places, history has always been a contested terrain for those who seek to mobilize knowledge of the past—of high-speed growth and of many other issues such as the Meiji Restoration, industrialization and Westernization, colonialism and imperialism, the wars, US occupation, and the postwar social movements—to create consent for specific political agendas, to ferment specific social atmospheres, and to reinforce specific cultural discourses. It has not been unusual for these contestations to be fueled by emotionally charged and intense conflicts and by exorbitant slander against those who do not share ideological, political, and spiritual beliefs. I hope that this book's argument will help clarify the importance of deliberating with reason and civility over which narratives make most sense when they are examined against their historical contexts and against available sources. I entrust to each reader the judgment of the validity of the narratives presented in this book.

Last, I want to acknowledge a very simple but extremely important fact: I have been moved, inspired, and pleasantly surprised by many, many films at every stage of the writing of this book. As I mentioned in the introduction, I conceived of this project while observing the representations of high-speed growth (or absence thereof) in films by such directors as Naruse Mikio, Imamura Shōhei, and Yamada Yōji between the 1950s and 1970s. They gave me an opportunity to delve into the discrepancy between the historical narratives that circulated widely and the heterogeneity of experiences that must have existed but had somehow been forgotten. In this book, I have dealt with only five films, and these are no doubt among the special films that I personally care for and respect, but it has not been my intention to privilege them as unique and exceptional. I have examined the significance of these five films within their synchronic and diachronic networks to demonstrate that they were by no means isolated works but rather parts of broader discourses that shaped the cultural landscape of contemporary Japan. There are many other fascinating, eye-opening, and insightful films that can be located within these networks and that helped me conceptualize, articulate, and reconsider my argument in each chapter. For example, Kawashima Yūzō's many other films made me recognize the centrality of the notion of *muen*, or "no ties," in the appreciation of *Susaki Paradise*. Various films on "going up to Tokyo" made in both prewar and postwar Japan, such as Ozu's *The Only Son* (1936), provided me with clues critical to discerning the representation of Tokyo as a land of opportunity and success in *Blue-Sky Girl*. The proliferation of Daiei films on industrial espionage and intrigue starring Tamiya Jirō—not only those in the "Black" series but many others—taken together taught me about Japanese society's anxiety over the growing opacity of the corporate world (and, of course, the seductive attraction of this actor). Films that explicitly addressed the violence committed by the US forces in "base towns" and Japanese complicity, such as Takechi Tetsuji's *Black Snow*, encouraged me to think in earnest about the political implications of *A Warm Misty Night*, a seemingly apolitical "mood action" film. Finally, the numerous films in the 1970s that addressed the themes of travel and drifting, such as Saitō Kōichi's *Weight of the Journey*, were the very reason that I decided to explore the meanings of Shiretoko and Africa in *The Light of Africa*. I have tried to reference as many of these other films as possible, but there are still many more that have gone unmentioned and that have escaped my attention. I would like to end this book by emphasizing that the narratives of high-speed growth that I have constructed here are deeply indebted to all these named and unnamed films (and other cultural texts, of course) that encouraged me to think.

Notes

Introduction

1. All the English translations of Japanese sources in this book are mine unless otherwise specified.

2. There is a rich accumulation of studies on the rise of extreme nationalist ideology and movement in the interwar years. Maruyama Masao's essays published in the early postwar years—"Chō-kokka shugi no ronri to shinri" ([1946] 1995) and "Nihon fashizumu no shisō to undō" ([1948] 1995), among others—are foundational texts. Ienaga Saburō ([1968] 2002), Matsuo Shōichi (1977), and Yoshimi Yoshiaki (1987) discuss the oppression of freedom and democracy during the fascist era, the right-wing political movement since the 1930s, and regular Japanese citizens' responses and participation, respectively. In English, Andrew Gordon (1992) explains the shift from "imperial democracy" to "imperial fascism" in the 1930s, while Alan Tansman (2009) explores fascism as a cultural response to the crisis of modernity.

3. For the application of modernization theory to the Japanese context, see John Whitney Hall (1965). Edwin Reischauer, a historian and US ambassador to Japan (1961–66), was probably one of the most vocal proponents of this theory. His writings, many of which targeted a general audience, allow us to see clearly the political agenda that it was expected to fulfill within the Cold War context. See Reischauer (1965, 1967).

4. Scott O'Bryan (2009) examines "growth" as an ideology, providing a fascinating overview of the process by which bureaucrats, economists, and specialists in other fields in postwar Japan consolidated a strong belief in it as a way to interpret the nation's economic conditions and to envisage its future.

5. Michael Schaller (1997) examines in detail how the US-Japanese diplomatic and economic relations evolved in the post–World War II era within the context of the Cold War.

6. On the Shōwa-era boom, see also Thompson (2011) and Anderson et al. (2016). For the critique of the "good old days" discourse of the Shōwa era, see Fuse (2006, 2007).

7. In this sense, I agree with Yasushi Yamanouchi (1998, 2011), who has examined how the total-war system established in both the Allied and Axis countries during World War II contributed to advancing social integration in the name of the national community and how this served as a foundation for the effective governance of society in the postwar era. One can argue that high-speed growth was one successful case of a national mobilization whose origin can be traced back to total war. Kobayashi Hideo (2004) makes a similar point and provides powerful empirical evidence for the continuity between total war and high-speed growth, particularly in the realm of economic planning, where the state played a crucial role in guiding private enterprise. Furthermore, Hiromi Mizuno, Aaron Moore, and John DiMoia (2018) extend the scope to Japan's economic aid for Asian countries during the Cold War and demonstrate how postwar Japan's government and corporations inherited a developmental ideology and practice from imperial Japan.

8. Two more works should be mentioned as sophisticated models for the use of films as historical sources. Sean D. O'Reilly (2018) analyzes the "lived experiences" of interwar and wartime Japanese society through the examination of films on Bakumatsu (late Tokugawa era) history. Jennifer Coates (2016) looks at the repetition of motifs and female representations observed in postwar Japanese films and thereby reveals the various concerns shared by people in the society that was recovering from wartime devastation.

9. Mitsuhiro Yoshimoto (2000) demonstrates how the discipline of film studies in the United States has come to resort to ahistorical and stereotypical "national character" to appreciate Japanese films since the 1960s, relating this trend to auteurism as a dominant form of studying cinema as well as the American governmental and military effort during and after World War II to understand the Japanese psyche.

10. For an elaborated version of this argument, see the scholarly essay published in the same year entitled "Chūsei to hangyaku" (Maruyama [1960] 1996a).

Chapter 1

1. On the link between Japan's economic recovery and America's Cold War international policy, see Forsberg (2000) and Schaller (1987). On Japan's position within the world system, see Cumings (1993). I have extensively discussed rearmament and the development of the Self-Defense Forces during the high-speed growth era elsewhere (T. Sasaki 2015).

2. In 1965, Kōtō Ward launched a large-scale address reform based on the 1962 Act on Indication of Residential Address. As a result, Susaki-Bentenchō was renamed Tōyōchō in 1967 (Kōtōku 1997, 173), and this name is no longer used officially. Although it is not uncommon to see the name of this neighborhood spelled Suzaki-Bentenchō (すざきべんてんちょう), the correct spelling is Susaki-Bentenchō (すさきべんてんちょう), and therefore I use the latter spelling throughout this book.

3. On Tosaka's concept of *fūzoku*, see Schäfer (2014) and Hirano (2014). Harootunian (2000) also helps better understand Tosaka's critical discussion of everydayness.

4. On the American military control of prostitution during the occupation era, see Takeuchi (2010). Mizoguchi Kenji's *Women of the Night* (*Yoru no onnatachi*, 1948), set in Osaka in the immediate postwar era, details the ways that a war widow (Tanaka Kinuyo) loses her only son due to poverty and ends up becoming the mistress of a drug dealer and then a street prostitute.

5. Satō Jun'ya's *Growing Up in a Brothel* (*Kuruwa sodachi*, 1964) is set in 1957, right before the full enforcement of the Anti-Prostitution Law, and tells a tragic story of the decline of Shimabara, a licensed quarter in Kyoto, through the eyes of a young geisha (Mita Yoshiko) with education and hopes for a middle-class family life. She struggles to escape a world dictated by the male desire to commodify women but has no effective means of changing her own fate and ends up killing her old patron out of resentment and despair.

6. Historian Fujime Yuki (1997) reveals the proponents' classist attitude toward prostitution and strongly criticizes the widespread discourse that praises the establishment of the Anti-Prostitution Law as an achievement in the history of the liberation of women. Kawashima's *A Woman Is Born Twice* (*Onna wa nido umareru*, 1961) allows us to observe how prostitution persisted after the enforcement of the law in the guise of a free encounter between the women who offered sexual services and the men who paid for them. In this film, low-end geisha Koen (Wakao Ayako), who also works as a prostitute under the table, sees her client (Frankie Sakai) at an inn where the owner facilitates their encounter by charging a margin. Under her gaudy kimono, she is wearing an ordinary dress. She plans to leave the inn in this dress the next morning and pretend that she and her client are just lovers to escape the attention of the police. Furthermore, right after the enforcement of the Anti-Prostitution Law, Shin-Tōhō released a series of mystery films depicting the clandestine world in which prostitution was controlled by criminal organizations. See, for example, *Call-Girl Territory* (*Hakusen himitsu chitai*, 1958) and *Black-Line District* (*Kurosen chitai*, 1960), both of which were directed by Ishii Teruo.

7. Mizoguchi's film is sometimes rendered as *Red Light District*, but in this book I use the more common English title, *Street of Shame*. On literary

and cinematic representations of Susaki Paradise and Yoshiwara around the time of the enforcement of the Anti-Prostitution Law, see Oshino (2014).

8. Shimizu Kazuhiko (2015) examines how the statement "no longer the 'postwar,'" which was originally meant to be cautionary, has come to be interpreted as embracing the beginning of high-speed growth and how that interpretation was established as part of postwar Japanese society's collective memory through negotiations between the media and the audience.

9. The results of these surveys and the other surveys conducted by the Prime Minister's Office (and later the Cabinet Office) are available on the Cabinet Office's website: https://survey.gov-online.go.jp/index-ko.html.

10. Indeed, in *Evening Stream* (*Yoru no nagare*, 1960), codirected by Kawashima and Naruse Mikio, Mihashi played a cook who was detained in Siberia and suffered permanent frostbite damage to one foot.

11. The economic white paper of the following year, with the subtitle "Expansion that was too rapid and its reflection" ("Hayasugita kakudai to sono hansei"), changed tone and focus quite dramatically and spent one section addressing unevenness between industries—the so-called "dual structure," or *nijū kōzō*: the coexistence of large companies with modern technologies, high productivity, and high wages on the one hand and small companies, family-run businesses, and agriculture with low wages and low productivity on the other. The white paper insisted that the resolution of this problem through the absorption of workers in the latter sector into modern industries with modern labor-management relations was indispensable for the continued growth of the Japanese economy. This change was no doubt a response to heavy criticism of the 1956 white paper. See Keizai Kikakuchō (1957, 33–42).

12. The Tokyo Metropolitan Government's Bureau of Port and Harbor also provided me with valuable information on the history of landfill in Tokyo Bay, for which I would like to express my gratitude.

13. By the 1960s, however, these landfill areas would manifest the contradiction of intense industrialization and urbanization blatantly. In 1957, the Tokyo metropolitan government designated one of the artificial islands located southeast of Susaki-Bentenchō—ironically named Yume-no-shima, or "Dream Island"—as a waste-disposal site for the ever-ballooning metropolis. In the summer of 1965, the enormous amount of garbage dumped there daily resulted in a large-scale infestation of flies that plagued residents in the surrounding areas for more than a month. The metropolitan government had to conduct aerial spraying of insecticide to suppress the infestation (Tōkyō Kyōshokuin Kumiai Kōtō Shibu 1987, 166–67).

14. David Harvey (2001, 2003b) employs the term "spatial fix" to explain the process by which capital expands to new territories (or restructures old territories) to absorb surplus capital and thereby to avoid the problem of overaccumulation—a problem immanent to the capitalist mode of production.

15. On liminal space, see van Gennep (1960); V. Turner (1969, 1974); and Thomassen (2014).

16. I want to point out that the places of *muen* have historical and functional commonalities with what Michel Foucault ([1967] 2008) has termed "heterotopia." Comparing it to a utopia, which exists only in the fanciful world, Foucault defines *heterotopia* as places created in the real world that are "written into the institution of society itself" and "a sort of counter-emplacements, a sort of effectively realized utopias in which the real emplacements, all the other real emplacements that can be found within culture, are simultaneously represented, contested and inverted" (17). Foucault's argument helps us discern the places of *muen* not necessarily as unique to Japan but more broadly as deriving from a human desire or need for "other places" that exist within society but are detached, physically and functionally, from the places of daily routine.

17. Tsutae says that she was born on an island called Yume-no-shima, or "dream island." But I was unable to locate such an island anywhere in this river. I would like to thank the management office for Tone River within the Kanto Regional Development Bureau of the Ministry of Land, Infrastructure, Transport, and Tourism for providing me with information on islands in the river.

18. On this play, see Tsunemitsu (2006). Miyazaki Hayao's *Spirited Away* (*Sen to Chihiro no kamikakushi*, 2000) offers probably one of the best-known uses of *engacho* in film. When Chihiro steps on the "bug of curse," whose black fluid covers her foot, Kama-ji instructs her to make a circle with her thumbs and index fingers and cuts that circle with his hand while shouting "engacho."

19. Marilyn Ivy (1995) analyzes the resurgence of *taishū engeki* in the 1980s as a cultural phenomenon that indicates marginality and loss within modern bourgeois culture. For cinematic representations of traveling troupes, see Ozu Yasujirō's *A Story of Floating Weeds* (*Ukikusa monogatari*, 1934) and self-remake *Floating Weeds* (*Ukikusa*, 1959) and Naruse Mikio's *Traveling Actors* (*Tabiyakusha*, 1940).

Chapter 2

1. Calculated from the data provided by the 1955 national census. See Sōrifu Tōkeikyoku (1959, 198).

2. Calculated from the data provided by the 1975 national census. See Sōrifu Tōkeikyoku (1977b, 206).

3. Tanabe Seiko ([1979] 1990) has translated this story into modern Japanese as *Princess Ochikubo* (*Ochikubo-hime*).

4. For an insightful analysis of Morishige Hisaya as a star whose quality derives from the locality of Osaka, see Cronin (2017, chap. 5). He particularly examines Morishige's performance in Kawashima Yūzō's *The Shop Curtain* (*Noren*, 1958). For a detailed text analysis of salaryman films, see Wada-Marciano (2012) and Nishimura (2012). The former examines them in the context of transwar history, pointing out postwar society's "discontinuity" and "continuity" with the prewar era, while the latter deals with the questions of economic capital, social capital (e.g., connection), and habitus in these films.

5. Note that the name Eburi Man puns on the English term *everyman*. Through this name, the author stressed the average nature of the protagonist, who was supposed to speak on behalf of many businessmen who belonged to the same class (the urban middle class) and generation (men who received school education before and during the war, like Nosaka Akiyuki and Kaikō Takeshi, as discussed in chapter 1).

6. In 1930, of the employed workforce of 29,619,640 in Japan (excluding the colonies), 14,699,461 people, or nearly 50 percent, engaged in agriculture and fishery (Naikaku Tōkeikyoku 1935, 248). In his fascinating book on the lives of "salarymen" in prewar Japan, Iwase Akira (2006) maintains that it is not easy to identify the exact number of white-collar workers in prewar Japan but suggests that they accounted for less than 10 percent of the employed population.

7. Okazaki Takeshi (2012) analyzes modern Japanese literature from the Meiji to the contemporary era with the theme of "going up to the capital." This unique work demonstrates the excitement, hope, and anxiety that the nation's capital inspired among various authors and how these feelings have been reflected in their literary works.

8. In the lyrics of "Share otoko," the setting has been switched to interwar Japan. While Frank Crumit's "A Gay Caballero" is about a man from Rio de Janeiro who tries to find a "fine señorita," "Share otoko" is about a man who is the best *mobo* (modern boy) in his village, wearing a blue shirt, a red tie, and Harold Lloyd–style round glasses. He moves to Tokyo full of anticipation, then develops an intimate relationship with a café waitress in Ginza but gets beaten up by her husband and realizes what a scary place Tokyo is.

9. While the phenomenon of mass employment is often understood as unique to the high-speed economic growth era, Yamaguchi highlights its historical continuity with other public and private attempts to expand the labor market or unify multiple labor markets for greater profits, such as the wartime state effort to balance labor supply and demand across regions and Japanese companies' searches for cheap labor beyond national borders in the 1970s and beyond. On "mass employment," see also Kase (1997).

10. As a result, there are abundant cinematic representations of maids in this era: for example, Ozu Yasujirō's *The Flavor of Green Tea over Rice* (*Ochazuke no aji*, 1952); Naruse Mikio's *Late Chrysanthemums* (*Bangiku*, 1954), *Flowing* (*Nagareru*, 1956), and *Daughter, Wife, and Mother* (*Musume, tsuma, haha*, 1960); Yoshimura Kōzaburō's *Time for Marriage* (*Konki*, 1961); and Toyoda Shirō's *A Kitchen Chronicle* (*Daidokoro taiheiki*, 1963; as well as the novel by Tanizaki Junichirō [(1963) 1974] from which it was adapted, available in English as *The Maids* [Tanizaki 2016]).

11. At the same time, in the postwar era, there have been numerous attempts by scholars and intellectuals from the region to overcome these imposed images by reclaiming Tohoku's cultural and historical identity. Nathan Hopson (2017) details this process.

12. Film scholar Saitō Ayako (2001, 2002, 2003, 2010a, 2010b) has extensively and meticulously analyzed the heroines Wakao played in Masumura's films, focusing on the issues of gender, sexuality, the body, and patriarchy and reading her films against the conventional readings that construe them predominantly as heterosexual romances.

13. A few years later, Wakao once again appeared in one of Mizoguchi's films: *Street of Shame* (*Akasen chitai*, 1956). In this film, working against her public star image as a girl next door, she plays a calculating prostitute who skillfully uses her youth and beauty to earn enough money to get out of Yoshiwara and start her own business.

14. Note that Wakao's success in *Blue-Sky Girl* as an unpretentious heroine led to her starring in another film adapted from a novel by Genji ([1959] 2016) and directed by Masumura—namely, *The Most Valuable Wife* (*Saikō shukun fujin*, 1959). In this film, Wakao plays a regular working woman in Tokyo named Kyōko (meaning "apricot girl"). Her two older sisters Momoko and Nashiko ("peach girl" and "pear girl," respectively) have managed to marry the president and executive manager of the company where they were working as secretaries. Their husbands are brothers, too, and have one more brother, who is single. Now, the two couples are trying to arrange a marriage between Kyōko and the youngest brother (Kawaguchi Hiroshi). The young woman and man initially resent this arranged marriage but gradually feel attracted to each other, and the film ends with their wedding. This is another variation of the Cinderella story, in that a girl from a humble family gets redeemed at the end with the arrival of a rich, handsome man.

15. In his seminal *Great Transformation*, Karl Polanyi ([1944] 2001) examined the development of the self-regulating market economy system from the nineteenth century and detailed what it meant for people to sell their labor power in the market as free individuals. Chapter 14, "Market and Man," is especially useful.

16. Michael Raine (2007) has discussed Masumura's critique of Japanese society in detail in his analysis of another Masumura film, *Giants and Toys* (*Kyojin to gangu*, 1958). Raine points out that Masumura was concerned about Japan's "(economic) modernization without (political) modernity" (157).

17. The rival of the Kōza school was the Rōnō school, which regarded post-Restoration Japan as a bourgeois capitalist society and thereby called for a socialist revolution as the next step. These two schools prepared the ideological bases for the Communist and Socialist Parties, respectively, in post-defeat Japan. Germaine Hoston (1990) offers the most thorough discussion of the debate between these two schools available in English. On modernism, or *kindai-shugi*, Hidaka (1964) gives a very informative overview.

18. For a thorough analysis of the intellectual movement in the early postwar years toward bourgeois democracy and the establishment of a modern subject capable of carrying out this project, see Koschmann (1996).

19. This would lead in 1964 to the famous Sumitomo Cement case, in which a woman who had been fired upon her marriage sued the company, demanding that the letter of intent that she had been forced to sign be nullified. In 1966, the Tokyo District Court ruled in the plaintiff's favor. It confirmed equality of the people under the law guaranteed by article 14 of the constitution and the prohibition of any gender-based discrimination that lacked rational reasons under article 90 of the civil code.

20. Jan Bardsley (2014) has detailed how Japanese society in the 1950s imagined the housewife as a symbol of the new era of postwar democracy and prosperity while engaging closely with the American notions of domesticity and gender roles that developed within the Cold War context.

21. For a critical examination of romantic love under capitalist patriarchy, see Ann Ferguson (2018). Her discussion of the affective economy—"the social relations and practices engaged in to meet affective needs such as love and sexuality and to care for children" (40)—shows how romantic love or a "voluntary love partnership" (43) can lead to sexual alienation.

Chapter 3

1. For a detailed analysis of the James Bond series within the sociocultural and political context of contemporary Britain, see also Chapman (2000).

2. *Shūkan Myōjō* had planned to publish this scoop article one week before, but Koizumi Shinzō, a well-known economist in charge of educating the crown prince, asked that publication be postponed. As a replacement, Kajiyama, under the pseudonym Kaji Kensuke, wrote a short, fictional story about a romance between the crown prince and a commoner woman, hinting at the crown prince's choice of Shōda Michiko among numerous candidates

(Kajiyama [1958] 2007). This process is explained in detail in the article that Kajiyama later wrote for *Bungei Shunjū* (Kajiyama [1968] 2007).

3. The literal translation of *keizai shōsetsu* is "economy novel," but in this book, relying on Tamae Prindle (1989), I use "business novels" to highlight the fact that authors within this genre covered a wide variety of industries within the corporate world. Prindle's book is one of very few works in English that have dealt with this enormously popular genre in Japan during high-speed growth. It includes English translations of several short stories by representative authors, including Shiroyama Saburō, Shimizu Ikkō, and Sakaiya Taichi.

4. For example, Masumura Yasuzō's *Giants and Toys* (1958) shows us a fierce advertisement war within the confectionary industry, starring Kawaguchi Hiroshi as a passionate employee eager to boost the sales of the caramel produced by his company, World, and Nozoe Hitomi as a regular young woman transformed into a celebrity for the promotion of World's caramel. The same director's *Black Test Car* (1962) depicts negative campaigns between two automobile companies, Pioneer and Yamato, concerning new sports cars.

5. Watanabe Osamu (2004) provides an overview of the process by which the Ikeda cabinet, in the aftermath of the Security Treaty protest, centered national politics on people's everyday economic lives in an effort to advance social integration of the working masses while at the same time mobilizing every aspect of society (e.g., school education) for the achievement of economic growth.

6. For his Marxist analysis of the history and contemporary structure of the Japanese economy, see also Ōuchi ([1962] 1970, [1963] 1970).

7. Tominaga's (1965) work explains how the theory of industrial society was received and developed in the Japanese context, starting with a discussion of Herbert Spencer, Ferdinand Tönnies, and Émile Durkheim and paying significant attention to *The Stages of Economic Growth* by Rostow (1960) and *Industrialism and Industrial Man* by Clark Kerr, John T. Dunlop, Frederick Harbison, and Charles A. Myers (1960). In contrast, the sociologist Kawamura Nozomu (1967) offers an effective critique pointing out how this theory, introduced to Japan by those aforementioned scholars, serves as an ideology for monopoly capitalism.

8. In Kajiyama's original novel *Shadow Weapon*, the background of the protagonist—named not Katayanagi but Katagiri—is quite different from in the film version. He was born in Shanghai, where his father was working for an intelligence agency. Although he passed the entrance exam for the First Higher School (the predecessor to the College of Arts and Sciences of Tokyo University), he was conscripted and sent to the Philippines during the war. He was captured by the Americans, but Major Walker discovered Katagiri's English skills and used him as an interpreter. After the war, he was

adopted by Walker, who was working for the US Army's Counter Intelligence Corps, and then moved to the United States with him. After graduating from Harvard, he earned a position at the William Burns Detective Agency, where he trained as an industrial spy (Kajiyama 1964). Note that while the novel emphasizes the organizational background of the protagonist, the film represents him as a complete loner who seemed to have built his career as a spy through his own effort.

9. Michael P. Cronin's (2017) work on Osaka is one of the rare studies in the English language to analyze cultural representations of Osaka as a modern city rivaling Tokyo.

10. This 1962 film was the third film adaptation of Hōjō's novel, following 1948 and 1955 versions. The song with the same title sung by Murata Hideo was used as a theme song for the film and sold more than one million records. A sequel was made in 1963. All of this attests to the enormous popularity of this novel in the early postwar years. Sakai Takashi (2011) offers a thorough examination of the life of Sakata Sankichi and the production of the discourse of this *shōgi* player within the context of the formation of modern Osaka.

11. On the history of Senri New Town, see Katayori (1979) and Yamaji (2002).

12. Discover Senri—an organization whose mission is to find and preserve historical sources on Senri New Town—kindly reviewed various images from the film and helped me identify exactly where location shooting was conducted.

13. In 1967, the station was renamed Minami-Senri ("South Senri") as the Hankyū line extended further north and built Kita-Senri ("North Senri") Station as its northern terminal. As for cinematic representations of Senri during the Osaka Expo, see the documentary film directed by Taniguchi Senkichi, *Japan Expo '70* (*Nihon bankoku-haku*, 1971). In Yamada Yōji's *Where Spring Comes Late* (*Kazoku*, 1970), the Kazami family visits the Expo on their migration from Nagasaki to Hokkaido. A more obscure example is Torii Motohiro's *Three Female Bees* (*Sanbiki no mesu-bachi*, 1970), a comedy about three delinquent women set at the Expo.

14. The Kintetsu's Nara line was extended further west to Namba in 1970 and connected to the Hanshin line for Kobe through Namba in 2009, but its Osaka line still uses Uehonmachi as its terminal. Although the station no longer enjoys the same bustling atmosphere as in the past, its bay platforms with eight tracks—six on the ground level and two underground—certainly allow visitors to extend their imagination back to the days when it functioned as one of the major terminals in the city. On the history of Kintetsu Railway, see Kinki Nihon Tetsudō Kabushiki-gaisha (1960, 2010).

15. On the history of Uemachi Daichi, see Ōtemon Gakuin Daigaku Uemachigaku Purojekuto (2015).

Chapter 4

1. The literal translation of the title would be *Evening Mist, Thank You Again for Tonight*, but because Nikkatsu instead uses *A Warm Misty Night* on their official website, I also use this title in this book.

2. Matsumoto Taira entered Nikkatsu in 1954 as a member of the art division. He held the positions of director of the union at the studio and director of the central executive committee for the union and then served as a board member for the company. His *Nikkatsu Shōwa seinshunki* is a rare account of Nikkatsu's financial struggle and the pressing issue of capital-labor relations in the film industry in the 1960s.

3. *The Penguin Encyclopedia of Popular Music* defines *mood music* as a "term loosely meaning background music" in the 1950s and explains that it "lived on in the USA in the form of insipid piped-in music in pretentious restaurants" and that "it used mostly strings but the best had what amounted to a symphony orchestra playing original arrangements of good songs, sometimes original tunes" (Clarke 1990, 820).

4. There are many studies on the foreign settlements in these port cities. As for Yokohama, see Yokohama Kaikō Shiryōkan and Yokohama Kyoryūchi Kenkyūkai (1996). As for Kobe, see Kōbe Gaikokujin Kyoryūchi Kenkyūkai (2005).

5. On the history of Yokohama's Chinese community and Chinatown, see Han (2014), who discusses the construction of Chinese residents' identity from the 1890s to the 1970s in relation to both China and Yokohama.

6. The Yokohama Bar Association investigated so-called "base problems," or *kichi mondai*, in Kanagawa Prefecture from legal perspectives and published a thorough report in the 1980s. See Yokohama Bengoshikai (1989).

7. Plenary session, no. 32, House of Representatives, Forty-Eighth Diet, April 15, 1965; plenary session, no. 15, House of Councilors, Forty-Eighth Diet, April 21, 1965. All the proceedings since the First Diet in 1947 under the Constitution of Japan are available at https://kokkai.ndl.go.jp.

8. *Watashi wa nani o hakonda no ka: Moto LST norikumiin ga mitsumeru Betonamu sensō*, made by NHK and aired October 11, 2015, is a rare documentary program that delves into this issue. According to this program, a total of about 1,400 Japanese men worked as crewmembers for the American LSTs.

9. The house band for Golden Cup attracted publicity, debuted in 1967 as the Golden Cups with the single record "Jezebel, My Love" ("Itoshi

no Jezebel") and successfully transformed into a nationally prominent "Group Sounds" band ("Densetsu no bā, kagayaki ima mo" 2014). On the relation between American bases and popular music, see Tsukada (2014). The genre of Group Sounds will be discussed in chapter 5.

10. On the same page, Russell further argues that "the normalcy of Caucasian whiteness" is accepted in Japan, pointing out that Japanese casts of American and European plays, such as *King Lear* and *A Streetcar Named Desire*, do not perform in whiteface. He states, "The whiteness of the characters they perform is invisible, unremarked, and ultimately unremarkable."

11. An *Asahi* newspaper article in 1952 also mentions a survey conducted by the Ministry of Health and Welfare around the same time. According to this survey, there were 5,013 mixed-race children nationwide. This number was far smaller than expected. The manager of the Elizabeth Saunders Home, an orphanage in Kanagawa, questioned the accuracy of the data, pointing out that the number included only those reported by Japanese midwives and gynecologists ("Konketsuji wa 5,013-nin" 1952).

12. Imai Tadashi's *Kiku and Isamu* (*Kiku to Isamu*, 1959) is a powerful film that sought to raise awareness of this issue through the portrayal of the racial and socioeconomic struggles of two siblings born to a Japanese mother and an African American GI and raised by their Japanese grandmother in a small village in Aizu. Takahashi Emiko and Okunoyama George, who played Kiku and Isamu respectively, were biracial children with no previous acting experience.

13. Later, Jō Akira successfully transitioned to the world of show business as a musician and actor. For example, he appeared in *Proof of the Man* (*Ningen no shōmei*, 1977), based on Morimura Seiichi's novel, as Johnny Heyward, a mixed-race man who comes to Japan from the United States looking for his Japanese mother. He also sang the theme song for this film, also called "Proof of the Man."

14. For a detailed analysis of Imamura's *Pigs and Battleships*, see Kitamura (2019). He explains the significance of this film in particular as well as the director's oeuvre broadly in relation to the Anpo protest, the politics of American bases, and anti-Americanism in postwar Japan.

15. It is not easy to determine exactly how much Japan earned in the war-related economy because of the different criteria that agencies use in their calculations. Michael Schaller, relying on data provided by the Ministry of International Trade and Industry, points out that Japan "earned at least $7 billion in 'extra' sales of goods and services related to Vietnam," including $1.77 billion in direct procurement, $2.83 billion in indirect procurement, and $2 billion in "additional exports to the United States made possible by the war" (1997, 198–99). See also Havens (1987, 92–97) and Shiomi et al. (1969, 438–40). Andō (1967) provides a comprehensive view of the procure-

ment boom in this period. Nihon Heiwa Iinkai (1968, 87–120) also discusses this issue extensively in one chapter.

16. In the Japanese original, Akiko also uses the English term *negro*, which is pronounced in a Japanese way: "niguro." Note that, as in the United States in the 1960s, in Japan at the time this word did not carry offensive or derogatory connotations.

17. Peter Kunze (2014) critiques the common reading of *Casablanca* that underlines romance between Rick and Ilsa and offers an alternative reading focusing on male friendship, homosocial interaction, and triangular relation: Rick, Ilsa, and Sam; Rick, Ilsa, and Victor; and Rick, Ilsa, and Renault.

18. On cultural representations of Korean-Japanese intimacy in the imperial era, see Kim (2020). In chapter 2, Kim discusses how the wedding between Un and Masako stimulated the proliferation of the discourse of intermarriage in the Korean media.

19. On Japan's economic relations with Southeast Asia, see Mizuno et al. (2018). On the historical transformations of the Japanese views of Asia, see Kobayashi Hideo (2012).

20. Mika Ko offers a close reading of *Sing a Song of Sex*. In Taniyama Takako's repeated remark about the shared origin of the Japanese and Koreans and Kaneko Sachiko's simultaneous silence, Ko (2020, 487) observes progressive intellectuals and activists' appropriation of the voice of *zainichi* Koreans and attempt to "use minority groups as an alibi to underwrite their political claims."

Chapter 5

1. On the detailed mechanism of this recession, see Nakamura Takafusa (1995, 205–18).

2. Michael Bourdaghs (2012) examines the development of Japanese popular music as forms of ideologies within the post–World War II geopolitical context. The book's chapter 4 discusses in detail Group Sounds music in relation to rebellious youth culture and the ideology of rock music that opposed commercialism and elitism in the late 1960s. In his book on Japanese rock 'n' roll music, Julian Cope (2008) also has one chapter on this genre (chap. 4).

3. Watanabe Osamu (2004) argues that the oil-crisis recession enabled the reinforcement of a "corporate-dominated society," or *kigyō shakai* in postwar Japan. As decisive factors, he points to not only the presence of cooperative labor unions but also the enhancement of the subcontracting of medium- and small-sized companies by large companies and the introduction of the corporate principle of competition into the public sector.

4. On the history of *roman poruno*, see Matsushima (2000). A 1972 roundtable discussion among three Nikkatsu directors—Kumashiro, Kurahara Koretsugu, and Yamaguchi Seiichirō—allows us to understand how these young directors took the imposition of this new genre from the Nikkatsu management as an opportunity to explore such issues as filmmaking within the corporate system dominated by market principles, sex as a way to explore human desire broadly, and freedom of expression. See Kumashiro et al. (1972).

5. In fact, during her final strip show before retirement in 1972, Ichijō was arrested by the Osaka Prefectural Police for violation of the Anti-Obscenity Law, her ninth arrest. When the film was released, she was in the midst of the trial. She appealed the case to the Supreme Court to dispute the definition of *obscenity* but lost and was jailed for a month. On this trial and its legal significance, see Sugiura (1981). On the cultural meanings of Ichijō Sayuri's performance, see Komada (1981). Sugiura was a member of defense team for Ichijō. Komada, as an author who wrote a novel on her (*Ichijō Sayuri no sei*; Komada 1971), gave testimony at the trial, arguing against the prosecutor, who saw her performance simply as a form of obscenity.

6. Marx ([1867] 1990) extensively discusses the ways capitalist accumulation produces and necessitates a relative surplus population in chapter 25 of *Capital*. Although the term *precariousness* is often used to refer to workers' conditions under the current neoliberal economic structure prevalent worldwide, I want to emphasize that this is by no means a new phenomenon but intrinsic to the system of market economy itself. In this sense, I agree with Ken Kawashima (2009), who has examined Korean migrant workers' struggle against the contingency of exchange in the labor market in interwar Japan. He writes, "The contemporary proliferation, maintenance, and exploitation of contingent labor should not blind us to the fact that contingent labor and the inexorable contingency inherent to the commodification of labor power are endemic to capitalist commodity economies, and that that has been true since the inception of industrial capital" (Ken Kawashima 2009, 7).

7. With the 1973 oil crisis as a turning point, the LDP initiated the revision of its promotion of the welfare state. Later in that decade, it established the new project of "Japanese-style welfare society," or *Nihon-gata fukushi shakai*, which deemphasized state responsibility for popular welfare and advocated instead self-help within family and community as a Japanese tradition. See Jiyū Minshutō (1979).

8. Here, we can recall Ozu Yasujirō's *Tokyo Twilight* (1957), mentioned in chapter 2. At the end of this film, Kikuko (Yamada Isuzu), heartbroken by the death of one of her daughters, leaves Tokyo for Hokkaido with her current husband. Their departure is treated as if it were a permanent farewell to Tokyo. Similarly, in Naruse's *Late Chrysanthemums* (1954), the son of Hosokawa Chikako's character, Tamae, also moves to Hokkaido for a new

job at the end of the film, and Tamae expresses her fear that she will never be able to see him again. These clearly demonstrate the peripheral position of Hokkaido within the national imaginary and the physical as well as psychological distance that Tokyo urbanites felt from this northern prefecture in 1950s Japan.

9. On another occasion, Katō gave a different explanation of her encounter with the song. According to this version, she first heard this song when political activist Fujimoto Toshio, then her boyfriend and later her husband, sang it for her on a date ("Shiretoko ryojō, Katō Tokiko-san" 2004).

10. For a detailed account of PR for the campaign, see Fujioka Wakao (1972). An employee at Dentsū, Fujioka presided over the project team dedicated to this campaign. Analyzing this campaign, Marilyn Ivy (1995, 34) demonstrates how "a generation's desire to escape to its origins" led to the cultural production of images of an authentic, discoverable Japan. Yoshikuni Igarashi (2021, chap. 4) examines the same campaign in relation to the work of the comic artist Tsuge Yoshiharu and argues that both mobilized the concept of nostalgia to explore the meanings of travel in an age of high mass consumption, though they greatly differed in the appraisal of the potential of tourism to offer an authentic experience.

11. Here are the original lyrics in Japanese:

Tabi no nasake ka, nomu hodo ni samayoi
Hama ni dete mireba tsuki wa teru nami no ue
Koyoi koso kimi o dakishimen to
Iwakage ni yoreba pirka ga warau

"Pirka" in the fourth line means "beautiful" or "pretty" in the Ainu language, which I have translated as a "pretty girl."

12. The original lyrics are as follows:

Jin jin jin jin, chi ga jin jin
Ume mo sakura mo hokorobite
Jin jin jin jin, chi ga jin jin
Hakoiri-musume wa nemure nai

13. *The Annual Report on the Family Income and Expenditure Survey* (*Kakei chōsa nenpō*) published by the Prime Minister's Office used the term "standard family" for the first time in 1969. It defined it as a nuclear family with an employed male head of household, a stay-at-home wife, and two unmarried children and used it as a model for the examination of income, savings, and consumption in Japanese society. Meanwhile, households engaged in agriculture (with 0.3 hectares of land or more in Hokkaido and 0.1 hectares of

land or more in the rest), forestry, and fishery; single-person households; and households with foreigners were deemed "inadequate" (*futekikaku*) households and excluded from the survey. The report translates *hyōjun kazoku* as "typical family" (35), but *hyōjun* in Japanese has not simply descriptive but prescriptive implications, and therefore I use "standard" instead. See Sōrifu Tōkeikyoku (1971).

Bibliography

Abe Shinzō. 2006. *Utsukushii kuni e*. Tokyo: Bungei Shunjū.
Agawa Hiroyuki, ed. 1970. *Ōzora o kakeru*. Vol. 7 of *Gendai no bōken*. Tokyo: Bungei Shunjū.
Althusser, Louis. (1970) 2001. "Ideology and Ideological State Apparatuses: Notes towards an Investigation." In *Lenin and Philosophy and Other Essays*, by Louis Althusser, translated by Ben Brewster, 85–126. New York: Monthly Review Press.
Amino Yoshihiko. (1978) 1996. *Muen, kugai, raku: Nihon chūsei no jiyū to heiwa*. Tokyo: Heibonsha.
Anderson, David, Hiroyuki Shimizu, and Chris Campbell. 2016. "Insights on How Museum Objects Mediate Recall of Nostalgic Life Episodes at a Shōwa Era Museum in Japan." *Curator: Museum Journal* 59 (1): 5–26.
Andō Shinzō. 1967. *Betonamu tokuju*. Tokyo: San'ichi Shobō.
Aoyagi Machiko, Hirano Ichirō, and Nagasawa Kazutoshi. 1968. *Minami-Taiheiyō no ōkoku Tonga, Iran/Afugan tankenki, Nepāru tanken kikō*. Vol. 4 of *Hikyō tanken*. Tokyo: Sannō Shobō.
"Aozora-musume roke hōkoku." 1957. *Myōjō* 6 (13): 76–77.
Appy, Christopher G. *Working-Class War: American Combat Soldiers and Vietnam*. 1993. Chapel Hill: University of North Carolina Press.
Ariyoshi Sawako. (1959) 2006. *Ki-no-kawa*. Tokyo: Shinchōsha.
"Ashidori mo karuku: Sendai kara chūsotsu no shūdan shūshoku daiichijin." 1957. *Asahi shimbun*, March 20, 1957, 3.
Avenell, Simon Andrew. 2010. *Making Japanese Citizens: Civil Society and the Mythology of the* Shimin *in Postwar Japan*. Berkeley: University of California Press.
Baran, Paul A., and Paul M. Sweezy. 1966. *Monopoly Capital: An Essay on the American Economic and Social Order*. New York: Monthly Review Press.
Bardsley, Jan. 2014. *Women and Democracy in Cold War Japan*. SOAS Studies in Modern and Contemporary Japan. London: Bloomsbury Academic.

"Bareta sangyō supai." 1961. *Shūkan Yomiuri* 20 (33): 19.
"Bōtō wa kyōran jōtai." 1974. *Asahi shimbun*, January 12, 1974, 1. Evening edition.
Bourdaghs, Michael K. 2012. *Sayonara Amerika, Sayonara Nippon: A Geopolitical Prehistory of J-Pop*. New York: Columbia University Press.
Bourdieu, Pierre. 1986. "The Forms of Capital." Translated by Richard Nice. In *Handbook of Theory and Research for the Sociology of Education*, edited by John G. Richardson, 241–58. Westport, CT: Greenwood Press.
Bresnan, John, ed. 1986. *Crisis in the Philippines: The Marcos Era and Beyond*. Princeton, NJ: Princeton University Press.
Cawelti, John G., and Bruce A. Rosenberg. 1987. *The Spy Story*. Chicago: University of Chicago Press.
Celoza, Albert F. 1997. *Ferdinand Marcos and the Philippines*. Westport, CT: Prager.
Chapman, James. 2000. *License to Thrill: A Cultural History of the James Bond Films*. New York: Columbia University Press.
Chiba Tetsuya and Kajiwara Ikki. (1968) 2000. *Ashita no Jō*. Vol. 1. Tokyo: Kōdansha.
"Chikayori-gatai yashinsaku: Keizai hakusho kaisetsu." 1956. *Yomiuri shimbun*, July 17, 1956, 3.
Chiyodaku. 1960. *Chiyodakushi*. Ge (vol. 3). Tokyo: Chiyoda-ku.
Clarke, Donald, ed. 1990. *The Penguin Encyclopedia of Popular Music*. London: Penguin Books.
Coates, Jennifer. 2016. *Making Icons: Repetition and the Female Image in Japanese Cinema, 1945–1964*. Hong Kong: Hong Kong University Press.
Cope, Julian. 2008. *Japrocksampler: How the Post-War Japanese Blew Their Minds on Rock'n'Roll*. London: Bloomsbury.
Cronin, Michael P. 2017. *Osaka Modern: The City in the Japanese Imaginary*. Cambridge, MA: Harvard University Asia Center.
Cumings, Bruce. 1993. "Japan's Position in the World System." In *Postwar Japan as History*, edited by Andrew Gordon, 34–63. Berkeley: University of California Press.
Daum, Andreas W., Lloyd C. Gardner, and Wilfried Mausbach, eds. 2003. *America, the Vietnam War, and the World: Comparative and International Perspectives*. Cambridge: German Historical Institute / Cambridge University Press.
Dazai Osamu. (1947) 2003. *Shayō*. Tokyo: Shinchōsha.
Denning, Michael. 1987. *Cover Stories: Narrative and Ideology in the British Spy Thriller*. London: Routledge / Kegan Paul.
"Densetsu no bā, kagayaki ima mo." 2014. *Asashi shimbun*, November 26, 2014, 11. Evening edition.
Donzelot, Jacques. 1991. "The Mobilization of Society." In *The Foucault Effect: Studies in Governmentality, with Two Lectures by and an Interview with Michel Foucault*, edited by Graham Burchell, Colin Gordon, and Peter Miller, 169–79. Chicago: University of Chicago Press.

Dyer, Richard. 1992. *Stars*. London: British Film Institute.
———. 2004. *Heavenly Bodies: Film Stars and Society*. London: Routledge.
Dower, John W. 1999. *Embracing Defeat: Japan in the Wake of World War II*. New York: W. W. Norton.
Elias, Norbert, and Eric Dunning. 1986. *Quest for Excitement: Sport and Leisure in the Civilizing Process*. Oxford: Basil Blackwell.
Enomoto, Satoru, and Matsuda Shūji. 2012. "Kōkoku sangyō no hatten to kōkoku dairiten." *Kokusaigaku kenkyū* 1:21–38.
Escobar, Arturo. 2011. *Encoutering Development: The Making and Unmaking of the Third Word*. Princeton, NJ: Princeton University Press.
Ezaki Mio, Nogami Tatsuo, and Ishimori Fumio. 1967. *Yogiri yo kon'ya mo arigatō*. Tokyo: Nikkatsu. Screenplay.
Ferguson, Ann. 2018. "Alienation in Love: Is Mutual Love the Solution?" In *Feminism and the Power of Love: Interdisciplinary Interventions*, edited by Anna García-Andrade, Lena Gunnarsson, and Anna G. Jónasdóttir, 36–54. New York: Routledge.
Ferro, Marc. (1977) 1988. *Cinema and History*. Translated by Naomi Greene. Detroit: Wayne State University Press.
Forsberg, Aaron. 2000. *America and the Japanese Miracle: The Cold War Context of Japan's Postwar Economic Revival, 1950–1960*. Chapel Hill: University of North Carolina Press.
Foucault, Michel. (1967) 2008. "Of Other Spaces." In *Heterotopia and the City: Public Space in Postcivil Society*, edited by Michiel Dahaene and Lieven De Cauter, 13–29. New York: Routledge.
"Frank Nagai no miryoku: Tokai no mūdo o sasayaku teion kashu." 1958. *Fujin kurabu* 39 (4): 146–49.
Frühstück, Sabine. 2003. *Colonizing Sex: Sexology and Social Control in Modern Japan*. Berkeley: University of California Press.
Fujime Yuki. 1997. *Sei no rekishigaku: Kōshō seido/dataizai taisei kara baishun bōshihō/yūsei hogohō taisei e*. Tokyo: Fuji Shuppan.
Fujioka Wakao. 1972. *Kareinaru shuppatsu: Disucabā Japan*. Tokyo: Mainichi Shimbunsha.
Fujitani, Takashi. 1996. *Splendid Monarchy: Power and Pageantry in Modern Japan*. Berkeley: University of California Press.
Fukada Hisaya, ed. 1970. *Higeki no yama, eikō no yama*. Vol. 2 of *Gendai no bōken*. Tokyo: Bungei Shunjū.
Fukuoka Tsubasa. 1973. "Sugawara Bunta, Takahashi Hideki, Hagiwara Ken'ichi no sannin ni kiku." *Kinema junpō* 612:114–17.
———. 1975. "Hagiwara Ken'ichi, jiko to eiga ni tsuite no subete o kataru." *Kinema junpō* 652:111–15.
Furuya Tatsuo. 1963. *Honkon gurūpu: Nihon o nerau gaikoku sangyō supai no soshiki*. Tokyo: Kōbunsha.
Fuse Katsuhiko. 2006. *Shōwa 33-nen*. Tokyo: Chikuma Shobō.

———. 2007. "'Shōwa wa yokatta' shindorōmu no kyoshoku." *Ekonomisuto* 85 (60): 84–85.
Garon, Sheldon. 1999. *Molding Japanese Minds: The State in Everyday Life*. Princeton, NJ: Princeton University Press.
Genji Keita. (1951) 1979. *Santō jūyaku*. Tokyo: Shinchōsha.
———. (1957) 1980. *Aozora musume*. Tokyo: Kōndansha.
———. (1959) 2016. *Saikō shukun fujin*. Tokyo: Chikuma Shobō.
Giddens, Anthony. (1981) 1995. *A Contemporary Critique of Historical Materialism*. 2nd ed. New York: Palgrave Macmillan.
———. 1987. *The Nation-State and Violence*. Vol. 2 of *A Contemporary Critique of Historical Materialism*. Berkeley: University of California Press.
———. 1991. *Modernity and Self-Identity: Self and Society in the Late Modern Age*. Stanford, CA: Stanford Univerity Press.
González, Irene. 2014. "Wakao Ayako and the Post-war Japanese Studio System: Celebrity and Performer." *Journal of Japanese and Korean Cinema* 6 (1): 39–54.
Gordon, Andrew. 1992. *Labor and Imperial Democracy in Prewar Japan*. Berkeley: University of California Press.
———. 1993. "Contests for the Workplace." In *Postwar Japan as History*, edited by Andrew Gordon, 373–94. Berkeley: University of California Press.
———. 1998. *The Wages of Affluence: Labor and Management in Postwar Japan*. Cambridge, MA: Harvard University Press.
Hagiwara Ken'ichi. 2008. *Shōken*. Tokyo: Kōdansha.
Hagiwara Ken'ichi and Suga Hidemi. 2010. *Nihon eiga (kantoku/haiȳu) ron: Kurosawa Akira, Kumashiro Tatsumi, soshite ōku no meikantoku/meiȳutachi no sugao*. Tokyo: Wani Bukkusu.
Hall, John Whitney. 1965. "Changing Conceptions of the Modernization of Japan." In *Changing Japanese Attitudes toward Modernization*, edited by Marius B. Jansen, 7–41. Princeton, NJ: Princeton University Press.
Hall, Stuart. 1981. "Notes on Deconstructing 'the Popular.'" In *People's History and Socialist Theory*, edited by Raphael Samuel, 227–40. London: Routledge / Kegan Paul.
———. 1982. "The Rediscovery of 'Ideology': Return of the Repressed in Media Studies." In *Culture, Society and the Media*, edited by Michael Gurevitch, Tony Bennett, James Curran, and Janet Woollacott, 52–86. London: Routledge.
Han, Eric. 2014. *Rise of a Japanese Chinatown: Yokohama, 1894–1972*. Cambridge, MA: Harvard University Press.
Hanamori Yasuji. 1956. "Keizai hakusho o yonde." *Asahi shimbun*, July 17, 1956, 4.
Hara Takeshi. 1998. *"Minto" Ōsaka tai "Teito" Tōkyō: Shisō to shite no Kansai shitetsu*. Tokyo: Kōdansha.

Harada Masahiko. 2018. *"Waga michi": Faitingu Harada*. Tokyo: Supōtsu Nippon Shimbunsha.
Harootunian, Harry D. 1993. "America's Japan / Japan's Japan." In *Japan in the World*, edited by Masao Miyoshi and H. D. Harootunian, 196–219. Durham, NC: Duke University Press.
———. 2000. *Overcome by Modernity: History, Culture, and Community in Interwar Japan*. Princeton, NJ: Princeton University Press.
Harvey, David. 1990. *The Condition of Postmodernity: An Enquiry into the Origins of Cultural Change*. Cambridge: Blackwell.
———. 2001. "Globalization and the 'Spatial Fix.'" *Geographische Revue* 3 (2): 23–30.
———. 2003a. "The Fetish of Technology: Causes and Consequences." *Macalester International* 13 (1), article 7. https://digitalcommons.macalester.edu/macintl/vol13/iss1/7.
———. 2003b. *The New Imperialism*. Oxford: Oxford University Press.
———. 2014. *Seventeen Contradictions and the End of Capitalism*. Oxford: Oxford University Press.
Havens, Thomas R. H. 1987. *Fire across the Sea: The Vietnam War and Japan 1965–1975*. Princeton, NJ: Princeton University Press.
Hayashi Fumiko. (1948–49) 1992. *Bangiku / Suisen / Shirasagi*. Tokyo: Kōdansha.
Hayden, Dolores. 1997. *The Power of Place: Urban Landscapes as Public History*. Cambridge, MA: MIT Press.
Hidaka Rokurō. 1964. "Sengo no 'kindai shugi.'" In *Kindai shugi*, edited by Hidaka Rokurō, 7–52. Gendai Nihon shisō taikei 34. Tokyo: Chikuma Shobō.
Higuchi Ichiyō. (1894–96) 2003. *Nigorie / Takekurabe*. Tokyo: Shinchōsha.
Hirano, Katsuya. 2014. "The Dialectic of Laughter and Tosaka's Critical Theory." In *Tosaka Jun: A Critical Reader*, edited by Ken C. Kawashima, Fabian Schäfer, and Robert Stolz, 176–93. Ithaca, NY: Cornell University Press.
Hitachi Seisakusho. 2010. *Kaitakushatachi no chōsen: Hitachi 100-nen no ayumi*. Tokyo: Hitachi Seisakusho.
Hopson, Nathan. 2017. *Ennobling Japan's Savage Northeast: Tōhoku as Postwar Thought, 1945–2011*. Cambridge, MA: Harvard University Asia Center.
Hoston, Germaine A. 1990. *Marxism and the Crisis of Development in Prewar Japan*. Princeton, NJ: Princeton University Press.
Ichikawa Kōichi. 2010. "Shōwa 30-nendai wa dō katarareta ka: 'Shōwa 30-nendai būmu' ni tsuite no oboegaki." *Masu komyunikēshon kenkyū* 76:7–22.
Ienaga Saburō. (1968) 2002. *Taiheiyō sensō*. Tokyo: Iwanami Shoten.
Igarashi, Yoshikuni. 2000. *Bodies of Memory: Narratives of War in Postwar Japanese Culture, 1945–1970*. Princeton, NJ: Princeton University Press.

———. 2021. *Japan, 1972: Visions of Masculinity in an Age of Mass Consumerism*. New York: Columbia University Press.
Ikeda Shin'ichi. 1975. "Ishizaka Kōji to Hagiwara Ken'ichi." *Gendai no me* 16 (2): 136–43.
Ishihara Shintarō. (1955) 2011. *Taiyō no kisetsu*. Tokyo: Shinchōsha.
———. (1956) 1980. *Kurutta kajitsu*. Tokyo: Kadokawa Shoten.
———, ed. 1970. *Sekai no kaiyō ni idomu*. Vol. 3 of *Gendai no bōken*. Tokyo: Bungei Shunjū.
Ishikawa Tatsuzō. 1968. *Seishun no satetsu*. Tokyo: Shinchōsha.
Isoda Tsutomu. 2001. *Kawashima Yūzō: Ranchō no bigaku*. Tokyo: Wides Shuppan.
Itokawa Hideo, ed. 1970. *Uchū e no tōi michi*. Vol. 4 of *Gendai no bōken*. Tokyo: Bungei Shunjū.
Ivy, Marilyn. 1995. *Discourses of the Vanishing: Modernity, Phantasm, Japan*. Chicago: University of Chicago Press.
Iwase Akira. 2006. *"Gekkyū hyakuen" sararīman: Senzen Nihon no "heiwa" na seikatsu*. Tokyo: Kōdansha.
Izumi Seiichi, ed. 1970. *Ushinawareta bunmei o motomete*. Vol. 8 of *Gendai no bōken*. Tokyo: Bungei Shunjū.
Jichi Daijin Kanbō Kikakushitsu. 1972. *Kaso chiiki taisaku kinkyū sochihō no kaisetsu*. Tokyo: Dai-Ichi Hōki.
Jinnai Hidenobu. 1985. *Tōkyō no kūkan jinruigaku*. Tokyo: Chikuma Shobō.
———. 1995. *Tokyo: A Spatial Anthropology*. Translated by Kimiko Nishimura. Berkeley: University of California Press.
Jiyū Minshutō [Liberal Democratic Party]. 1966. *Jiyū minshutō jūnen no ayumi*. Tokyo: Jiyū Minshutō.
———. 1979. *Nihon-gata fukushi shakai*. Jiyū Minshutō kenkyū sōsho 8. Tokyo: Jiyū Minshutō Kōhō Iinkai Shuppankyoku.
———. 2006. *Jiyū Minshutō gojūnenshi*. 2 vols. Tokyo: Jiyū Minshutō.
"Jochū-san no kai, Kikōkai." 1955. *New Age* 7 (10): 36–41.
Jones, Phil, and James Evans. 2012. "Rescue Geography: Place Making, Affect and Regeneration." *Urban Studies* 49 (11): 2315–30.
Johnson, Chalmers. 1982. *MITI and the Japanese Miracle: The Growth of Industrial Policy, 1925–1975*. Stanford, CA: Stanford University Press.
Kaikō Takeshi and Nosaka Akiyuki. 1968. "Warera yakeato/yamiichi-ha." *Bungakukai* 22 (12): 146–58.
Kajiyama Toshiyuki. 1958. "Kōtaishi-hi naitei!? Shōda Michiko-san." *Shūkan Myōjō* 1 (18): 8–12.
———. (1958) 2007. "Wadai shōsetu: Kōtaishi no koi." In *Rupo sengo ōdan: Toppu-ya wa mita*, 16–31. Tokyo: Iwanami Shoten.
———. 1962a. *Kuro no shisōsha*. Tokyo: Kōbunsha.

———. 1962b. *Akai daiya*. Jō (vol. 1). Tokyo: Shūeisha.
———. 1963a. *Akai daiya*. Ge (vol. 2). Tokyo: Shūeisha.
———. 1963b. *Yume no chōtokkyū*. Tokyo: Kadokawa Shoten.
———. 1963c. "Sangyō supai." In *Kigyō kyōsō*, 247–60. Shin-bijinesuman kōza 2. Tokyo: Chikuma Shobō.
———. 1964. *Kage no kyōki*. Tokyo: Kōdansha.
———. (1968) 2007. "Kōtaishi-hi sukūpu no ki." In *Rupo sengo ōdan: Toppu-ya wa mita*, 1–15. Tokyo: Iwanami Shoten.
Kajiyama Toshiyuki Kinen Jigyō Iinkai. 2007. *Botsugo 33-nen kinen jigyō: Jidai o sakidori shita sakka Kajiyama Toshiyuki o ima minaosu*. Hiroshima: Chūgoku Shimbunsha.
Kamata Satoshi. (1973) 1983. *Jidōsha zetsubō kōjō: Aru kisetsukō no nikki*. Tokyo: Kōdansha.
Kamion'yu Takashi. 1975a. *Sahara ni kaketa seishun: Kamion'yu Takashi no shuki*. Tokyo: Jiji Tsūshinsha.
———. 1975b. *Sahara ni shisu: Kamion'yu Takashi no isshō*. Tokyo: Jiji Tsūshinsha.
Kamura Masamitsu. 1974. "Nihonjin tanken: Hagiwara Ken'ichi." *Shūkan posuto* 6 (36): 185–87.
Kase Kazutoshi. 1997. *Shūdan shūshoku no jidai: Kōdo seichō no ninaitetachi*. Tokyo: Aoki Shoten.
Katagiri Shinji. 2007. "'Shōwa būmu' no kyōshū." *Ekonomisuto* 85 (60): 77–81.
Katayori Toshihide. 1979. *Senri Nyū Taun no kenkyū: Keikaku-teki toshi kensetsu no kiseki, sono gijutsu to shisō*. Tokyo: Sanpō Shuppan.
Katō Tokiko. (1971) 1994. *Nihon aikashū: Shiretoko ryojō*. Tokyo: Polydor. Compact disc.
Kawabata Yasunari. (1927) 2003. *Izu no odoriko*. Tokyo: Shinchōsa.
Kawakita Jirō, ed. 1970. *Mikai no tochi no buzoku*. Vol. 6 of *Gendai no bōken*. Tokyo: Bungei Shunjū.
Kawamura Nozomu. 1967. "'Sangyō shakai'-ron to 'marukusu shugi shakai-gaku': Shakaigaku no bun'ya ni okeru tōmen suru futatsu no mondai." *Nihon no kagakusha* 1 (6): 24–31.
Kawanishi Hidemichi. 2001. *Tōhoku: Tsukurareta ikyō*. Tokyo: Chūō Kōron Shinsha.
———. 2007. *Zoku Tōhoku: Ikyō to genkyō no aida*. Tokyo: Chūō Kōron Shinsha.
Kawashima Kurabu, ed. 2014. *Kantoku Kawashima Yūzō: Shōchiku jidai*. Tokyo: Wides Shuppan.
———. 2018. *Gizen e no chōsen: Eiga kantoku Kawashima Yūzō*. Tokyo: Wides Shuppan.
Kawashima, Ken C. 2009. *Proletarian Gamble: Korean Workers in Interwar Japan*. Durham, NC: Duke University Press.

Kawashima Takeyoshi. (1948) 2000. *Nihon shakai no kazokuteki kōsei*. Tokyo: Iwanami Shoten.
Kayaoğlu, Turan. 2010. *Legal Imperialism: Sovereignty and Extraterritoriality in Japan, the Ottoman Empire, and China*. Cambridge: Cambridge University Press.
Kazami Takehide, Suzuki Keiko, and Fujki Takane. 1967. *Hitokui jinshu no kuni, Kirimanjaro no yuki, Indio no hikyō*. Vol. 1 of *Hikyō tanken*. Tokyo: Sannō Shobō.
Keizai Kikakuchō [Economic Planning Agency]. 1956. *Keizai hakusho*. Shōwa 31-nendo. Tokyo: Shiseidō.
———. 1957. *Keizai hakusho*. Shōwa 32-nendo. Tokyo: Shiseidō.
———. 1960. *Keizai hakusho*. Shōwa 35-nendo. Tokyo: Ōkurashō Insatsukyoku.
———. 1997. *Sengo Nihon keizai no kiseki: Keizai Kikakuchō 50-nenshi*. Tokyo: Keizai Kikakuchō.
Kerr, Clark, John T. Dunlop, Frederick Harbison, and Charles A. Myers. 1960. *Industrialism and Industrial Man: The Problems of Labor and Management in Economic Growth*. Cambridge, MA: Harvard University Press.
Kikuchi Kan. (1920) 2002. *Shinju-fujin*. Tokyo: Bungei Shunjū.
Kim, Su Yun. 2020. *Imperial Romance: Fictions of Colonial Intimacy in Korea, 1905–1945*. Ithaca, NY: Cornell University Press.
Kimura Bunpei. 1963. *Kaisha tai kaisha: Kigyō shihai kono kyōfu no bōryaku*. Tokyo: Seishun Shuppan.
Kinki Nihon Tetsudō Kabushiki-gaisha. 1960. *Kinki Nihon Tetesudō 50-nen no ayumi*. Osaka: Kinki Nihon Tetsudō Kabushiki-gaisha.
———. 2010. *Kinki Nihon Tetsudō 100-nen no ayumi: 1910–2010*. Osaka: Kinki Nihon Tetsudō Kabushiki-gaisha.
"Kinkyū daitokushū, 74 kyōfu no mainasu seichō." 1974. *Sandē Mainichi* 53 (1): 12–16.
Kitamura, Hiroshi. 2019. "Confronting America: *Pigs and Battleships* and the Politics of US Bases in Postwar Japan." In *Killers, Clients and Kindred Spirits: The Taboo Cinema of Shohei Imamura*, edited by Lindsay Coleman and David Desser, 41–55. Edinburgh: Edinburgh University Press.
Ko, Mika. 2020. "Minority Culture: Whose Song Is It? Korean and Women's Voice in Ōshima Nagisa's *Sing a Song of Sex* (1967)." In *The Japanese Cinema Book*, edited by Hideaki Fujiki and Alastair Phillips, 479–88. London: British Film Institute.
Kobayashi Daiji, Mochizuki Noboru, and Ishizaka Kinji. 1967. *Hadakazoku Gabion, Onborogō bōkenki, dōran no Kongo o iku*. Vol. 2 of *Hikyō tanken*. Tokyo: Sannō Shobō.
Kobayashi Hideo. 2004. *Teikoku Nihon to sōryokusen taisei*. Tokyo: Yūshisha.
———. 2012. *Nihonjin no Ajia-kan no hensen: Mantetsu chōsabu kara kaigai kigyō shinshutsu made*. Tokyo: Bensei Shuppan.

Kōbe Gaikokujin Kyoryūchi Kenkyūkai. 2005. *Kōbe to kyoryūchi: Tabunka kyōsei toshi no genzō*. Kobe: Kōbe Shimbun Sōgō Shuppan Sentā.
Kojima Takao, ed. 2011. *Nihon Keizai no kiroku: Dai-2-ji sekiyu kiki e no taiō kara baburu hōkai made*. Vol. 1. Tokyo: Naikakufu Keizai Shakai Sōgō Kenkyūjo.
Komada Shinji. 1971. *Ichijō Sayuri no sei*. Tokyo: Kōdansha.
———. 1981. "Sutorippu to seiteki buyō." In *Sarasu: Sutorippu no sekai*, edited by Minami Hiroshi, Nagai Hiroo, and Ozawa Shōichi, 5–37. Geisōsho 3. Tokyo: Hakusuisha.
"Konketsuji wa 5,013-nin: Yosōgai ni sukunai kōseishō chōsa." 1952. *Asahi shimbun*, December 24, 1952, 7.
Kosaka Tomoko and Hamaguchi Sumako. 1974. *Afurika bikkuri bōkenki*. Tokyo: M. I. C. Shuppan.
Koschmann, J. Victor. 1996. *Revolution and Subjectivity in Postwar Japan*. Chicago: University of Chicago Press.
Kōtō Kuyakusho. 1967. *Kōtōku nijūnenshi*. Tokyo: Kōtō Kuyakusho.
Kōtōku. 1997. *Kōtōkushi*. Chū (vol. 2). Tokyo: Kōtōku.
Ku Mina. 2018. "Shisō kara no sekkyokuteki tōhi: Kawashima Yūzō to fūzoku eiga." In *Kawashima Yūzō wa nido umareru*, edited by Kawasaki Kōhei, Kitamura Kyōhei, and Shimura Miyoko, 34–56. Tokyo: Suiseisha.
Kumashiro Tatsumi, Kurahara Koretsugu, and Yamaguchi Seiichirō. 1972. "Zadankai: Roman poruno no kyozō to jitsuzō." *Shinario* 28 (6): 38–45.
Kumazawa Makoto. 1981. *Nihon no rōdōshazō*. Tokyo: Chikuma Shobō.
———. 1986. *Shokubashi no shura o ikite: Sairon Nihon no rōdōshazō*. Tokyo: Chikuma Shobō.
———. 1996. *The Portraits of the Japanese Workplace: Labor Movements, Workers, and Managers*. Translated by Andrew Gordon and Mikiso Hane. Boulder, CO: Westview Press.
Kunimitsu Shirō. (1962) 1985. *Shagai gokuhi*. Tokyo: Shūeisha.
Kunze, Peter. 2014. "Beautiful Friendship: Masculinity and Nationalism in *Casablanca*." *Studies in Popular Culture* 37 (1): 19–37.
Kurihara Genta. 1989. *Nihon shihon shugi no nijū kōzō*. Tokyo: Ochanomizu Shobō.
Kurita Hisaya, ed. 2011. *Beigun kichi to Kanagawa*. Yokohama: Yūrindō.
Lang, Robert. 2002. *Masculine Interests: Homoerotics in Hollywood Film*. New York: Columbia University Press.
Lefebvre, Henri. (1974) 1991. *The Production of Space*. Translated by Donald Nicholson-Smith. Malden, MA: Blackwell Publishing.
Lenin, Vladimir I. (1917) 1987. "Imperialism, the Highest Stage of Capitalism." In *Essential Works of Lenin: "What Is to Be Done?" and Other Writings*, edited by Henry M. Christman, 177–270. New York: Dover Publications.
Maeda Ai. 1982. *Toshi kūkan no naka no bungaku*. Tokyo: Chikuma Shobō.

———. (1982) 2004. "Their Time as Children: A Study of Higuchi Ichiyō's *Growing Up (Takekurabe)*." Translated by Edward Fowler. In *Text and the City: Essays on Japanese Modernity*, by Maedi Ai, edited by James A. Fujii, 109–43. Durham, NC: Duke University Press.

Mansfield, Nick. 2000. *Subjectivity: Theories of the Self from Freud to Haraway*. New York: New York University Press.

Marcuse, Herbert. 1964. *One-Dimensional Man: Studies in Ideology in Advanced Industrial Society*. Boston: Beacon Press.

———. (1965) 1968. "The Affirmative Character of Culture." Translated by Jeremy J. Shapiro. In *Negations: Essays in Critical Theory*, 88–133. Boston: Beacon Press.

Maruyama Kenji. 1974. *Afurika no hikari*. Tokyo: Kawade Shobō.

Maruyama Masao. (1946) 1995. "Chō-kokka shugi no ronri to shinri." In *Maruyama Masao-shū*, vol. 3, edited by Matsuzawa Hiroaki and Uete Michiari, 17–36. Tokyo: Iwanami Shoten.

———. (1948) 1995. "Nihon fashizumu no shisō to undō." In *Maruyama Masao-shū*, vol. 3, edited by Matsuzawa Hiroaki and Uete Michiari, 259–322. Tokyo: Iwanami Shoten.

———. (1952) 1995. "Seiji no sekai." In *Maruyama Masao-shū*, vol. 5, edited by Matsuzawa Hiroaki and Uete Michiari, 125–91. Tokyo: Iwanami Shoten.

———. (1960) 1996a. "Chūsei to hangyaku." In *Maruyama Masao-shū*, vol. 8, edited by Matsuzawa Hiroaki and Uete Michiari, 163–277. Tokyo: Iwanasmi Shoten.

———. (1960) 1996b. "Sentaku no toki." In *Maruyama Masao-shū*, vol. 8, edited by Matsuzawa Hiroaki and Uete Michiari, 347–50. Tokyo: Iwanasmi Shoten.

———. (1960) 1996c. "Fukusho no setsu." In *Maruyama Masao-shū*, vol. 8, edited by Matsuzawa Hiroaki and Uete Michiari, 351–58. Tokyo: Iwanasmi Shoten.

———. (1961) 1996. "Shisōshi no kangaekata ni tsuite." In *Maruyama Masao-shū*, vol. 9, edited by Matsuzawa Hiroaki and Uete Michiari, 45–82. Tokyo: Iwanasmi Shoten.

Marx, Karl. (1867) 1990. *Capital*. Vol. 1. Translated by Ben Fowkes. New York: Penguin Books.

———. (1894) 1991. *Capital*. Vol. 3. Translated by David Fernbach. New York: Penguin Books.

Masumura Yasuzō. (1958) 2014a. "Eiga no supīdo ni tsuite." In *Eiga kantoku Masumura Yasuzō no sekai*, ge (vol. 2), edited by Fujii Hiroaki, 26–34. Tokyo: Wides Shuppan.

———. (1958) 2014b. "Aru benmei." In *Eiga kantoku Masumura Yasuzō no sekai*, ge (vol. 2), edited by Fujii Hiroaki, 34–40. Tokyo: Wides Shuppan.

———. (1958) 2014c. "Watashi no shuchō suru engi." In *Eiga kantoku Masumura Yasuzō no sekai*, ge (vol. 2), edited by Fujii Hiroaki, 41–47. Tokyo: Wides Shuppan.

———. (1967) 2014. "Itaria de hakken shita 'kojin.'" In *Eiga kantoku Masumura Yasuzō no sekai*, jō (vol. 1), edited by Fujii Hiroaki, 31–40. Tokyo: Wides Shuppan.

"Mata fueta miuri: Ukeirechi wa Tōkyō ga ōi." 1951. *Asahi shimbun*, September 22, 1951, 3.

Matsumoto Taira. 2012. *Nikkatsu Shōwa seishunki: Nihon de mottomo nagai rekishi o motsu eiga-gaisha no kōbōshi*. Tokyo: WAVE Shuppan.

Matsuo Shōichi. 1977. *Nihon fashizumu shiron*. Tokyo: Hōsei Daigaku Shuppankai.

Matsushima Toshiyuki. 2000. *Nikkatsu roman poruno zenshi: Meisaku, meiyū, meikantoku-tachi*. Tokyo: Kōdansha.

McGowan, Todd. 2016. *Capitalism and Desire: The Psychic Cost of Free Markets*. New York: Columbia University Press.

Minami Hiroshi, Ōi Kashiko, and Yanagi Masako. 1956. "Fan retā no kenkyū." *Kinema junpō* 141:105–12.

Mishima Yukio. (1953) 1970. *Manatsu no shi*. Tokyo: Shinchōsha.

———. (1960) 2010. *Ojōsan*. Tokyo: Kadokawa Shoten.

Misono Ryōko. 2012. *Eiga to kokumin kokka: 1930-nendai Shōchiku merodorama eiga*. Tokyo: Tokyo Daigaku Shuppankai.

Mizuno, Hiromi, Aaron S. Moore, and John DiMoia, eds. 2018. *Engineering Asia: Technology, Colonial Development and the Cold War Order*. SOAS Studies in Modern and Contemporary Japan. London: Bloomsbury Academic.

Morinaga Takurō. 2007. "Ōita, Bungo-Takada ga fukkatsu saseta 'aimai na yasashisa.'" *Ekonomisuto* 85 (60): 82–83.

"Morishige Hisaya, Katō Tokiko no 3-jikan." 1971. *Shūkan heibon* 13 (8): 52–55.

Muramatsu Shunkichi. 1972. *Tabishibai no seikatsu*. Tokyo: Yūzankaku Shuppan.

Murayama Masami, ed. 1970. *Shiroi tairiku ni kakeru hitobito*. Vol. 5 of *Gendai no bōken*. Tokyo: Bungei Shunjū.

Muroo Saisei. (1918) 1995. *Jojō shōkyokushū / Ai no shishū*. Tokyo: Kōdansha.

Naikaku Tōkeikyoku. 1935. *Kokusei chōsa*. Shōwa 5-nen, vol. 2. Tokyo: Tōkyō Tōkei Kyōkai.

Nakae Katsumi. 1963. *Nihon himitsu jōhō*. Tokyo: Arechi Shuppan.

Nakamura, Takafusa. 1993. *Nihon keizai: Sono seichō to kōzō*. Tokyo: Tōkyō Daigaku Shuppankai.

———. 1995. *The Postwar Japanese Economy: Its Development and Structure, 1937–1994*. Translated by Jacqueline Kaminski. Tokyo: University of Tokyo Press.

Nakamura Takeshi. 1954. *Sararīman Mejiro Sanpei: Shōsetu*. Tokyo: Kōbunsha.
Nakayama Ichirō and Ōhara Sōichirō. 1962. "Sangyō shakai no yōsei suru ningen." *Chūō kōron* 77 (12): 90–99.
Natsumei Sōseki. (1908) 2011. *Sanshirō*. Tokyo: Shinchōsha.
Nihon Heiwa Iinkai. 1968. *Nihon no kokusho*. Tokyo: Rōdō Junpōsha.
Nihon Kokuyū Tetsudō. 1974. *Nihon kokuyū tetsudō hyakunenshi*. Vol. 13. Tokyo: Nihon Kokuyū Tetsudō.
"Nihonjin sen'in zokuzoku ōbo." 1965. *Asahi shimbun*, April 10, 1965, 15.
"Nihonjū o roke suru." 1957. *Asahi shimbun*, March 8, 1957, 5. Evening edition.
Nikkatsu Kabushiki-gaisha. 2014. *Nikkatsu 100-nenshi*. Tokyo: Nikkatsu.
Nishimura Hiroshi. 2012. "Shachō shirīzu kara sengo o miru: Shihon, jinmyaku, mi no narai." In *Sengo Nihon eigaron: 1950-nendai o yomu*, edited by Mitsuyo Wada-Marciano, 50–77. Tokyo: Seikyūsha.
Nishiyama Chiaki. 1974. *Jiyū keizai: Sono seisaku to genri*. Tokyo: Chūō Kōransha.
Nishiyama Tadashi. 1974. "Konchikushō kuso kuso!! 'satetsu' no nai 'sasurai': Shōken to Hagiwara Ken'ichi." *Sandē Mainichi* 53 (32): 116–19.
Nitta Jirō. 1974. "Nihonjin no tanken to bōken: Saikin no hon o megutte." *Asahi shimbun*, September 16, 1974, 11.
Niven, John. 1987. *The American President Lines and Its Forebears, 1848–1984: From Paddlewheelers to Containerships*. Newark, NJ: University of Delaware Press.
Nkrumah, Kwame. 1966. *Neo-colonialism: The Last Stage of Imperialism*. New York: International Publishers.
Nosaka Akiyuki. (1968) 1972. *Amerika hijiki / Hotaru no haka*. Tokyo: Shinchōsha.
———. (1999) 2011. *Zesshō! Nosaka Akiyuki*. Tokyo: P-Vine. Compact disc.
O'Bryan, Scott. 2009. *The Growth Idea: Purpose and Prosperity in Postwar Japan*. Honolulu: University of Hawaii Press.
Odaka Kunio. 1958. *Sangyō shakaigaku*. Tokyo: Daiyamondosha.
Oguma Eiji. 1995. *Tan'itsu minzoku shinwa no kigen: Nihonjin no jigazō*. Tokyo: Shin'yōsha.
Ogura Fumi. 2006. "'Fūzoku eiga' to 'genzai' no mobiritī." *Hyōshō bunkaron kenkyū* 5: 98–123.
Ōhara Shakai Mondai Kenkyūjo. 1951. *Nihon rōdō nenkan*. Vol. 23. Tokyo: Jiji Tsūshinsha.
———. 1976. *Nihon rōdō nenkan*. Vol. 46. Tokyo: Rōdō Junpōsha.
Okada Yutaka. 1975. "Gentō no minatomachi no otoko no roman." *Shinario* 31 (6): 30–31.
Okakura Koshirō. 1967. *Ajia Afurika mondai nyūmon*. 2nd ed. Tokyo: Iwanami Shoten.
Okazaki Takeshi. 2012. *Jōkyō suru bungaku: Sōseki kara Haruki made*. Tokyo: Shin-Nihon Shuppansha.

Okiura Kazuteru. 2006. *"Akusho" no minzokushi: Iromachi, shibaimachi no toporojī.* Tokyo: Bungei Shunjū.

Okui Tomoyuki. 1996. *Ajīru to shite no Tōkyō: Nichijō no naka no seiiki.* Tokyo: Kōbundō.

Ōmori Sakae, Sekine Yoshirō, and Kimura Hisao. 1967. *Chōsō no Himaraya, Afurika ōdan ichimankiro, Chibetto senkō jūnen.* Vol. 3 of *Hikyō tanken.* Tokyo: Sannō Shobō.

O'Reilly, Sean D. 2018. *Re-Viewing the Past: The Uses of History in the Cinema of Imperial Japan.* New York: Bloomsbury Academic.

Oshino Takeshi. 2014. "Susaki Paradaisu no shōmetsu: Sengo Nihon ni okeru akasen chitai." *Sō: Eizō to hyōgen* 7:108–20.

Ōtemon Gakuin Daigaku Uemachigaku Purojekuto. 2015. *Uemachigaku o sōzō suru: Yomigaeru koto Ōsaka.* Ibaraki, Osaka: Ōtemon Gakuin Daigaku Shuppankai.

Ōuchi Tsutomu. (1962) 1970. *Nihon keizairon.* Jō (vol. 1). Tokyo: Tōkyō Daigaku Shuppankai.

———. (1963) 1970. *Nihon keizairon.* Ge (vol. 2). Tokyo: Tōkyō Daigaku Shuppankai.

———. 1970. *Kokka dokusen shihon-shugi.* Tokyo: Tōkyō Daigaku Shuppankai.

Ozaki Kōyō. (1898–1903) 1969. *Konjiki yasha.* Tokyo: Shinchōsha.

Polanyi, Karl. (1944) 2001. *The Great Transformation: The Political and Economic Origins of Our Time.* Boston: Beacon Press.

Pratt, Mary Louise. 1992. *Imperial Eyes: Travel Writing and Transculturation.* London: Routledge.

Prindle, Tamae K, ed. and trans. 1989. *Made in Japan and Other Japanese "Business Novels."* Armonk, NY: M. E. Sharpe.

Raine, Michael. 2001. "Ishihara Yūjirō: Youth, Celebrity, and the Male Body in Late-1950s Japan." In *Word and Image in Japanese Cinema*, edited by Dennis Washburn and Carole Cavanaugh, 202–25. Cambridge: Cambridge University Press.

———. 2007. "Modernization without Modernity: Masumura Yasuzō's *Giants and Toys* (1958)." In *Japanese Cinema: Texts and Contexts*, edited by Alastair Phillips and Julian Stringer, 152–67. London: Routledge.

Reischauer, Edwin O. 1965. *Nihon kindai no atarashii mikata.* Tokyo: Kōdansha.

———. 1967. *Beyond Vietnam: The United States and Asia.* New York: Knopf.

Reitan, Richard. 2012. "Narratives of 'Equivalence': Neoliberalism in Contemporary Japan." *Radical History Review* 2012 (112): 43–64.

Relph, Edward. 1976. *Place and Placelessness.* London: Pion.

Richie, Donald. 2001. *A Hundred Years of Japanese Film: A Concise History, with a Selective Guide to Videos and DVDs.* Tokyo: Kodansha International.

Roquet, Paul. 2016. *Ambient Media: Japanese Atmospheres of Self.* Minneapolis: University of Minnesota Press.

Rose, Nikolas. 1999. *Powers of Freedom: Reframing Political Thought*. Cambridge: Cambridge University Press.
Rostow, W. W. (1960) 1971. *The Stages of Economic Growth: A Non-Communist Manifesto*. 2nd ed. Cambridge: Cambridge University Press.
Ruoff, Kenneth J. 2001. *The People's Emperor: Democracy and the Japanese Monarchy, 1945–1995*. Cambridge, MA: Harvard University Asia Center.
Russell, Catherine. 2011. *Classical Japanese Cinema Revisited*. New York: Continuum.
Russell, John G. 2011. "Race as Ricorso: Blackface(s), Racial Representation, and the Transnational Apologetics of Historical Amnesia in the United States and Japan." In *Racial Representations in Asia*, edited by Yasuko Takezawa, 124–47. Kyoto / Melbourne: Kyoto University Press / Trans Pacific Press.
———. 2015. "Historically, Japan is no stranger to blacks, nor to blackface." *Japan Times*, April 19, 2015. https://www.japantimes.co.jp/community/2015/04/19/voices/historically-japan-is-no-stranger-to-blacks-nor-to-blackface/.
"Saikin no ryūkō mūdo myūjikku." 1956. *Swing Journal* 10 (5): 22–23.
Saitō Ayako. 2001. "Wakao Ayako shiron I." *Meiji Gakuin Daigaku geijutsugaku kenkyū* 11:1–18.
———. 2002. "Wakao Ayako shiron II." *Meiji Gakuin Daigaku geijutsugaku kenkyū* 12:1–13.
———. 2003. "Joyū wa teikō suru." In *Eiga joyū Wakao Ayako*, edited by Saitō Ayako and Yomota Inuhiko, 111–249. Tokyo: Misuzu Shobō.
———. 2010a. "The Melodramatic Body as a Discursive Critique of Patriarchy in Masumura Yasuzō's Films of the 1960s." *Meiji Gakuin Daigaku geijutsugaku kenkyū* 20:1–11.
———. 2010b. "Reading as a Woman: The Collaboration of Ayako Wakao and Yasuzo Masumura." In *Reclaiming the Archive: Feminism and Film History*, edited by Vicki Callahan, 154–75. Detroit: Wayne State University Press.
Saitō Masaharu. 1975. "*Kushi no hi* kara *Afurika no hikari* e: Kumashiro Tatsumi ni okeru shinario no kaitai." *Shinario* 31 (6): 32–38.
Saitō Masaharu and Ono Kōsei. 1975. "Kumashiro Tatsumi kantoku no *Afurika no hikari*: Futeikei na serifu to futeikei na engi ni yotte." *Kinema junpō* 663:142–43.
Sakai Takashi. 2011. *Tsūtenkaku: Shin Nihon shihon-shugi hattatsushi*. Tokyo: Seidosha.
Sandokai, Kajiyama Gurūpu, ed. 1981. *Sekiran'un to tomo ni: Kajiyama Toshiyuki tsuitō bunshū*. Tokyo: Kisetsusha.
"Sangyō supai no keiji sekinin." 1964. *Hōritsu kōron* 13 (132): 41–47.
"Sangyō supai to himitsu hogohō." 1964. *Jitsugyō ōrai* 152:28–29.

Saotome Katsumoto. 1971. *Tōkyō daikūshū: Shōwa 20-nen 3-gatsu 10-ka no kiroku*. Tokyo: Iwanami Shoten.
Sasaki Shun'ichi. 1972. "Atarashii tabi no sōzō o mezashite." *Kokuyū tetsudō* 30 (1): 5–7.
Sasaki, Tomoyuki. 2015. *Japan's Postwar Military and Civil Society: Contesting a Better Life*. SOAS Studies in Modern and Contemporary Japan. London: Bloomsbury Academic.
Sasaki-Uemura, Wesley. 2001. *Organizing the Spontaneous: Citizen Protest in Postwar Japan*. Honolulu: University of Hawaii Press.
Sasakura Akira. 1999. *Shōwa no chanpu: Tako Hachirō monogatari*. Fukuoka: Ashi Shobō.
Satō Nobuyuki, Yabuuchi Yoshihiko, and Yamamoto Reiko. 1968. *Jujutsu no teikoku, Porineshia no rakuen, tsurugi to katatsumuri no kuni*. Vol. 5 of *Hikyō tanken*. Tokyo: San'nō Shobō.
Satō Kōjirō. 1984. "Machi to eiga to ningen to: Yokohama o totta eiga kantoku-tachi." *Shimin gurafu Yokohama* 48: 44-45.
Satō Tadao. 1972. "Kumashiro Tatsumi-ron." *Eiga hyōron* 29 (12): 26–32, 96.
———. 2012. "Taishūteki ninki o enagara kyoshō no sōsaku iyoku o shigeki shita eiga kunan no jidai no dai-joyū." In *Joyū Wakao Ayako*, edited by Harada Masaaki and Aoki Shinya, 28–40. Tokyo: Kineme Junpōsha.
Schäfer, Fabian. 2014. "The Actuality of Journalism and the Possibility of Everyday Critique." In *Tosaka Jun: A Critical Reader*, edited by Ken C. Kawashima, Fabian Schäfer, and Robert Stolz, 150–75. Ithaca, NY: Cornell University Press.
Schaller, Michael. 1987. *The American Occupation of Japan: The Origins of the Cold War in Asia*. New York: Oxford University Press.
———. 1997. *Altered States: The United States and Japan since the Occupation*. New York: Oxford University Press.
Sedgwick, Eve Kosofsky. 1985. *Between Men: English Literature and Male Homosocial Desire*. New York: Columbia University Press.
"Sengo yonjūnen no Nihon, kokumin no mikata: Honshi seron chōsa." 1985. *Asahi shimbun*, July 9, 1985, 11.
Shah, Nayan. 2011. *Stranger Intimacy: Contesting Race, Sexuality, and the Law in the North American West*. Berkeley: University of California Press.
Sharp Kabushiki-gaisha. 1992. *Seii to sōi: 80-nen no ayumi*. Osaka: Sharp Kabushiki-gaisha.
Shibaki Yoshiko. (1941) 1997. "Seika no ichi." In *Shibaki Yoshiko meisakusen*, jō (vol. 1), 7–36. Tokyo: Shinchōsha.
———. (1955) 1994. *Susaki Paradaisu*. Tokyo: Shūeisha.
Shilling, Chris. 2018. "Physical Capital and Situated Action: A New Direction for Corporeal Sociology." In *Physical Culture, Ethnography and the Body:*

Theory, Method and Praxis, edited by Michael D. Giardina and Michele K. Donnelly, 47–62. London: Routledge.
Shimizu Ikkō. 1974. "Sengo saiaku no keizai hakyoku o kakugo seyo." *Gendai* 8 (1): 74–84.
Shimizu Ikutarō. (1966) 1993. *Gendai shisō*. Vol. 12 of *Shimizu Ikutarō chosakushū*. Tokyo: Kōdansha.
Shimizu Kazuhiko. 2015. "'Mohaya *sengo* dewa nai' to iu shakaiteki kioku no kōsei katei." *Edogawa Daigaku kiyō* 25:195–206.
Shimizu Michiko. 2004. *Jochū imēji no katei bunkashi*. Kyoto: Sekai Shisōsha.
Shiomi Toshitaka, Yamada Akira, and Hayashi Shigeo, eds. 1969. *Anpo kokusho*. Tokyo: Rōdō Junpōsha.
"Shiretoko ryojō, Katō Tokiko-san: Shiretoko to watashi 1." 2004. *Asahi shimbun*, Feburary 12, 2004, 20. Hokkaido edition.
Shiroyama Saburō. (1959) 1963. *Sōkaiya Kinjō*. Tokyo: Shinchōsha.
"Shūdan shūshoku shita nenshō rōdōsha no taikenki." 1958. *Shokugyō antei kōhō* 9 (10): 16–21.
"Shūdan shūshoku shita wakōdo no gekirei to eiga *Hitotsubu no mugi* no tokubetsu shisha." 1958. *Shokugyō antei kōhō* 9 (10): 14–15.
"Shūdan shūshoku tsuzuite nyūkyō." 1957. *Asahi shimbun*, March 23, 1957, 8.
Silverberg, Miriam. 2006. *Erotic Grotesque Nonsense: The Mass Culture of the Japanese Modern Times*. Berkeley: University of California Press.
Smith, Neil. (1984) 2008. *Uneven Development: Nature, Capital, and the Production of Space*. 3rd ed. Athens: University of Georgia Press.
Sōrifu Tōkeikyoku [Statistics Bureau, Prime Minister's Office]. 1959. *Kokusei chōsa*. Shōwa 30-nen, vol. 3, part 2. Tokyo: Sōrifu Tōkeikyoku.
———. 1971. *Kakei chōsa nenpō*. Shōwa 44-nen. Tokyo: Nihon Tōkei Kyōkai.
———. 1977a. *Kokusei chōsa*. Shōwa 50-nen, vol. 1. Tokyo: Sōrifu Tōkeikyoku.
———. 1977b. *Kokusei chōsa*. Shōwa 50-nen, vol. 2. Tokyo: Sōrifu Tōkeikyoku.
Stoler, Ann Laura. 2002. *Carnal Knowledge and Imperial Power: Race and the Intimate in Colonial Rule*. Berkeley: University of California Press.
Sugden, John. 1996. *Boxing and Society: An International Analysis*. Manchester: Manchester University Press.
Sugino Isamu and Yonemura Chiyo. 2000. "Sengyōshufu no keisei to henyō." In *Kindaika to shakai kaisō*, vol. 1 of *Nihon no kaisō shisutemu*, edited by Hara Junsuke, 177–95. Tokyo: Tōkyō Daigaku Shuppankai.
Sugiura Seiken. 1981. "Ichijō Sayuri saiban o kangaeru." In *Sarasu: Sutorippu no sekai*, edited by Minami Hiroshi, Nagai Hiroo, and Ozawa Shōichi, 181–239. Geisōsho 3. Tokyo: Hakusuisha.
Sukarno, Ratna Sari Dewi. 2010. *Dewi Sukarno kaisōki*. Tokyo: Sōshisha.
Takaoka Hiroyuki. 2011. *Sōryokusen taisen to "fukushi kokka": Senjiki Nihon no "shakai fukushi" kōsō*. Tokyo: Iwanami Shoten.

Takeuchi, Michiko. 2010. "'Pan-Pan Girls' Performing and Resisting Neocolonialism(s) in the Pacific Theater: U.S. Military Prostitution in Occupied Japan, 1945–1952." In *Over There: Living with the U.S. Military Empire from World War Two to the Present*, edited by Maria Höhn and Seungsook Moon, 78–108. Durham, NC: Duke University Press.

Tanabe Seiko. (1979) 1990. *Ochikubo-hime*. Tokyo: Kadokawa Shoten.

Tanaka Kakuei. 1972. *Nihon rettō kaizō-ron*. Tokyo: Nikkan Kōgyō Shimbunsha.

Tanizaki Jun'ichirō. (1924) 1985. *Chijin no ai*. Tokyo: Shinchōsha.

———. (1963) 1974. *Daidokoro taiheiki*. Tokyo: Chūō Kōronsha.

———. 2016. *The Maids*. Translated by Michael P. Cronin. New York: New Directions.

"Tanomi no tsuna wa 'kikyūhei.'" 1967. *Asahi shimbun*, July 28, 1967, 7.

Tansman, Alan. *The Aesthetics of Japanese Fascism*. Berkeley: University of California Press.

"Terenchefu ni sannen: Sangyō supai zen'in ni yūzai hanketsu." 1965. *Asahi shimbun*, June 27, 1965, 15.

Thomassen, Bjørn. 2014. *Liminality and the Modern: Living through the In-Between*. Burlington, VT: Ashgate.

Thompson, Christopher S. 2011. "Japan's Showa Retro Boom: Nostalgia, Local Identity, and the Resurgence of *Kamadogami* Masks in the Nation's Northeast." *Journal of Popular Culture* 44 (6): 1307–32.

Tōkyō Kyōshokuin Kumiai Kōtō Shibu. 1987. *Kōtō no rekishi*. Tokyo: Ayumi Shuppan.

Tominaga Ken'ichi. 1965. *Atarashii sangyō shakai: Sangyōka to shakai hendō*. Tokyo: Kashima Kenkyūjo Shuppankai.

Tosaka Jun. (1936) 1966. "Shisō to fūzoku." In *Tosaka Jun zenshū*, vol. 4, 269–469. Tokyo: Keisō Shobō.

Tsukada Shūichi. 2014. "Kichi bunka to popyurā ongaku: Yokohama/Yokosuka o firudo to shite." *Mita shakaigaku* 19:80–93.

Tsunemitsu Tōru. 2006. *Shigusa no minzokugaku: Yōjutsuteki sekai to shinsei*. Kyoto: Mineruva Shobō.

Tuan, Yi-Fu. 1977. *Space and Place: The Perspective of Experience*. Minneapolis: University of Minnesota Press.

Turner, Bryan S. 1984. *The Body and Society: Explorations in Social Theory*. Oxford: B. Blackwell.

Turner, Victor. 1969. *The Ritual Process: Structure and Anti-Structure*. Chicago: Aldine Publishing.

———. 1974. "Liminal to Liminoid, in Play, Flow, and Ritual: An Essay in Comparative Symbology." *Rice University Studies* 60 (3): 53–91.

Umesao Tadao, ed. 1970. *Sabaku to mitsurin o koete*. Vol. 1 of *Gendai no bōken*. Tokyo: Bungei Shunjū.

———. 1972. "Asahi kōza *Tanken to bōken* ni tsuite." In *Tanken to bōken: Asahi kōza*, vol. 1, edited by Asahi Shimbunsha, 11–21. Tokyo: Asahi Shimbunsha.
Unoki Kenta. 2012. "Sengo Nihon no 'kindaika' to shin-seikatsu undō." *Seisaku kagaku* 19 (4): 177–94.
van Gennep, Arnold. 1960. *The Rites of Passage*. Translated by Monika B. Vizedom and Gabrielle L. Caffee. Chicago: University of Chicago Press.
Vogel, Ezra F. 1979. *Japan as Number One: Lessons for America*. Cambridge, MA: Harvard University Press.
Wada-Marciano, Mitsuyo. 2008. *Nippon Modern: Japanese Cinema of the 1920s and 1930s*. Honolulu: University of Hawaii Press.
———. 2012. "(Sai)teigi sareru rōdōryoku: Kansenshi de no sararīman eiga." In *Sengo Nihon eigaron: 1950-nendai o yomu*, edited by Mitsuyo Wada-Marciano, 24–49. Tokyo: Seikyūsha.
Wager, Jans B. 2005. *Dames in the Driver's Seat: Rereading Film Noir*. Austin: University of Texas Press.
Wallerstein, Immanuel. 1991. *Geopolitics and Geoculture: Essays on the Changing World-System*. Cambridge: Cambridge University Press.
———. 1995. *After Liberalism*. New York: New Press.
Watanabe Osamu, ed. 2004. *Kōdo seichō to kigyō shakai*. Nihon no jidaishi 27. Tokyo: Yoshikawa Kōbunkan.
Watanabe Osamu and Gotō Michio, eds. 1997. *Nihon shakai no taikō to kōsō*. Kōza gendai Nihon 4. Tokyo: Ōtsuki Shoten.
Watanabe Takenobu. 1981. *Nikkatsu akushon no karei na sekai*. Jō (vol. 1). Tokyo: Miraisha.
———. 1982a. *Nikkatsu akushon no karei na sekai*. Chū (vol. 2). Tokyo: Miraisha.
———. 1982b. *Nikkatsu akushon no karei na sekai*. Ge (vol. 3). Tokyo: Miraisha.
Watashi wa nani o hakonda no ka: Moto LST norikumiin ga mitsumeru Betonamu sensō. 2015. BS1 Special, NHK, October 11, 2015.
Yamaguchi Hitomi. (1963) 1996. *Eburi Man-shi no karei na seikatsu*. Tokyo: Kadokawa Shoten.
———. (1963) 2009. *Eburi Man-shi no yūga na seikatsu*. Tokyo: Chikuma Shobō.
Yamaguchi Satoshi. 2016. *Shūdan shūshoku to wa nan de atta ka: "Kin no tamago" no jikūkan*. Kyoto: Mineruva Shobō.
Yamaji Hideo. 2002. *Atarashiki furusato: Senri Nyū Taun no 40-nen*. Osaka: NGS.
Yamanaka, Jō. 2001. *Akashi: Eien no shauto*. Tokyo: Tokuma Shoten.
Yamanouchi, Yasushi. 1998. "Total War and System Integration: A Methodological Introduction." In *Total War and "Modernization,"* edited by Yasushi Yamanouchi, J. Victor Koschmann, and Ryūichi Narita, 1–39. Ithaca, NY: Cornell University Press.
———. 2011. *Shisutemu shakai no gendaiteki isō*. Tokyo: Iwanami Shoten.
Yamasaki Toyoko. 1965. *Shiroi kyotō*. Tokyo: Shinchōsha.

———. 1969. *Zoku shiroi kyotō*. Tokyo: Shinchōsha.
———. 1973. *Karei naru ichizoku*. 3 vols. Tokyo: Shinchōsha.
Yokohama Bengoshikai. 1989. *Kichi to jinken*. Tokyo: Nihon Hyōronsha.
Yokohama Kaikō Shiryōkan and Yokohama Kyoryūchi Kenkyūkai. 1996. *Yokohama kyoryūchi to ibunka kōryū: Jūkyū-seiki kōhan no kokusai toshi o yomu*. Tokyo: Yamakawa Shuppan.
Yokohamashi Furusato Rekishi Zaidan. 2014. *Senryō-gun no ita machi: Sengo Yokohama no shuppatsu*. Yokohama: Yokohamashi Shiryōshitsu.
Yokohamashi Sōmukyoku Shishi Henshūshitu. 2000. *Yokohamashishi*. Vol. 2, part 2, book 2 (ge). Yokohama: Yokohamashi.
Yokohamashi Sōmukyoku Shōgaibu. 1973. *Yokohamashi to beigun kichi*. Yokohoma: Yokohamashi.
Yomota Inuhiko. 2003. "Yokubō to minshushugi." In *Eiga joyū Wakao Ayako*, edited by Saitō Ayako and Yomota Inuhiko, 9–110. Tokyo: Misuzu Shobō.
Yoshimi Yoshiaki. 1987. *Kusa no ne no fashizumu*. Tokyo: Tōkyō Daigaku Shuppankai.
Yoshimoto, Mitsuhiro. 2000. *Kurosawa: Film Studies and Japanese Cinema*. Durham, NC: Duke University Press.
———. 2002. "Questions of Japanese Cinema: Disciplinary Boundaries and the Invetion of the Scholarly Object." In *Leaning Places: The Afterlives of Area Stuies*, edited by Masao Miyoshi and H. D. Harootunian, 368–401. Durham, NC: Duke University Press.
Yoshiyuki Junnosuke. 1966. *Shūu / Genshoku no machi*. Tokyo: Shinchōsha.
Yuki Shigeko. (1955) 1968. *Jochūkko*. Tokyo: Mugi Shobō.
"Zadankai: *Afurika no hikari* Kumashiro satsuei butai, Shiretoko hōdan." 1975. *Shinario* 31 (6): 26–29.
Žižek, Slavoj. 2009. *The Sublime Object of Ideology*. London: Verso.

Online Databases

Asahi newspaper archive, https://database.asahi.com
Cabinet Office consumer confidence surveys (including the penetration rates of durable consumer goods), https://www.esri.cao.go.jp/jp/stat/shouhi/shouhi.html
Cabinet Office economic white papers, https://www5.cao.go.jp/keizai3/keizaiwp/index.html
Cabinet Office public opinion surveys on citizens' daily lives, https://survey.gov-online.go.jp/index-ko.html
National Diet proceedings, https://kokkai.ndl.go.jp
Statistics Bureau national censuses, https://www.stat.go.jp/data/kokusei/2010/users-g/kako.html

Filmography

The films mentioned in this book are listed here, ordered alphabetically by their English titles, followed by the original Japanese titles.

Always: Sunset on Third Street (*Always san-chōme no yūhi*; Always 三丁目の夕日). Dir. Yamazaki Takashi. Japan: ROBOT, 2005.
Black Bills (*Kuro no satsutaba* 黒の札束). Dir. Murayama Mitsuo. Japan: Daiei, 1963.
Black Challenger (*Kuro no chōsensha* 黒の挑戦者). Dir. Murayama Mitsuo. Japan: Daiei, 1964.
Black Hit-by-Pitch (*Kuro no shikyū* 黒の死球). Dir. Mizuho Shunkai. Japan: Daiei, 1963.
Black-Line District (*Kurosen chitai* 黒線地帯). Dir. Ishii Teruo. Japan: Shin-Tōhō, 1960.
Black Parking (*Kuro no chūshajō* 黒の駐車場). Dir. Yuge Tarō. Japan: Daiei, 1963.
Black Report (*Kuro no hōkokusho* 黒の報告書). Dir. Masumura Yasuzō. Japan: Daiei, 1963.
Black River (*Kuroi kawa* 黒い河). Dir. Kobayashi Masaki. Japan: Ninjin Kurabu, 1957.
Black Runaway (*Kuro no bakusō* 黒の爆走). Dir. Tomimoto Sōkichi. Japan: Daiei, 1964.
Black Scar (*Kuroi kizuato no burūsu* 黒い傷あとのブルース). Dir. Nomura Takashi. Japan: Nikkatsu, 1961.
Black Snow (*Kuroi yuki* 黒い雪). Dir. Takechi Tetsuji. Japan: Kokuei/Nikkatsu, 1965.
Black Strait (*Kuroi kaikyō* 黒い海峡). Dir. Ezaki Mio. Japan: Nikkatsu, 1964.
Black Super-Express (*Kuro no chōtokkyū* 黒の超特急). Dir. Masumura Yasuzō. Japan: Daiei, 1964.
Black Test Car (*Kuro no tesutokā* 黒の試走車). Dir. Masumura Yasuzō. Japan: Daiei, 1962.

Black Trademark (*Kuro no torēdo māku* 黒の商標). Dir. Yuge Tarō. Japan: Daiei, 1963.

Black Trump Card (*Kuro no kirifuda* 黒の切り札). Dir. Inoue Umetsugu. Japan: Daiei, 1964.

Black Weapon (*Kuro no kyōki* 黒の凶器). Dir. Inoue Akira. Japan: Daiei, 1964.

Blue-Sky Girl (*Aozora musume* 青空娘). Dir. Masumura Yasuzō. Japan: Daiei, 1957.

Bonchi (ぼんち). Dir. Ichikawa Kon. Japan: Daiei, 1960.

Burden of Love (*Ai no onimotsu* 愛のお荷物). Dir. Kawashima Yūzō. Japan: Nikkatsu, 1955.

The Call of the Foghorn (*Muteki ga ore o yonde iru* 霧笛が俺を呼んでいる). Dir. Yamazaki Tokujirō. Japan: Nikkatsu, 1960.

Call-Girl Territory (*Hakusen himitsu chitai* 白線秘密地帯). Dir. Ishii Teruo. Japan: Shin-Tōhō. 1958.

Casablanca. Dir. Michael Curtiz. United States: Warner Bros., 1942.

A Cat, a Man, and Two Women (*Neko to Shōzō to futari no onna* 猫と庄三と二人のをんな). Dir. Toyoda Shirō. Japan: Tōkyō Eiga, 1956.

Clothes of Deception (*Itsuwareru seisō* 偽れる盛装). Dir. Yoshimura Kōzaburō. Japan: Daiei, 1951.

Company President with a Secret Stash (*Hesokuri shachō* へそくり社長). Dir. Chiba Yasuki. Japan: Tōhō, 1956.

Crazed Fruit (*Kurutta kajitsu* 狂った果実). Dir. Nakahira Kō. Japan: Nikkatsu, 1956.

Creatures That Live at the End of the World (*Chi no hate ni ikiru mono* 地の涯に生きるもの). Dir. Hisamatsu Seiji. Japan: Tōhō, 1960.

Daughter, Wife, and Mother (*Musume, tsuma, haha* 娘・妻・母). Dir. Naruse Mikio. Japan: Tōhō, 1960.

Death by Hanging (*Kōshikei* 絞死刑). Dir. Ōshima Nagisa. Japan: Sōzōsha and ATG, 1968.

Elegant Beast (*Shitoyaka na kedamono* しとやかな獣). Dir. Kawashima Yūzō. Japan: Daiei, 1962.

The Elegant Life of Mr. Everyman (*Eburi Man-shi no yūga na seikatsu* 江分利満氏の優雅な生活). Dir. Okamoto Kihachi. Japan: Tōhō, 1963.

Evening Stream (*Yoru no nagare* 夜の流れ). Dir. Kawashima Yūzō and Naruse Mikio. Japan: Tōhō, 1960.

The Failure of Youth (*Seishun no satetsu* 青春の蹉跌). Dir. Kumashiro Tatsumi. Japan: Tōkyō Eiga / Watanabe Kikaku, 1974.

The Flavor of Green Tea over Rice (*Ochazuke no aji* お茶漬けの味). Dir. Ozu Yasujirō. Japan: Shōchiku, 1952.

Floating Weeds (*Ukikusa* 浮草). Dir. Ozu Yasujirō. Japan: Daiei, 1959.

Flowing (*Nagareru* 流れる). Dir. Naruse Mikio. Japan: Tōhō, 1956.

Foundry Town (*Kyūpora no aru machi* キューポラのある街). Dir. Urayama Kirio. Japan: Nikkatsu, 1962

Front-Row Life (*Kaburitsuki jinsei* かぶりつき人生). Dir. Kumashiro Tatsumi. Japan: Nikkatsu, 1968.

A Geisha (*Gion bayashi* 祇園囃子). Dir. Mizoguchi Kenji. Japan: Daiei, 1953.

Giants and Toys (*Kyojin to gangu* 巨人と玩具). Dir. Masumura Yasuzō. Japan: Daiei, 1958.

A Grain of Wheat (*Hitotsubu no mugi* 一粒の麦). Dir. Yoshimura Kōzaburō. Japan: Daiei, 1958.

Growing Up in a Brothel (*Kuruwa sodachi* 廓育ち). Dir. Satō Jun'ya. Japan: Tōei, 1964.

History of Postwar Japan as Told by a Bar Hostess (*Nippon sengoshi: Madamu Onboro no seikatsu* にっぽん戦後史マダムおんぼろの生活). Dir. Imamura Shōhei. Japan: Nippon Eiga Shinsha / Tōhō, 1970.

Home from the Sea (*Kokyō* 故郷). Dir. Yamada Yōji. Japan: Shōchiku, 1972.

Hooray for Marriage, or Sweet Beans for Two (*Meoto zenzai* 夫婦善哉). Dir. Toyoda Shirō. Japan: Tōhō, 1955.

The Husband Witnessed (*Otto ga mita* 夫が見た). Dir. Masumura Yasuzō. Japan: Daiei, 1964.

I Am Waiting (*Ore wa matteru ze* 俺は待ってるぜ). Dir. Kurahara Koreyoshi. Japan: Nikkatsu, 1957.

I Was Born, But . . . (*Umarete wa mita keredo* 生まれてはみたけれど). Dir. Ozu Yasujirō. Japan: Shōchiku, 1932.

Immortal Love (*Eien no hito* 永遠の人). Dir. Kinoshita Keisuke. Japan: Shōchiku, 1961.

The Insect Woman (*Nippon konchūki* にっぽん昆虫記). Dir. Imamura Shōhei. Japan: Nikkatsu, 1963.

The Izu Dancer (*Koi no hana saku Izu no odoriko* 恋の花咲く 伊豆の踊り子). Dir. Gosho Heinosuke. Japan: Shōchiku, 1933.

The Izu Dancer (*Izu no odoriko* 伊豆の踊り子). Dir. Nishikawa Katsumi. Japan: Nikkatsu, 1963.

Japan Expo '70 (*Nihon bankoku-haku* 日本万国博). Dir. Taniguchi Senkichi. Japan: Nyūsu Eiga Seisakusha Renmei, 1971.

Japanese Girls at the Harbor (*Minato no Nihon-musume* 港の日本娘). Dir. Shimizu Hiroshi. Japan: Shōchiku, 1933.

Ki River (*Ki-no-kawa* 紀の川). Dir. Nakamura Noboru. Japan: Shōchiku, 1966.

Kiku and Isamu (*Kiku to Isamu* キクとイサム). Dir. Imai Tadashi. Japan: Daitō Eiga, 1959.

The Kiss Thief (*Seppun dorobō* 接吻泥棒). Dir. Kawashima Yūzō. Japan: Tōhō, 1960.

Kisses (*Kuchizuke* くちづけ). Dir. Masumura Yasuzō. Japan: Daiei, 1957.

A Kitchen Chronicle (*Daidokoro taiheiki* 台所太平記). Dir. Toyoda Shirō. Japan: Tōkyō Eiga, 1963.

Late Chrysanthemums (*Bangiku* 晩菊). Dir. Naruse Mikio. Japan: Tōhō, 1954.

The Light of Africa (*Afurika no hikari* アフリカの光). Dir. Kumashiro Tatsumi. Japan: Tōhō / Watanabe Kikaku, 1975.

Maid's Boy (*Jochūkko* 女中っ子). Dir. Tasaka Tomotaka. Japan: Nikkatsu, 1955.

Man Who Causes a Storm (*Arashi o yobu otoko* 嵐を呼ぶ男). Dir. Inoue Umetsugu. Japan: Nikkatsu, 1957.

Matriarchal Family (*Nyokei kazoku* 女系家族). Dir. Misumi Kenji. Japan: Daiei, 1963.

Midday Trap (*Mahiru no wana* 真昼の罠). Dir. Tomimoto Sōkichi. Japan: Daiei, 1962.

Midnight Cowboy. Dir. John Schlesinger. USA: United Artists, 1969.

The Most Valuable Wife (*Saikō shukun fujin* 最高殊勲夫人). Dir. Masumura Yasuzō. Japan: Daiei, 1959.

My Town (*Waga machi* わが町). Dir. Kawashima Yūzō. Japan: Nikkatsu, 1956.

My Way (*Waga michi* わが道). Dir. Shindō Kaneto. Japan: Kindai Eiga Kyōkai, 1974.

Ninja in a Suit (*Sebiro no ninja* 背広の忍者). Dir. Yuge Tarō. Japan: Daiei, 1963.

The Only Son (*Hitori musuko* 一人息子). Dir. Ozu Yasujirō. Japan: Shōchiku, 1936.

Osaka Elegy (*Naniwa erejī* 浪華悲歌). Dir. Mizoguchi Kenji. Japan: Daiichi Eigasha, 1936.

Ōshō (王将). Dir. Itō Daisuke. Japan: Daiei, 1962.

Our Neighbor, Miss Yae (*Tonari no Yae-chan* 隣の八重ちゃん). Dir. Shimazu Yasujirō. Japan: Shōchiku, 1934.

The Petrified Forest (*Kaseki no mori* 化石の森). Dir. Shinoda Masahiro. Japan: Tōkyō Eiga, 1973.

Pigs and Battleships (*Buta to gunkan* 豚と軍艦). Dir. Imamura Shōhei. Japan: Nikkatsu, 1961.

Portrait of Madame Yuki (*Yuki-fujin ezu* 雪夫人絵図). Dir. Mizoguchi Kenji. Japan: Shin-Tōhō / Takimura Puro, 1950.

Preparation for the Festival (*Matsuri no junbi* 祭りの準備). Dir. Kuroki Kazuo. Japan: Sōeisha / Eiga Dōjinsha / ATG, 1975.

A Promise (*Yakusoku* 約束). Dir. Saitō Kōichi. Japan: Saitō Production / Shōchiku, 1972.

Proof of the Man (*Ningen no shōmei* 人間の証明). Dir. Satō Jun'ya. Japan: Kadokawa, 1977.

The Rambler with a Guitar (*Gitā o motta wataridori* ギターを持った渡り鳥). Dir. Saitō Buichi. Japan: Nikkatsu, 1959.

Red Angel (*Akai tenshi* 赤い天使). Dir. Masumura Yasuzō. Japan: Daiei, 1966.

Red Diamond (*Akai daiya* 赤いダイヤ). Dir. Konishi Michio. Japan: Tōei, 1964.

Red Handkerchief (*Akai hankachi* 赤いハンカチ). Dir. Masuda Toshio. Japan: Nikkatsu, 1964.

Room for Rent (*Kashima ari* 貸間あり). Dir. Kawashima Yūzō. Japan: Takarazuka Eiga, 1959.

Salaryman Mejiro Sanpei (*Sararīman Mejiro Sanpei* サラリーマン目白三平). Dir. Chiba Yasuki. Japan: Tōei, 1955.

Sayuri Ichijō: Following Desire (*Ichijō Sayuri: Nureta yokujō* 一条さゆり濡れた欲情). Dir. Kumashiro Tatsumi. Japan: Nikkatsu, 1972.

Scarecrow. Dir. Jerry Schatzberg. USA: Warner Bros., 1973.

Season of the Sun (*Taiyō no kisetsu* 太陽の季節). Dir. Furukawa Takumi. Japan: Nikkatsu, 1956.

Seisaku's Wife (*Seisaku no tsuma* 清作の妻). Dir. Masumura Yasuzō. Japan: Daiei, 1965.

The Shop Curtain (*Noren* 暖簾). Dir. Kawashima Yūzō. Japan: Takarazuka Eiga, 1958.

Sing a Song of Sex (*Nihon shunkakō* 日本春歌考). Dir. Ōshima Nagisa. Japan: Sōzōsha, 1967.

Sisters of Gion (*Gion no kyōdai* 祇園の姉妹). Dir. Mizoguchi Kenji. Japan: Daiichi Eigasha, 1936.

Spirited Away (*Sen to Chihiro no kamikakushi* 千と千尋の神隠し). Dir. Miyazaki Hayao. Japan: Studio Ghibli, 2001.

A Story of Floating Weeds (*Ukikusa monogatari* 浮草物語). Dir. Ozu Yasujirō. Japan: Shōchiku, 1934.

Street of Shame (*Akasen chitai* 赤線地帯). Dir. Mizoguchi Kenji. Japan: Daiei, 1956.

The Sun in the Last Days of the Shogunate (*Bakumatsu taiyōden* 幕末太陽傳). Dir. Kawashima Yūzō. Japan: Nikkatsu, 1957.

Sunset Hill (*Yūhi no oka* 夕陽の丘). Dir. Matsuo Akinori. Japan: Nikkatsu, 1964.

Susaki Paradise Red Light (*Susaki Paradaisu aka-shingō* 洲崎パラダイス赤信号). Dir. Kawashima Yūzō. Japan: Nikkatsu, 1956.

Tales of Ginza (*Ginza nijūyonchō* 銀座二十四帖). Dir. Kawashima Yūzō. Japan: Nikkatsu, 1955.

Temple of the Wild Geese (*Gan no tera* 雁の寺). Dir. Kawashima Yūzō. Japan: Daiei, 1962.

Third-Rate Executives (*Santō jūyaku* 三等重役). Dir. Sunohara Masahisa. Japan: Tōhō, 1952.

Three Female Bees (*Sanbiki no mesu-bachi* 三匹の牝蜂). Dir. Torii Motohiro. Japan: Tōei, 1970.

Time for Marriage (*Konki* 婚期). Dir. Yoshimura Kōzaburō. Japan: Daiei, 1961.

Times of Joy and Sorrow (*Yorokobi mo kanashimi mo ikutoshitsuki* 喜びも悲しみも幾歳月). Dir. Kinoshita Keisuke. Japan: Shōchiku, 1957.

Tokyo Story (*Tōkyō monogatari*). Dir. Ozu Yasujirō. Japan: Shōchiku, 1953.

Tokyo Twilight (*Tōkyō boshoku* 東京暮色). Dir. Ozu Yasujirō. Japan: Shōchiku, 1957.

Tora-san, Our Lovable Tramp (*Otoko wa tsurai yo* 男はつらいよ). Dir. Yamada Yōji. Japan: Shōchiku, 1969.

Traveling Actors (*Tabiyakusha* 旅役者). Dir. Naruse Mikio. Japan: Tōhō, 1940.

Tsugaru Jongara-bushi (津軽じょんがら節). Dir. Saitō Kōichi. Japan: Saitō Production / ATG, 1973.
Twisted Path of Love (*Koibitotachi wa nureta* 恋人たちは濡れた). Dir. Kumashiro Tatsumi. Japan: Nikkatsu, 1973.
Twenty-Four Eyes (*Nijūshi no hitomi* 二十四の瞳). Dir. Kinoshita Keisuke. Japan: Shōchiku, 1954.
The Wanderers (*Matatabi* 股旅). Dir. Ichikawa Kon. Japan: ATG. 1974.
Warm Current (*Danryū* 暖流). Dir. Masumura Yasuzō. Japan: Daiei, 1957.
A Warm Misty Night (*Yogiri yo kon'ya mo arigatō* 夜霧よ今夜も有難う). Dir. Ezaki Mio. Japan: Nikkatsu, 1967.
Weight of the Journey (*Tabi no omosa* 旅の重さ). Dir. Saitō Kōichi. Japan: Shōchiku, 1972.
The Wharf of No Return (*Kaerazaru hatoba* 帰らざる波止場). Dir. Ezaki Mio. Japan: Nikkatsu, 1966.
When a Woman Ascends the Stairs (*Onna ga kaidan o agaru toki* 女が階段を上がる時). Dir. Naruse Mikio. Japan: Tōhō, 1960.
Where Spring Comes Late (*Kazoku* 家族). Dir. Yamada Yōji. Japan: Shōchiku, 1970.
A Wife Confesses (*Tsuma wa kokuhaku suru* 妻は告白する). Dir. Masumura Yasuzō. Japan: Daiei, 1961.
A Woman Is Born Twice (*Onna wa nido umareru* 女は二度生まれる). Dir. Kawashima Yūzō. Japan: Daiei, 1961.
Women of the Night (*Yoru no onnatachi* 夜の女たち). Dir. Mizoguchi Kenji. Japan: Shōchiku, 1948.
Women's Medal (*Onna no kunshō* 女の勲章). Dir. Yoshimura Kōzaburō. Japan: Daiei, 1961.
A World for Two (*Futari no sekai* 二人の世界). Dir. Matsuo Noriaki. Japan: Nikkatsu, 1966.
Yearning (*Midareru* 乱れる). Dir. Naruse Mikio. Japan: Tōhō, 1964.
A Young Miss (*Ojōsan* お嬢さん). Dir. Yuge Tarō. Japan: Daiei, 1961.

Index

Abe Shinzō, 8, 142
Africa, 143, 179–80, 184, 187–88, 192, 195, 209; as fantasy, 200–206; neocolonialism in, 166–67
Agawa Hiroyuki, 200
Akagi Keiichirō, 145, 154
akasen chitai (red-line district), 32–33
Akihabara, 19, 45–50, 115, 128, 144, 214
Akutagawa Prize, 32, 144, 187
All-Japan Seamen's Union, 157
Althusser, Louis, 91
Always: Sunset on Third Street (*Always san-chōme no yūhi*, 2005), 8
American President Lines, 151, 163, 166, 169
Amino Yoshihiko, 52, 54
Anpo, *see* US-Japan Security Treaty
Anti-Prostitution Law, 19, 27, 32–33, 43, 69, 221n5, 221n6, 222n7
Aoyama (in Tokyo), 72–73, 90–92, 115, 128
Aratama Michiyo, 21, 27, 65
Articles of Agreement of International Monetary Fund, 104, 125
Arima Ineko, 94–95

Ariyoshi Sawako, 17
Asahi newspaper, 6, 17, 72, 157, 162, 200–201, 230n11
Asaoka Ruriko, 22, 146, 148–49, 151, 154
Ashikawa Izumi, 51, 146, 154
Asia-Pacific War, 30, 38, 134, 174, 194
Atsumi Kiyoshi, 17
auteurism, 220n9

Balibar, Étienne, 174
Bardsley, Jan, 226n20
Beatles, 181
Black Bills (*Kuro no satsutaba*, 1963), 110
Black Challenger (*Kuro no chōsensha*, 1964), 110
Black Hit-by-Pitch (*Kuro no shikyū*, 1963), 110
Black-Line District (*Kurosen chitai*, 1960), 221n6
Black Parking (*Kuro no chūshajō*, 1963), 110
Black Report (*Kuro no hōkokusho*, 1963), 110
Black River (*Kuroi kawa*, 1957), 14
Black Runaway (*Kuro no bakusō*, 1964), 110

Black Scar (*Kuroi kizuato no burūsu*, 1961), 154
Black Snow (*Kuroi yuki*, 1965), 161, 217
Black Strait (*Kuroi kaikyō*, 1964), 149
Black Super-Express (*Kuro no chōtokkyū*, 1964), 108, 110
Black Test Car (*Kuro no tesutokā*, 1962), 110, 227n4
Black Trademark (*Kuro no torēdo māku*, 1963), 110
Black Trump Card (*Kuro no kirifuda*, 1964), 110
Black Weapon (*Kuro no kyōki*, 1964); home appliances in, 114–16; industrial society in, 120–21; spies in, 122, 127; and Osaka, 128–30, 133, 135, 137, 140; as part of "Black" series, 104, 109–11
blackface, 158–59
Blue-Sky Girl (*Aozora musume*, 1957); body in, 96–97; and Genji Keita, 64–66; and Izu, 78–79; and Tokyo, 68–69, 72, 75; subjectivity in, 89, 91; Wakao Ayako in, 82–84
body, 22, 64, 96–97, 100–101, 170, 173, 225n12
Bogart, Humphrey, 143
Bonchi (1960), 128
Bourdaghs, Michael, 231n2
Bourdieu, Pierre, 93
Breton Woods system, 178
bubble economy, 1, 214–15
Bungei Shunjū, 107, 200, 227n2
Burden of Love (*Ai no onimotsu*, 1955), 28
business novel, 106, 108–109, 227n3

Call of the Foghorn, The (*Muteki ga ore o yonde iru*, 1960), 154

Call-Girl Territory (*Hakusen himitsu chitai*, 1958), 221n6
capital; accumulation of, 215, 222n14, 232n6; flow of, 44–45; physical, 96, 101; social; 93, 96, 224n4; violence of, 2, 69
capitalism, 16, 116–19, 131, 189, 191; advanced, 130; expansion of, 9, 44–45, 69; global, 155; industrial, 140, 189; Japanese, 71, 87, 105; monopoly, 117, 227n7
Casablanca (1942), 143, 170, 231n17
Cat, a Man, and Two Women, A (*Neko to Shōzō to futari no onna*, 1956), 129
Chiba Tetsuya, 160
China, 4, 13, 126, 229n5
Chinatown, 150, 229n5
cinematography, 12, 21, 62
class; -based discrimination, 74, 83; conflict, 131, 188; consciousness, 99; difference, 35, 148; as social category, 18, 82, 118; *see also* middle class *and* working class
close-up, 169, 173
Clothes of Deception (*Itsuwareru seisō*, 1951), 81
Coates, Jennifer, 220n8
Cold War, 5, 57, 142, 144, 161, 219n3, 219n5, 220n1, 226n20; in Asia, 9, 26, 165, 176, 220n7; geopolitics, 142, 165
colonialism, 11, 167, 216; *see also* neocolonialism
Communist Party, *see* Japan Communist Party
Company President with a Secret Stash (*Hesokuri shachō*, 1956), 64
Constitution of Japan, 4, 8, 69, 89, 117, 142, 226n, 229n
contact zone, 144, 155, 157–58, 161–62

cosmopolitanism; and spies, 121–22, 138; of Yokohama, 151, 153, 155, 157, 161, 163
Counter Intelligence Corps (US Army), 124, 228n8
Crazed Fruit (*Kurutta kajitsu*, 1956), 145
Creatures That Live at the End of the World (*Chi no hate ni ikiru mono*, 1960), 193
Cronin, Michael, 228n9
cronyism, 16
Crumit, Frank, 224n8

Daiei, 77, 82–84, 120, 122, 130, 145, 217; and "Black" series, 104, 107, 109, 111, 125; president of, 81, 84
Daiki (Osaka Electric Railroad Company), 138–40
Daionjimae (in Tokyo), 41–43
Dan Reiko, 28
Daughter, Wife, and Mother (*Musume, tsuma, haha*, 1960), 225n10
Dazai Osamu, 79
Death by Hanging (*Kōshikei*, 1968), 14
democracy, 15, 21, 39, 63, 87, 219n2; American-style, 85; bourgeois, 87, 226n18; liberal, 91; parliamentary, 38; pluralist, 5; postwar, 82, 226n20; Taishō, 4
denkigai, *see* electric town
Denning, Michael, 105–106
depopulation, 196–97, 199
Diamond Line (Nikkatsu), 145–46
Diet (of Japan), 15, 32, 43, 157, 197, 229n7
DiMoia, John, 220n7
"Discover Japan," 19, 193–95, 199, 202–203

Dodge Plan, 26
Dream Island (Yume-no-shima, Tokyo), 222n13
Dunning, Eric, 100
Dyer, Richard, 82

"economic miracle," 6, 63
Economic Planning Agency, 7, 21, 27, 33–34
economic white paper (1956), 21, 27, 33–37, 41, 44, 145
Eighth Army (US Army), 156, 160
"electric town," 19, 46, 128
Elegant Beast (*Shitoyaka na kedamono*, 1962), 81
The Elegant Life of Mr. Everyman (*Eburi Man-shi no yūga na seikatsu*, 1963), 65
Elias, Norbert, 100
emperor (of Japan), 4–5, 10, 26, 85, 87, 107, 171, 184
empire (of Japan), 4, 26, 71, 95, 127, 151, 171, 175
employment security office, 71, 189
engacho, 54, 56, 223n18
espionage, 22, 104, 120, 124, 126–27, 217; clandestine world of, 111; in industrialized countries, 135; war on, 105, 107
ethnicity, 18, 82, 176
Etō Jun, 17
Evening Stream (*Yoru no nagare*, 1960), 222n10
exoticism, 150–51
exploration (*tanken*), 200–203
Ezaki Mio, 19, 22, 143, 154

Failure of Youth, The (*Seishun no satetsu*, 1974), 185–86, 208
family, *see* middle class, nuclear family, *and* "standard family"
fantasy, 23, 75, 85, 90, 180, 203

Index

Ferguson, Ann, 226n21
Ferro, Marc, 12
fetishism, 115–16, 176
feudalism, 15, 63, 85, 87, 184
Fichte, Johann, 174
Flavor of Green Tea over Rice, The (Ochazuke no aji, 1952), 225n10
Fleming, Ian, 105
Floating Weeds (*Ukikusa*, 1959), 223n19
Flowing (*Nagareru*, 1956), 2, 225n10
Foucault, Michel, 223n16
Foundry Town (*Kyūpora no aru machi*, 1962), 14
Friedman, Milton, 191
friendship, 143, 173, 210; male-male, 206–208, 231n17
Front-Row Life (*Kaburitsuki jinsei*, 1968), 185
Fuji Tatsuya, 188
Fujime Yuki, 221n6
Fujioka Wakao, 233n10
Fukuda Takeo, 179
Furuya Tatsuo, 125–26
Futamura Teiichi, 68
fūzoku, 28–30, 33, 59, 106, 221n3

GDP (Gross Domestic Product), 5, 22, 178
Geisha, A (*Gion bayashi*, 1953), 81–82
gender, 14, 48, 69, 101, 131, 211; in 1950s Japan, 92–93, 101; -based discrimination, 32, 131, 174, 215, 226n19; division of labor, 210; roles, 58, 225n20; as social category, 18, 82–83, 225n12
Genji Keita, 62–66, 77–79, 82, 108, 225n14
Giants and Toys (*Kyojin to gangu*, 1958), 226n16, 227n4
Giddens, Anthony, 4, 100

Ginza, 17, 28, 97, 224n8
GNP (Gross National Product), 5, 117, 142, 162
Gō Eiji, 158–59
"going up to the capital," 67–68, 72, 224
Golden Cups, 229n1
González, Irene, 81
Gordon, Andrew, 219n2
Grain of Wheat, A (*Hitotsubu no mugi*, 1958), 83–84
Great Depression, 38–39, 117
Growing Up in a Brothel (*Kuruwa sodachi*, 1964), 221n5
Group Sounds, 181, 183, 230n9, 231n2

Hagiwara Ken'ichi, 192, 207–209, 211; as cultural icon in 1970s, 180–87
Hakodate, 149–50
Hall, John, 5
Hall, Stewart, 3
Hamada Yūko, 112
Han, Eric, 229n5
Hanamori Yasuji, 34
Hankyū (railway company), 1, 131, 133, 136, 139, 228n13
Hanshin (railway company), 131, 136, 185, 228n14
Hanshin-kan, 18, 131
Hara Setsuko, 95
Harootunian, Harry D., 5, 221n3
Harvey, David, 115, 190, 222n14
Hasegawa Kazuhiko, 192
Hayashi Fumiko, 94
Hayden, Dolores, 136
Hayek, Friedrich, 191
Heibon, 66
heterosexuality, 180, 208, 210–11, 225n12
heterotopia, 223n16

Hidari Sachiko, 69, 76, 89
Higashi-Nakano, 90, 92
Higashiyama Chieko, 69, 97
high-speed growth; anxieties and tensions of, 14, 16; beginning of, 34, 43, 47, 57; demographic change brought by, 62, 70–71; as a disciplinary discourse, 6–8; end of, 178–80, 198; height of, 103–104; as historical fact, 6; home appliances as a symbol of, 115; as massive capitalist development, 9; and modernization, 118–19; problems caused by 196, 206; views of Asia during, 175
Higuchi Ichiyō, 41
Himeda Shinsaku, 192
Hiroshima, 12, 69, 78, 193, 201
historical narratives, 2–4, 59, 63, 142; alternative, 8, 10, 166, 213; competing, 215–18; and Maruyama Masao's methodology, 12–16; of postwar Japan, 5–8, 22, 27, 34–35, 104, 111, 142, 178–79, 211
historicity, 15, 213
historicization, 10–11, 14, 19, 143, 213–14, 216
History of Postwar Japan as Told by a Bar Hostess (*Nippon sengoshi: Madamu onbroro no seikatsu*, 1970), 161
Hitachi, 114
Hitchcock, Alfred, 152, 155
Hodaka Noriko, 91
Hōjō Hideji, 128, 228n10
Hokkaido, 149, 187–88, 192, 211, 228n13; depopulation in, 199; as frontier, 95, 232n8; visual representations in *The Light of Africa*, 23, 179, 203, 205
Home from the Sea (*Kokyō*, 1972), 2

homosexuality, 208–11
homosociality, 15, 143, 170–71, 176, 231n17
Honda, 5
Hong Kong, 125–26
Hooray for Marriage, or Sweet Beans for Two (*Meoto zeinzai*, 1955), 129
Hopson, Nathan, 225n11
Hori Kyūsaku, 146
Hoston, Germaine, 226n17
Husband Witnessed, The (*Otto ga mita*, 1964), 80
hybridity, 151, 175

I Am Waiting (*Ore wa matteru ze*, 1957), 145
I Was Born, But... (*Umarete wa mita keredo*, 1932), 65
Ibuse Masuji, 56
Ichijō Sayuri, 185, 232n5
Ichikawa Kon, 128, 182–83
ideology, 63, 84, 219n2, 227n7, 231n2; in capitalist society, 89–92; developmental, 220n7; emperor-centered, 10; growth as, 219n4; neoliberalism as, 15
Ienaga Saburō, 219n2
Igarashi, Yoshikuni, 10, 233n10
Ikeda Hayato, 2, 69, 117, 142, 227n5
Ikeda Shin'ichi, 184–85
Imai Tadashi, 230n12
Imamura Shōhei, 2, 69, 161, 185, 217, 230n14
Immortal Love (*Eien no hito*, 1961), 16
Imperial University, *see* Tokyo University
imperialism, 11, 38, 117, 144, 150, 171, 216
income doubling plan, 2, 5, 9, 69, 117, 142

individualism, 85–89
industrial society, 122, 127, 148, 182, 185, 202–203; mass production in, 140; standardization in, 106, 135, 139–40; theory of, 118–21, 227n7
industrial spy, 105, 107, 109, 111–13, 135, 202, 214; as cosmopolitan urbanite, 121–27
industrialization, 11, 128, 197, 216; in postwar Japan, 2, 63, 66, 70, 118, 200, 206, 223n13; of rural Japan, 197
infertility, 144, 170–75
Inland Sea, 16, 62, 77, 196
Inoue Akira, 19, 22, 104, 109–10
Inoue Takayuki, 181
Inoue Umetsugu, 109–10
Insect Woman, The (*Nippon konchūki*, 1963), 2, 69, 185
intelligence, 121, 125–26, 135, 166, 227n8
intertextuality, 63, 79, 80, 84, 127, 135, 143, 161, 213; *see also* Wakao Ayako
intimacy, 50, 180, 206–11, 231n18
Isayama Hiroko, 185
Ise, 135–38
Ishihara Shintarō, 28, 144–45, 200
Ishihara Yūjirō, 143, 162, 169, 185; in early career, 145; and "mood action" films, 146–51
Ishii Teruo, 221n6
Ishikawa Tatsuzō, 186
Ishizaka Kōji, 184
Itō Daisuke, 128
Itokawa Hideo, 200
Ivy, Marilyn, 223n19, 233n10
Iwase Akira, 224n6
Iwashita Shima, 17
Izu, 19, 21, 62–63, 67, 75, 92, 96, 128; national image of, 78–79

Izu Dancer, The (*Koi no hana saku Izu no odoriko*, 1933), 79
Izu Dancer, The (*Izu no odoriko*, 1963), 79

James Bond, 105, 226n1
Jansen, Marius, 5
Japan AALA (Asia, Africa, and Latin America) Solidarity Committee, 167
Japan Association of Corporate Executives, 119
Japan Communist Party, 184, 226n17
Japan Expo '70 (*Nihon bankoku-haku*, 1971), 228n13
Japan Productivity Center, 57
Japan Socialist Party, 32, 57, 157, 184, 226n17
Japanese Girls at the Harbor (*Minato no Nihon-musume*, 1933), 150–51
Japanese style management, 178, 191
Jinmu boom, 21, 26
Jinnai Hidenobu, 52, 55
Jō Akira, *see* Yamanaka Akira
jōkyō, *see* "going up to the capital"

Kaikō Takeshi, 38, 224n5
Kajiyama Toshiyuki, 105–109, 125, 226n2, 227n8
Kamata Satoshi, 215
Kamion'yu Takashi, 201
Kanda (in Tokyo), 46, 146
Kanda River, 48, 53
Kanō Junko, 130
Kansai, 18, 78, 129–30, 136
katagi, 50–51, 58
Katō Tokiko, 193–94, 233n9
Katsura Kokinji, 56
Kawabata Yasunari, 79, 106
Kawaguchi Hiroshi, 77, 89, 225n14, 227n4

Kawamura Nozomu, 227n7
Kawamura Reikichi, 64
Kawarasaki Kenzō, 208
Kawasaki Keizō, 79, 109–10
Kawashima, Ken C., 232n6
Kawashima Takeyoshi, 87
Kawashima Yūzō, 27–28, 36, 38, 40–41, 45, 128–29, 191, 222n10, 224n4; and *fūzoku* film, 28–29, 32–33; location shooting of Akihabara by, 46; and *muen*, 56; and Wakao Ayako, 81, 221n6
Kawazu Seizaburō, 47–48
Kayaoğlu, Turan, 150
keizai shōsetsu, see business novel
Keynesian economics, 117, 189
Ki River (*Ki-no-kawa*, 1966), 16–17
Kiku and Isamu (*Kiku to Isamu*, 1959), 230n12
Kikuchi Kan, 79
Kim, Su Yun, 231n18
Kinema junpō, 81, 182, 185, 207, 209
Kinoshita Keisuke, 16–17
Kintetsu (railway company), 112, 135–39, 228n14
Kintetsu Department Store, 136, 139
Kirishima Noboru, 68
Kishi Keiko, 182
Kishi Nobusuke, 117
Kiss Thief, The (*Seppun dorobō*, 1960), 28
Kisses (*Kuchizuke*, 1957), 62, 89
Kitahara Mie, 146
Kitamura Hiroshi, 230n14
Kitchen Chronicle, A (*Daidokoro taiheiki*, 1963), 225n10
Ko, Mika, 231n20
Kobayashi Akira, 17, 145, 154
Kobayashi Hideo, 220n7
Kobayashi Keiju, 65
Kobayashi Masaki, 14

Kobe, 1, 62, 71, 78, 163–64, 170–71, 228n14; as exotic port city, 125–26, 149–51, 229n4; image of, 18; suburban development of, 131, 134
kokutai, see national polity
Kokutetsu, *see* National Railways
Konishi Michio, 107
Korea, 157, 162–63, 171, 175–76, 231n18
Korean Japanese, 14, 18, 175–76, 231n20, 232n6
Korean War, 6, 26, 69, 162
Kōza school, 87, 226n17
Koyama Akiko, 176
Kubo Masao, 171
Kumashiro Tatsumi, 22, 179, 180, 182, 187, 192, 208; and "roman porno," 185–86, 199, 232n4
Kumazawa Makoto, 215
Kunimitsu Shirō, 108
Kunze, Peter, 231n17
Kurahara Koretsugu, 232n4
Kuroki Kazuo, 17
Kurosawa Akira, 182
Kwantung Army, 38, 171
Kyō Machiko, 81, 130
Kyoto, 78, 111, 130, 136, 184, 194, 221n
Kyoto University, 201

labor market, 71, 76, 83, 191, 224n9, 232n6
labor power, 51, 118, 188, 225n15, 232n6
Labor Standards Act, 39, 74
labor union, 120, 124, 178, 182, 231n3; in early postwar years, 57; at Nikkatsu, 146, 229n2
Letchworth Garden City, 131
Late Chrysanthemums (*Bangiku*, 1954), 94–95, 225n10, 232n8

Lenin, Vladimir I., 117
Liberal Democratic Party (LDP), 7–9, 57, 93, 179, 182, 184, 191, 197; and cronyism, 16; and US-Japan Security Treaty, 15, 117; and Vietnam War, 157; and welfare state, 118, 142, 190, 232n7
Light of Africa, The (*Afurika no hikari*, 1975); Africa in, 205–206; intimacy in, 206–208, 211; and Maruyama Kenji's novel, 186–87; precariousness in, 191–92; representations of rural Japan in, 192, 195–99; as response to oil crisis recession, 180–81
liminal space, 50, 54, 56, 58, 151, 155, 223n15
liminality, 28, 52, 151, 154, 191
location shooting, 14, 16; for *Black Weapon*, 133, 137, 228n12; for *Blue-Sky Girl*, 78; of Kinoshita Keisuke, 17; for *The Light of Africa*, 179, 192–93; for Nikkatsu "mood action" films, 148, 151, 172; for *Susaki Paradise Red Light*, 40, 46
LST (tank-landing ship, US Navy), 156–57, 229n8

MacArthur, Douglas, 156
Maeda Ai, 41–42
Maid's Boy (*Jochūkko*, 1955), 77
Mainichi newspaper, 186
Man Who Causes a Storm (*Arashi o yobu otoko*, 1957), 145
Manchuria, 4, 33, 38, 67, 94–95, 131, 176
Marcos, Ferdinand Emmanuel, 236
Marcuse, Herbert, 6, 121
Maruyama Kenji, 186–87

Maruyama Masao, 13–15, 87, 121, 216, 219n2
Marx, Karl, 117, 232n6
Marxism, 5, 87, 90, 117, 119, 227n6
Marunouchi, 92, 146
mass consumption, 118, 121, 135, 203, 233n10
"mass employment," 9, 71, 74, 83–84, 224n9
mass production, 111, 113, 121, 135, 140, 185, 203, 215
Masumura Yasuzō, 62–63, 78, 80, 82, 89, 104, 225n12, 225n14, 227n4; and "Black" series, 104, 107–10; and individualism 85–89, 96, 226n16
Matriarchal Family (*Nyokei kazoku*, 1963), 128, 130
Matsumoto Seichō, 106
Matsumoto Taira, 229n2
Matsuo Kazuko, 147
Matsuo, Shōichi, 219n2
McGowan, Todd, 116
Meiji Restoration, 15, 56, 216
melodrama, 62, 146, 148
Mickey Curtis & the Samurai, 181
Midday Trap (*Mahiru no wana*, 1962), 120
middle class, 12, 66, 83, 104, 108, 113, 176, 193, 200, 211, 224n; American life, 147; domesticity, 58; consciousness, 6; family, 69, 73–74, 76, 93–94, 122, 144, 180, 210, 221n; life, 22, 72, 120, 147, 203; sexual morals, 58; suburban commuters, 139; youth culture, 185
Midnight Cowboy (1969), 208
Mihashi Tatsuya, 21, 27–28, 38–39, 47, 222n10
Miike struggle, 84

Mikawa Ken'ichi, 147
Mimasu Aiko, 32
Minami Hiroshi, 81
Ministry of Health and Welfare, 57, 230n11
Ministry of Labor, 40, 71, 84
Minobe Ryōkichi, 184
Minobe Tatsukichi, 4, 184
mise-en-scène, 14, 155
Mishima Yukio, 77, 79
Misono Ryōko, 11
Misumi Kenji, 128
Mita Yoshiko, 221n5
Miyakawa Kazuko, 77
Miyake Kuniko, 93
Miyazaki Hayao, 223n18
Mizoguchi Kenji, 29, 32–33, 40, 79, 81, 130, 221n4, 221n7, 225n13
Mizuho Shunkai, 109–10
Mizuno, Hiromi, 220n7
Mochizuki Yūko, 65, 94
modernity, 11, 100, 196, 219n2
modernization, 5, 33–34, 77, 215; theory of, 5, 118, 166, 219n3
Momoi Kaori, 186, 195
"mood action" films, 144–48, 159, 176, 217; set in port cities, 148–51
mood music, 146–47, 229n3
"mood popular song," 147–48, 152–53
Moore, Aaron, 220n7
Morishige Hisaya, 64–65, 129, 193, 224n4
Most Valuable Wife, The (*Saikō shukun fujin*, 1959), 225n14
mūdo kayōkyoku, see "mood popular song"
muen (no ties), 28, 58–59, 217, 223n16; in Kawashima Yūzō's films, 52, 54, 56; in premodern Japan, 50–52

Murata Hideo, 228n10
Murayama Mitsuo, 109–10
Muroo Saisei, 68
Mutual Security Act, 9, 26
My Town (*Waga machi*, 1956), 128
My Way (*Waga michi*, 1974), 199
Myōjō, 66, 79, 82

Nagai, Frank, 147
Nagasaki, 148–50, 157, 228n13
Nagata Masaichi, 81, 84
Nagoya, 62, 71, 83, 112, 130, 134, 136–37, 193–94
Nakagawa Rie, 185
Nakajima Takehiro, 17
Nakamura Ganjirō, 129–30
Nakamura Noboru, 16
Nakamura Takeshi, 65
Nakamura Tamao, 130
Nakayama Ichirō, 119
Namba, 133, 228n14
Naniwa Chieko, 56, 129–30
Nanjō Agency (Imperial Navy), 126
Nara, 136–37, 194, 228n14
narrative, *see* historical narratives
Naruse Mikio, 2, 94–95, 217, 222n10, 223n19, 225n10, 232n8
Nashimoto Masako, 171
national pension, 57, 117, 142
national polity (*kokutai*), 4
National Railways, 46, 65, 67, 90, 193–94
nationalism, 3–4, 39, 173, 219n2
nationality, 174–75
nation-state, 17, 68, 76–77, 129, 175, 197, 203, 211, 214–15; as framework for historical narratives, 3–4; "interior frontier" within, 174; Osaka in, 138; periphery of, 196
Natsume Sōseki, 68

Negishi Housing Complex, 156, 158
Nemoto Naoko, 171, 174
neocolonialism, 159, 163, 166–68
neoliberalism, 8, 15–16, 82, 190–91, 215, 232n6
New Life campaign, 9, 57
Nikkatsu, 17, 144–46, 159, 185–86, 229n1, 229n2; action films, 146, 148, 154–55; "roman porno," 185–86, 232n4
Ninja in a Suit (Sebiro no ninja, 1963), 121
Nintendo, 5
Nishimura Hiroshi, 224n4
Nishiyama Chiaki, 191
Nitani Hideaki, 22, 163
Nitta Jirō, 200
Nixon, Richard, 178
Nkrumah, Kwame, 166–67
North Dock (in Yokohama), 156, 158
Nosaka Akiyuki, 38, 195, 224n5
Nozoe Hitomi, 89, 227n4
nuclear family, 73, 93–94, 180, 209–11, 233n13

O'Bryan, Scott, 219n4
Ochanomizu, 46
Oda Sakunosuke, 128
Odaka Kunio, 118
Ōhara Institute for Social Research, 40
oil crisis (1973), 26, 62, 106, 191, 197, 232n7; in narrative of economic history, 178–79; recession caused by, 182, 187, 189, 192, 203, 214, 231n3
Okada Yutaka, 192
Okakura Koshirō, 167
Okamoto Kihachi, 65
Okazaki Takeshi, 224n7

Organisation for Economic Co-operation and Development, 104
Only Son, The (Hitori musuko, 1936), 68, 217
Ono Kōsei, 209
Onomichi, 12, 69
O'Reilly, Sean, 220n8
Osaka; dialect of, 129–30; films set in, 128–29; and Genji Keita 64, 78; as metropolis, 62, 70–71, 76, 83, 104; suburban development of, 131–35; train network in, 135–40
Osaka Castle, 130, 136
Osaka Elegy (Naniwa erejī, 1936), 130–31
Osaka Expo, 133, 193, 228n13
Ōshima Nagisa, 14, 175
Ōshō (1962), 128, 228n10
Otowa Nobuko, 56
Ōtsuka Zenshō, 122
Ōuchi Hyōe, 117
Ōuchi Tsutomu, 117–18
Our Neighbor, Miss Yae (Tonari no Yae-chan, 1934), 65
Ozaki Kōyō, 79
Ozawa Shōichi, 51
Ozu Yasujirō, 29, 65, 68, 94–95, 217, 223n19, 225n10, 232n8; and *Tokyo Story*, 12, 69, 79

Pacific Ocean, 62, 67, 78, 90, 152, 165, 196
Pacific War, *see* Asia-Pacific War
pan-Asianism, 22, 171, 174–75, 214
Panasonic, 46, 83
patriarchy, 14, 93, 131, 225n12, 226n21
performativity, 99–100
Petrified Forest, The (Kaseki no mori, 1973), 184

Philippines, The, 149, 162, 165, 227n8
Pigs and Battleships (*Buta to gunkan*, 1961), 2, 161, 230n14
place; as analytical category, 16–20; authentic, 139–40
placelessness, 19, 131, 134–35, 138
Polanyi, Karl, 225n15
Portrait of Madame Yuki (*Yuki-fujin ezu*, 1950), 79
Pratt, Mary Louise, 144, 157
precariousness, 2, 9, 21, 23, 70, 180, 188–89, 198, 214; in neoliberalism, 232n6; representations of, 191
Preparation for the Festival (*Matsuri no junbi*, 1975), 17
Presley, Elvis, 181
Prindle, Tamae, 227n3
procurement, 26, 142, 162, 230n15
Promise, A (*Yakusoku*, 1972), 181–83
Proof of the Man (*Ningen no shōmei*, 1977), 230n13
prostitution, 30–33, 40, 51, 69, 221n4
Pujie, 171
Puyi, 171
PYG, 181

race, 18, 152, 159–61, 168, 173–74, 230n11
Raine, Michael, 145, 226n16
Rambler with a Guitar, The (*Gitā o motta wataridori*, 1959), 17
Rausu, 179–80, 192–93, 195, 198–99, 205–206
Red Angel (*Akai tenshi*, 1966), 80
Red Diamond (*Akai daiya*, 1964), 107
Red Handkerchief (*Akai hankachi*, 1964), 148–49
reflexivity, 96, 100
Reinanzaka Church, 172

Reischauer, Edwin, 5, 219n3
Reitan, Richard, 191
relative surplus population, 71, 232n6
Relph, Edward, 19, 134
revolution, 5, 15, 22, 26, 144, 162–64, 167–69, 173–74; during Cold War, 165–66; industrial, 118; socialist, 226n17
Rolling Stones, 181
roman porno, 185, 232n4
romantic love, 21, 91, 93, 226n21
Room for Rent (*Kashima ari*, 1959), 56
Roquet, Paul, 148
Rose, Nikolas, 58
Rostow, W. W., 118, 227n7
Russell, John G., 159, 230n10
Ryū Chishū, 65, 69

Saga Hiro, 171
Saitama, 14, 70, 180, 184
Saitō Kōichi, 181, 183, 199, 217
Saitō Masaharu, 187
Sakai, Frankie, 56, 221n6
Sakai Takashi, 228n10
Sakaiya Taichi, 227n3
Sakata Sankichi, 129, 228n10
salaryman, 63–66, 108–109, 224n4, 224n6
Salaryman Mejiro Sanpei (*Sararīman Mejiro Sanpei*, 1955), 65
Sandē Mainichi, 64
Sasebo, 157–58
Satakedai (in Osaka), 132–33
Satō Eisaku, 142
Satō Jun'ya, 221n5
Satō Tadao, 62–63, 185
Sawada Kenji, 181
Sawamura Sadako, 73
Sayuri Ichijō: Following Desire (*Ichijō Sayuri: Nureta yokujō*, 1972), 185–86

Sazanka Kyū, 56
Scarecrow (1973), 208
Schaller, Michael, 219n5, 230n15
Schumpeter, Joseph, 119
Season of the Sun (*Taiyō no kisetsu*, 1956), 144–45
Second Sino-Japanese War, 38
Seisaku's Wife (*Seisaku no tsuma*, 1965), 80
Self-Defense Forces, 26, 220n1
Senri New Town, 106, 128, 131–36, 228n11, 228n12
sexual orientation, 18, 82, 208
sexuality, 208–10, 225n12, 226n21
Shah, Nayan, 209–10
Shanghai, 126, 151, 227n
Sharp, 46, 114
Shiba Ryōtarō, 106
Shibaki Yoshiko, 32–33, 38, 45
Shiga Naoya, 79
Shimazu Yasujirō, 65
Shimizu Hiroshi, 150
Shimizu Ikkō, 227n3
Shimizu Ikutarō, 118
Shimizu Kazuhiko, 222n8
Shin Kinzō, 97
Shindō Kaneto, 199
Shinjuku, 74, 90
Shinkansen, 22, 103, 106–108, 110, 193–94
Shinoda Masahiro, 182, 184
Shin-Osaka, 103–104, 108, 194
Shinsaibashi, 130, 133
Shin-Senri-yama, 133, 228n13
Shin-Tōhō, 109, 221n6
Shiretoko, 22–23, 177, 179, 192–96, 218
Shiroyama Saburō, 108–109, 227n3
Shizuoka, 21, 62, 78, 150, 158
Shōchiku, 11, 65, 88
Shōda Michiko, 107, 226n2
Shōken, *see* Hagiwara Ken'ichi

Shop Curtain, The (*Noren*, 1958), 129, 224n4
Shōsetsu Shinchō, 76
Shōwa retro boom, 8
shūdan shūshoku, see "mass employment"
Shūkan Bunshun, 107
Shūkan Myōjō, 107, 226n2
Silverberg, Miriam, 10
Sing a Song of Sex (*Nihon shunkakō*, 1967), 175–76, 231n20
Sisters of Gion (*Gion no kyōdai*, 1936), 81
Smith, Neil, 44
social relations, 11, 30, 57, 87, 91, 115
Socialist Party, *see* Japan Socialist Party
Sony, 5, 47, 83
Southeast Asia, 143–44, 163, 166–68, 170–74; during Cold War, 165; Japan's economic aid to, 231n19; solidarity for 174
Spiders, 181
Spirited Away (*Sen to Chihiro no kamikakushi*, 2001), 223n18
spy, *see* industrial spy
"standard family," 210–11, 233n13
Stoler, Ann Laura, 174
Story of Floating Weeds, A (*Ukikusa monogatari*, 1934), 223n19
Street of Shame (*Akasen chitai*, 1956), 32–33, 40, 221n7, 225n13
subjectivity, 63, 66, 85, 89, 96
Sugawara Kenji, 67, 79, 83–84
Sukarno (president of Indonesia), 171
Sukarno, Ratna Sari Dewi, *see* Nemoto Naoko
Sumiyoshi Shrine, 130, 136
Sun in the Last Days of the Shogunate, The (*Bakumatsu taiyōden*, 1957), 56

Sunset Hill (*Yūhi no oka*, 1964), 146, 149
Susaki (Susaki-Bentenchō), 37, 46, 48, 50, 53, 54, 128, 214, 222n13; address change of, 221n2; history of, 27, 30, 45; representations of, 40
Susaki Paradise, 27, 33, 37, 41–42, 47, 50–54, 58; and Anti-Prostitution Law, 43; on artificial island, 44–45; history of 30–31; literary representations of, 32
Susaki Paradise Red Light (*Susaki Paradise aka-shingō*, 1956); and 1956 economic white paper, 33, 36–37; home appliances in, 115; in Kawashima Yūzō's oeuvre, 29–30, 56; and Mizoguchi Kenji's *Street of Shame*, 33; precariousness in, 191–92; representations of children in, 42; traveling actors in, 55; uneven development in, 44, 47, 63

tabiyakusha (traveling actor), 54–55
Taishō democracy, 4, 38, 85
taiyōzoku (sun tribe), 145
Takahashi Yōko, 198
Takamine Hideko, 16
Takarada Akira, 28
Takechi Tetsuji, 161, 217
Tales of Ginza (*Ginza nijūyonchō*, 1955), 28
Tamiya Jirō, 105, 109–11, 120–21, 129, 185, 217
Tanabe Seiko, 223n3
Tanaka Kakuei, 178, 190, 197
Tanaka Kinuyo, 221n4
Tanaka Kunie, 23, 187
Taniguchi Senkichi, 228n13
Tanizaki Jun'ichirō, 68, 78, 225n10
Tansman, Alan, 219n2

Tasaka Tomotaka, 76
Temple of the Wild Geese (*Gan no tera*, 1962), 81
Tempters, 181
Tennōji, 56, 129, 133, 136
Terentyef, George, 124
Third World, 165–67
Third-Rate Executives (*Santō jūyaku*, 1952), 64
Three Female Bees (*Sanbiki no mesubachi*, 1970), 228n13
"three sacred treasures," 9, 113–14
Tigers (music band), 181
Time for Marriage (*Konki*, 1961), 225n10
Time of Joy and Sorrow (*Yorokobi mo kanashimi mo ikutoshitsuki*, 1957), 17
Toake Yukiyo, 149
Tobita (in Osaka), 43
Todoroki Yukiko, 28, 37
Tōhō, 64, 65, 179, 186
Tohoku, 69–72, 76–77, 83, 85, 225n11
tokuingai (special restaurant area), 31–32, 43
Tokyo; cultural representations of, 68–69; growth of, 70; labor migration to, 76–77; landfill in, 30, 45; licensed quarters in 30; and "mass employment," 71–72, 74, 83–84; uneven development in, 28, 63; US bombing of, 40, 46
Tokyo Bay, 30, 45, 56, 222n
Tokyo Metropolitan Government, 45, 222n12
Tokyo Station, 46, 67, 72, 89, 92, 142
Tokyo Story (*Tōkyō monogatari*, 1953), 12–13, 69, 79
Tokyo Summer Olympics (1964), 2, 22, 45, 103–104, 106, 114

Tokyo Twilight (*Tōkyō boshoku*, 1957), 94, 232n8
Tokyo University, 30, 78, 86, 184, 227n8
Tokugawa era, 4, 45, 52, 54, 78, 220n8
Tokutomi Sohō, 79
Tomimoto Sōkichi, 109–10, 120
Tominaga Ken'ichi, 118–19, 227n7
Tone River, 53, 223n
toppu-ya (top shop), 107
Tora-san, Our Lovable Tramp (*Otoko wa tsurai yo*, 1969), 17
Torii Motohiro, 228n13
Tosaka Jun, 29–30, 221n3
Toyoda Shirō, 129, 225n10
Toyota, 5, 76, 83, 215
Toyotomi clan, 128, 136
Traveling Actors (*Tabiyakusha*, 1940), 223n19
Tsugaru Jongara-bushi (1973), 181, 199
Tsuge Yoshiharu, 233n10
Tsukasa Yōko, 17
Tsuruoka Masayoshi and Tokyo Romantica, 147
Tsūtenkaku, 56, 130
Twisted Path of Love (*Koibitotachi wa nureta*, 1973), 185, 199
Twenty-Four Eyes (*Nijūshi no hitomi*, 1954), 16

Uchiyamada Hiroshi and Cool Five, 148
Uehonmachi, 106, 135–40, 228n14
Uemachi Daichi, 136, 229n15
Umeda, 1, 133
Umesao Tadao, 200–202
unemployment, 26, 179, 189–90, 215
uneven development, 19, 28, 37, 44–50, 59, 179, 197, 214–15

unevenness, 12, 17, 45, 48, 63, 69, 194, 222n11
United Red Army, 182
universal health care, 57, 117, 142
Uno Kōzō, 117
Urayama Kirio, 14
urbanization, 63, 66, 70, 106, 118, 128, 135, 200, 222n13
US forces, 144, 156–57, 159, 161, 168, 170, 175; and bar and nightclub industry, 158; and Japanese economy, 142, 162
US occupation of Japan, 26, 46, 64, 104, 147, 156, 168, 175; mixed-race children during, 159–61; policies of, 85; and prostitution, 31, 221n4
US-Japan Security Treaty (Anpo), 9, 15, 116, 156–57, 165, 182; protest against, 5, 142, 184, 186, 227n5, 230n14
Utsui Ken, 109–10

Ventures, 181
Vietnam War, 5, 22, 142–44, 156–58, 162–63, 165, 175, 182
Voight, John, 208

Wada Hiroshi and Mahina Stars, 147
Wada Kōji, 145
Wada-Marciano, Mitsuyo, 11, 150, 224n4
Wakao Ayako, 62–63, 77, 79, 96, 130, 221n6, 225n13, 225n14; intertextuality of 80–85
Wanderers, The (*Matatabi*, 1973), 184
Warm Current (*Danryū*, 1957), 89
Warm Misty Night, A (*Yogiri yo kon'ya mo arigatō*, 1967); absent presence of US forces in, 157–58; blackface in, 159; dual attitude toward Asia in, 174–76; friendship

in, 207; image of Yokohama in, 154; representations of Third World in, 167; trafficking in a woman in, 171; triangular relation in, 170–71
Watanabe Osamu, 227n5, 231n3
Watanabe Takenobu, 146, 148, 151
Weight of the Journey (*Tabi no omosa*, 1972), 181, 217
welfare state, 57–58, 118, 142, 191, 232n7
Westernization, 11, 216
Wharf of No Return, The (*Kaerazaru hatoba*, 1966), 154
When a Woman Ascends the Stairs (*Onna ga kaidan o agaru toki*, 1960), 2
Where Spring Comes Late (*Kazoku*, 1970), 2, 228n13
white-collar worker, 64–66, 83, 93, 106, 108, 125, 224n6
Wife Confesses, A (*Tsuma wa kokuhaku suru*, 1961), 80
Woman Is Born Twice, A (*Onna wa nido umareru*, 1961), 81, 221n6
Women of the Night (*Yoru no onnatachi*, 1948), 221n4
Women's Medal (*Onna no kunshō*, 1961), 130
working class, 63, 66, 80–82, 160, 185, 211, 214; neighborhood, 14, 55, 92, 128; women, 32, 64, 69, 76, 131
World for Two, A (*Futari no sekai*, 1966), 149
World War II, 33, 87, 117, 126, 143, 220n7; defeat in, 4, 6, 26; post-, 2, 30, 105, 134, 166–67, 189, 219n5, 231n2

yakeato yamiichi-ha (faction of the ruins and black market), 38
Yamada Isuzu, 81, 94, 131, 232n8
Yamada Yōji, 2, 17, 217, 228n13
Yamaguchi Hitomi, 65
Yamaguchi Satoshi, 71, 224n9
Yamaguchi Seiichirō, 232n4
Yamamura Sō, 28
Yamanaka Akira, 160–61, 230n13
Yamanouchi, Yasushi, 220n7
Yamasaki Toyoko, 108, 128
Yamate Catholic Church, 151
Yearning (*Midareru*, 1964), 2
Yi Un, 171
Yokohama; cosmopolitan, 151–52, 154–55; as exotic port city, 125–26, 144, 149–51; as neocolonial port city, 159–61; and Vietnam War, 156–58; US occupation of; 152–56
Yokohama Harbor, 143, 152, 155, 168, 207
Yokosuka, 156–58, 161
Yomiuri newspaper, 35
Yoshida Hideko, 175
Yoshida Tadashi, 147
Yoshimi Yoshiaki, 219n2
Yoshimoto, Mitsuhiro, 220n9
Yoshimura Kōzaburō, 81, 83, 225n10
Yoshinaga Sayuri, 14, 154
Yoshiwara, 32–33, 41–43, 222n7, 225n13
Yoshiyuki Junnosuke, 32
Young Miss, A (*Ojōsan*, 1961), 77
Yuge Tarō, 77, 109–10, 121
Yūhigaoka (in Osaka), 56
Yuki Shigeko, 76

www.ingramcontent.com/pod-product-compliance
Lightning Source LLC
Chambersburg PA
CBHW030530230426
43665CB00010B/828